The Indians of the Paraguayan Chaco

THE INDIANS
OF THE
PARAGUAYAN
CHACO

Identity and Economy

John Renshaw

University of Nebraska Press

Lincoln and London

Portions of chapter 5 have been previously published
as "Property, Resources, and Equality among
the Indians of the Paraguayan Chaco," *Man* 23, no. 2 (1988).
All photographs are courtesy of the author.

Library of Congress Control Number: 2002108050
ISBN 0-8032-3938-6 (cloth)
ISBN 0-8032-8991-x (paper)

Contents

Photographs

Figures and Maps

Tables

Preface

THIS STUDY is based on a doctoral thesis that I presented at the London School of Economics in 1986. Some of the information has been updated, but the study follows the general argument and structure of the original. I have expanded the introduction to provide more detail about the context in which the original fieldwork was carried out, and I have added a section on indigenous organizations at the end of the chapter on the political system. I would like to thank the Rights Department of Blackwell for permission to reprint the material in chapter 5 that was previously published in *Man* 23, no. 2 (June 1988) as "Property, Resources, and Equality among the Indians of the Paraguayan Chaco."

The original fieldwork was financed from 1975 to 1979 with a generous grant from the Social Science Research Council of Great Britain (now ESRC), and the photographic and recording equipment was provided by the Central Research Fund of the University of London. While writing up, I was also assisted by a grant from the Radcliffe Brown Memorial Fund.

I owe a great debt of gratitude to Dr. Joanna Overing, my supervisor at the London School of Economics, who gave me both practical and intellectual support at every stage of the study, and to James Woodburn, who for a time acted as my supervisor. Barbara Bentley and Stephen Corry of Survival International also provided invaluable help, particularly during the difficult year of 1976, when it seemed unlikely I would be able to return to Paraguay.

In Paraguay I received help and hospitality from a great number of people. All the members of the Marandú team, particularly Dr. Miguel Chase Sardi, were of great assistance and provided me with an invaluable introduction to the Chaco when I first visited Paraguay in 1975, and these friendships were renewed when I later worked with API. It was through

API that I met Ramón Fogel, who not only became a good friend but also helped focus my attention on many of the themes covered in this study.

From 1980 to 1983 I worked with the Instituto Nacional del Indígena (INDI), and I am particularly grateful for the companionship and support of the people who worked in INDI, especially Colonel Oscar Centurion, Graciela Ocariz, and General Marcial Samaniego. One of the main achievements of INDI was to have carried out the first census of the Indian population of Paraguay. This would not have been possible without the unstinting support we received from the Paraguayan census office (DGEC), in particular from David Vera, and from the United Nations Fund for Population Activities (UNFPA), whose representatives, George Walmesley and Leslie McTyre, provided moral support as well as financial backing. It was under the auspices of INDI that I was later able to work in Mistolar and Pedro P. Peña, and I must thank the Inter-American Indigenist Institute and its then director, Dr. Oscar Arce Quintanilla, for the funding that made the study possible.

During the time I lived in Asunción I enjoyed the company and ideas of a number of anthropologists who worked in Paraguay, and I must especially thank Norman Anderson, Kim Hill, and Richard Reed, whose ideas helped me greatly in the elaboration of this study. Richard Reed and Harriet Klein later reviewed the first draft of this study and offered many useful comments and ideas, which I have tried to incorporate into the final version. I must also thank David Angus, who prepared all the maps and diagrams for the study.

In the Chaco I received help and hospitality from a great many people, among whom I would like to mention Paul Wyma and his family, with whom I stayed in Puesto Paz; Santiago Pucherai, my teacher and assistant in Maria Auxiliadora; Luís Franco Goiburu and Captain Rolón of Bahía Negra; Bruno Barra and Pedro Ozuna of Puerto Diana; Achón Mallero and Guillermo Mallero, Pablo Romero and their families in Buena Vista; Cirilo Pinto, who worked with me in Mistolar and Pedro P. Peña; Siriaco Pérez and his family, with whom we stayed in Mistolar; and Comisario Inspector Pedro Ignacio Moran and Nery Calderón, our hosts in Pedro P. Peña. I must also mention my gratitude to all those who worked on the 1981 census, especially the supervisors and enumerators, who included Severo Flores, Pablo Flores, Alejandro López, Bruno Barra, Wilmar Stahl, Peter Faulkner, and Andrés Chemjai, not to mention our illustrious drivers Adolfo Mongelos, Justo Pastor Benítez, and Chopetito.

My greatest debt, however, is to my family. My wife, Graciela, and her family in Cerrito have not only provided continual support but have taught me more than I could otherwise have known about the Chaco. Indeed, without the help of my wife's parents, Francisco Ramírez and Isabel García, and her kin, especially Damian García, Catalino García, Olegario García, Felipe Coronel, Marcelino Coronel, Saturnino García, and Antonio Caballero, this book could never have been written. I must also thank my own parents, who provided years of moral and financial support, for which I am eternally grateful, and who never questioned the rationality of this enterprise that took up so many years of our lives.

The Indians of the Paraguayan Chaco

Introduction

THIS BOOK has three main aims. First, it is intended as an ethnographic description of contemporary Indian life in the Paraguayan Chaco. There is little reliable information available on the region, in English or indeed in any other language, and this book is the first attempt to offer an overview of the Chaco since Alfred Metraux's "Ethnography of the Chaco" was published in the *Handbook of South American Indians* in 1963.

The second and related aim is to develop a methodological approach that will allow an honest description of contemporary indigenous societies like those found in the Chaco. This goes beyond the familiar problems of ethnography, of trying to generalize about a group of people who may be very diverse in their beliefs, attitudes, behavior, and even their sense of ethnic or group identity. The study is an attempt to describe societies that have a historical sense of their own autonomy and yet are all to some extent integrated into the social and economic life of a nation. This requires the ethnographer to address the issue of social change and the nature of ethnic identity.

This is obvious but needs to be stressed because it offers the opportunity to move beyond the conventional descriptions of "acculturated" societies. Most descriptions are phrased in terms of the "ethnographic present" and refer to some past era when these societies suffered little or no interference from outside, an era that in the context of the Chaco bears little or no relation to any historical reality. Or else they consider indigenous societies in terms of the economic and social relations imposed by the national society but offer little insight into the values, organization, or culture of the societies they are describing.

Here I shall focus on the values that underlie the Indians' economy. This is not because I regard the economy or the Indians' economic values as being more significant than any other aspect of these societies. For

1

the societies of the Chaco, the "economy" is in any case nothing more than an analytical abstraction. It is, in Marshall Sahlins's words, "not a distinct or specialized organization, but something that generalized social groups and relations, notably kinship groups and relations, *do*" (1974:76). Rather, I have chosen to concentrate on the economy because, unlike, for example, religious values, the economy is readily observable. It provides an area where it is fairly easy to move between the description of what people actually do and what they say—and perhaps think—about what they are doing. The economy is, moreover, an area where the issue of social change is manifest at its clearest. As I shall describe in the chapters that follow, the Indians' economy operates in a context that is largely determined by forces outside their immediate control. This does not imply, however, that their system of economic values is also shaped by outside forces. Indeed, I shall argue precisely the opposite—that the Indians' perception of their economy cannot simply be assumed on the basis of an outsider's supposedly "objective" understanding of their situation within the regional economy.

This leads directly to the final and perhaps most ambitious aim of the study. I would like to move beyond descriptive ethnography and touch on issues relating to development and the reduction of poverty. The most difficult question is whether it is really possible to envisage a program of social and economic development that would respect and strengthen the Indians' sense of identity—what Victor Hugo Cárdenas (1997) talks of as "development with identity."[1] There is no doubt that most of the Indian peoples of the Paraguayan Chaco live in conditions of poverty and deprivation. Many communities have no rights to land, and even those that do have land of their own have little or no income and are largely dependent on poorly paid wage labor outside their communities. Indeed, when judged by any of the conventional criteria for defining poverty—levels of income, infant mortality, access to health services or education—the Indians of the Chaco can be counted among the very poorest sectors of the Paraguayan population.[2] They are not, however, simply an underclass or an undifferentiated rural proletariat, but a clearly defined population who have a sense of their ethnic identity, both as Indians and as members of particular ethnic and linguistic groups.

Any serious social or economic development program for the Indians of the Chaco has to confront formidable obstacles. The political and social structure of the region is dominated by powerful, well-organized interest groups: the cattlemen, represented by the Asociación Rural del Paraguay, the Mennonite cooperatives, and the military and the missionary organizations, all of which to some extent depend on the Indians as a cheap and submissive workforce. The environment is harsh and offers little in the way of economic opportunities, and the Indians themselves are disorganized and lack the technical, political, or organizational capacity necessary to transform their social and economic situation. Even before attempting to address these issues, though, I believe we have to come to an understanding of what "development with identity" might look like, and consider how far the value systems of the Indians of the Chaco are indeed compatible with conventional notions of social and economic development.

Many Indian communities have been involved in development projects. These have varied considerably, both in their general aims and in the degree of control vested with the communities. But, almost invariably—and this is true even of those projects specifically intended to foster self-determination—the projects have assumed an understanding of the Indians' economic aspirations that has later proved to be unfounded. Often this has led to the project's failure, certainly in terms of the planners' original aims, and in more than a few cases has provoked crises and divisions within the Indian communities themselves. This has led some anthropologists to question whether the economic development of the Chaco societies is a legitimate objective.[3] As a result, most of the development-focused nongovernmental organizations (NGOs), and even the more enlightened missionary organizations, have tended to concentrate their efforts almost exclusively on land titling.

It is not my intention to offer a particular model or methodology for ethnodevelopment. Rather, my aim is to examine the economy, values, and social organization of the Indian societies of the Chaco, and to try to clarify the questions that need to be asked before setting out any program of social and economic development.

Theoretical Considerations

This study, like so many ethnographies, started life as a doctoral thesis. The thesis was largely based on my experiences in Paraguay between 1975 and 1983 and was presented at the London School of Economics (LSE) in June 1986. The original version offered a tighter, more academic argument, and it deliberately played down some of the practical issues that affect the lives of the indigenous peoples it tried to portray. Since it was an academic thesis, I was unable to question the validity of the ethnographic enterprise, and I deliberately passed over much of the day-to-day development work in which I was engaged between 1975 and 1983. The study took a long time to write and was only completed after a number of false starts. In part this was due to the tension between the academic anthropological discourse and the realities of my development work in Paraguay.

One of the greatest difficulties I faced was the lack of a suitable theoretical framework in which to place my experiences. In the early 1970s I was an undergraduate at Cambridge, and in 1975 I started graduate studies at the LSE with Joanna Overing. At that time British social anthropology was beginning to take a more serious interest in Lowland South America, an interest inspired by Claude Lévi-Strauss's structuralism and, I think incidentally, one that coincided with the final demise of British colonialism. A lot of good ethnography was coming into print, and there was a sense of excitement, of pushing forward our understanding, particularly of the relation between social organization, myth, and cosmology. In 1976 I attended the symposium "Time and Social Structure in Lowland South America" at the Congress of Americanists in Paris, where scholars from Britain, France, the United States, and Brazil presented a wealth of new information, particularly on the societies of the Guianas, the Western Amazon, and Central Brazil. The emphasis, however, was on describing traditional societies before they disappeared. Indeed, at the time it was every graduate student's dream to work with a recently contacted tribe, to personally experience an utterly different way of life, and to salvage information on their culture before it disappeared. In retrospect, this idea seems very dated.[4] The anthropological literature on social change was conceptually much weaker, although on the fringes of academia there was concern about the destruction of the indigenous societies of Lowland South America, which appeared in the press and in the publications of NGOs like Survival International, IWGIA, and Cultural Survival.

4

Much of the academic literature on social change had been produced during the 1950s and 1960s, mainly by American scholars, and implicitly drew on an evolutionary model that parallels the archaeological record. These studies tended to present social change ("acculturation") as a two-way exchange of cultural traits in which the socially and technologically dominant societies eventually impose their culture on simpler societies. This is in line with a tradition of cultural anthropology that owes its inspiration to Franz Boas. It is a tradition that views culture as an eclectic mixture of traits—myths, songs, handicrafts, dances, dress, kinship terms, marriage rules, hunting equipment, tools, and so on—without really assigning priority to any particular area. As societies come into contact, traits are adopted or rejected until both societies are eventually merged or assimilated.

Although there are no studies of the Paraguayan Chaco from this period, there are two publications on the wider region that reflect this approach. Elman and Helen Service's *Tobatí: Paraguayan Town* (1954), a study of a small town in the department of Cordillera, is an attempt to understand how the Spanish colonial and Guaraní influences merged to produce a distinctly Paraguayan society. This study is still the subject of debate in Paraguay, since it concludes that Paraguayan culture is largely Hispanic in origin and that the continued use of the Guaraní language is something of an anomaly. James Watson's *Cayua Culture Change* (1952) is an ethnographic description of a Brazilian Guaraní community closely related to the Chiripa-Guaraní communities of the department of Canindeyú.[5] Watson's study is interesting in that it highlights the conceptual weakness of acculturation theory. He describes the Cayua as a neo-Brazilian peasant population who have lost virtually all their traditional culture, but meanwhile he provides tantalizing hints of a world he has missed—the religion of the Guaraní having been reduced to a few songs and dances on a Saturday night. This is essentially the same society as described in the classic studies of Nimuendajú (1914/1978), Cadogan (1971), and Melia (1991), but here the anthropologist has been deceived by his theoretical assumptions about what the society should look like. As I shall describe when I come to my own fieldwork, Watson is by no means the only anthropologist to have been misled in this way.

Darcy Ribeiro's study of the Indians of Brazil, published in Spanish in

1971 as *Fronteras indígenas de la civilización,* offers a radical critique of acculturation theory. Ribeiro's study, originally carried out for UNESCO, examines the situation of the Brazilian Indians over the previous century. It demonstrates that rather that being assimilated into the national society, the Indians of Brazil have been either physically exterminated or reduced to an underclass living in poverty on the margins of Brazilian society. Ribeiro describes a process that he calls *ethnic transfiguration,* whereby indigenous peoples are reduced through the loss of their lands and the destruction of their natural resources and are forced into dependence on the regional economy. At the same time they are pressured to reject or hide those aspects of their culture that are incompatible with the values of the national society.

Ribeiro's study was the only theoretical approach that provided a coherent framework for understanding the processes that affected the indigenous peoples of Lowland South America during the 1960s and 1970s. It seems to have provided the theoretical basis for Miguel Chase Sardi's "La situación actual de los indígenas del Paraguay" (1971), a study that was important not only as an analysis of the situation in Paraguay but also as a charter for action. It was one of the studies that lead to the Declaration of Barbados and to initiatives such as the Marandú Project. But Ribeiro's work is not so well known in English, and as far as I am aware, Paul Henley's study of the Panare (1982) is the only work that has specifically acknowledged a debt to Ribeiro.

Ribeiro offers a convincing model of the process of ethnic transfiguration that occurs as tribal societies are drawn into the orbit of the modern nation state. He is not entirely convincing, however, when he tries to explain the persistence of Indian ethnic identity exclusively in terms of their marginality vis-à-vis the national society. In one passage, for example, he remarks:

> Once the bonds of economic dependence are fixed within the regional context, the tribe can only conserve those elements of its original culture that are compatible with the condition of Indians who are integrated yet not assimilated. This results in an acculturation that leaves them as generic Indians who conserve almost nothing of their original patrimony, but who remain defined as Indians and who identify themselves as such. The relations between these generic Indians and the Brazilian population are me-

diated by a body of reciprocal representations, each conceiving of the other in the most disparaging manner possible, which are more conducive to isolation than communication, and which perpetuate their condition of alternates in opposition. (1971:346, my translation)

Personally I have not found that even the most obviously "acculturated" of the Chaco societies conforms to the picture presented above, and the notion of "generic Indians" has been of little use when trying to understand the basis of the Indians' ethnic identity. Some of the Chaco peoples, such as the Angaité and the Guaná, no longer speak their own languages and since the beginning of the twentieth century have worked as wage laborers in the tannin factories, logging camps, and ranches of the Alto Paraguay. Their material culture is virtually identical to that of the poorest sectors of the Paraguayan population. Even so, they still maintain values and aspirations that are quite distinct from those of the national society. These values are not exactly the same as they were over a century ago, but as I shall discuss in the following chapters, they still conform to a vision of society, and of man's relation to the natural world, that is in many respects peculiar to the Indian societies of the Chaco.

A theoretical approach that I found more useful is that presented by Michael Taussig in *The Devil and Commodity Fetishism in South America* (1980) and by June Nash in *We Eat the Mines and the Mines Eat Us* (1979). Both authors are concerned with the description of societies situated on the margins of global capitalism, and both develop an analysis of the conflict between the reciprocity-based value systems of traditional societies and what Taussig, drawing on Marx, calls *commodity fetishism,* or the predominance of capitalist economic relations over social relationships. The conflict between these value systems is an explicit topic of discussion in some of the Indian communities of the Chaco and is not even mediated by the sort of iconography — of largely Hispanic origin — that the bulk of Taussig's book is devoted to. The contradictions between the traditional, community-focused values of indigenous societies and the individualism characteristic of capitalist systems generate tensions within indigenous societies which may lead to patterns of social and economic behavior that at first sight appear dysfunctional.

I read Taussig's book during the early 1980s, when I was trying to organize the material I had collected in Mistolar and Pedro P. Peña. I found

7

that Taussig's ideas closely reflected the Nivaclé's critique of life in the Mennonite Colonies, and his approach was useful in helping develop the framework of my thesis, although I explicitly referred to his work only in a separate article that was later published in the journal *Man* (Renshaw 1988).

The problems with the conceptual framework of my study extended to other issues besides social change. In retrospect, one of my greatest difficulties was to have been laboring under the illusion that I was working with "acculturated" societies. Much of my reading had focused on the social organization and cosmology of the societies living in the Amazon Basin and the Guianas, and I wasted a lot of time looking for evidence of a more structured social organization that I assumed had somehow fallen into disuse. This problem was exacerbated by the fact that much of my early fieldwork was carried out among the Zamuco-speaking societies: the Ayoreo and the Chamococo. Both these societies have a more highly elaborated formal social organization than the rest of the Chaco societies, and in some ways are reminiscent of the Bororo and the Gê-speaking societies of Central Brazil.

As an undergraduate I had read Pierre Clastres's study of Aché leadership, "Échange et pouvoir: Philosophie de la chefferie indienne" (1962), and was familiar with the sort of unstructured, highly egalitarian political leadership characteristic of hunter-gatherer societies. However, it was only when I read James Woodburn's (1982) article on egalitarian societies—which draws heavily on Claude Meillassoux's work (1981)— that I began to fully appreciate how the Chaco societies fit into a broader model of hunter-gatherer societies. Even though most of the Chaco societies do have some tradition of agriculture, they are in many ways typical of Woodburn's model of egalitarian societies. They are characterized by individualistic production, a reliance on immediately available resources, and the absence of any clearly defined, enduring corporate groups that exercise control over natural or any other resources. Once I had grasped the importance of this idea, it became easier to understand the essential features of Chaco social organization and appreciate that the elaborate system of Ayoreo and Chamococo patriclans is an ideological superstructure that has been grafted onto a very simple system of social organization.

The study that follows is divided into seven main chapters. Chapter 1 provides a general background and considers the ecology, the regional economy, and the recent history of the Chaco, as well as basic information about the ethnic division of the Indian population, their numbers and location. The next three chapters provide a detailed description of the Indians' economic activities: Chapter 2 looks at hunting, fishing, and gathering; chapter 3 at agriculture and stock raising. Chapter 4 looks at the Indians' participation in the market economy as wage laborers and as independent producers—cultivating cash crops, trapping, and manufacturing handicrafts. In addition to describing these activities, I consider some of the reasons for the Indians' marked dependence on wage labor, and I examine the ecological and socioeconomic factors that restrict the potential of agriculture and other forms of independent production for the market. I also look briefly at the impact or lack of impact that economic development projects have had in the Chaco.

In the following chapter, chapter 5, I have tried to describe the economy from the Indians' standpoint. I examine their ideas about sharing, their notions of property, and their attitudes to natural resources, and I consider how these ideas can explain the importance attached to wage labor. Some of these themes are elaborated in chapter 6, where I examine the Indians' social organization and describe the household and the extended kin and residential group, and consider how these levels of organization function in regard to production, consumption, and exchange. In chapter 7, I look at the community and territorial group and focus on the nature of political leadership, paying particular attention to how the notion of personal autonomy, described in the context of the economy, is manifest in the political sphere. Finally, I discuss the experiences of the Indian organizations that have developed over the last twenty years, and consider their importance for economic and social development.

Definitions and Scope of the Study

The Indians of the Paraguayan Chaco number around forty-five thousand people and constitute about a third of the region's population. They are divided into thirteen distinct named ethnic groups, which on linguistic grounds can be divided into five major linguistic families. Despite this ethnic and linguistic diversity, the Chaco is a relatively homogeneous cultural area, and in this study I shall try to develop a general model of the Chaco societies' economic and social organization. On the whole, the Indians of the Chaco, who are referred to in Spanish as *indígenas,* or more popularly as *paisanos,* are a clearly defined population, and there is rarely any doubt whether an individual is or is not an Indian.[6]

In practice, an individual is considered to be Indian rather than "Paraguayan" (in the sense of ethnic Paraguayan) or Mennonite on the basis of residence and descent.[7] Of the two, residence is perhaps the most important. The Indians of the Chaco generally live apart from the rest of the population, in distinct colonies, communities, and *barrios,* and even when they live in close proximity to Paraguayans — as, for instance, on the ranches of the Lower Chaco, this segregation is informally, although usually quite clearly, marked. There are, however, a very small number of people who reside in Indian communities and are regarded as Paraguayans. These are almost invariably men born and brought up as Paraguayans who have married Indian wives and have chosen to reside in their wives' communities. These men continue to be regarded as Paraguayans, although their children, provided they are brought up in the mother's community, are considered Indians.

Descent is a rather more confusing criterion, as the majority of the population who consider themselves to be "Paraguayan" are in fact descended from the aboriginal Guaraní inhabitants of Eastern Paraguay and continue to speak the Guaraní language. In some Indian communities, on the other hand, a certain proportion of the population show traces of Paraguayan or even European ancestry, being the illegitimate children or descendants of Paraguayans. At times this racial intermixture makes it difficult to distinguish Indians from Paraguayans on the basis of their physical appearance alone.

A few people do leave their communities to settle in urban areas, particularly in Asunción. They include girls who have been taken to work as domestic servants, and some families, mainly from the Alto Paraguay, who have migrated to the city in search of work. However, they continue to be regarded and indeed regard themselves as Indians.[8] In fact, unless they have been taken to the city as small children, the migrants to the city lose their Indian identity only through intermarriage, and even then it is the children, rather than the spouses, who will be unambiguously identified as Paraguayans.

Introduction

Although the Indians of the Chaco are a homogeneous population in the context of the national society, they are, as I shall describe in the next chapter, divided into thirteen ethnic groups. These ethnic groups are not normally sociopolitical units, although two of the smallest, the Guaná and the Mak'a, are in effect little more than single communities. These ethnic groups can best be conceived of as cultural categories that reflect, not always entirely accurately, certain distinctive cultural features. Of these, language is generally the most significant. There are some exceptions, however. Both the Guaraní Ñandeva (Tapieté) and the Guaraní Occidentales (Guarayos) speak Guaraní and, certainly today, do not even seem to show any difference in dialect. The languages of the Lengua-Maskoy linguistic family—particularly Lengua, Angaité, and Sanapaná —also appear to be mutually intelligible and could perhaps be considered dialects of a single language.

The definition of ethnic groups is further complicated by the fact that they are not necessarily endogamous, and there are no clearly defined rules for determining the ethnic affiliation of the children of mixed marriages. In practice, children whose parents belong to different ethnic groups tend to adopt the identity of whichever group is predominant in the locality where they are raised. Thus, the children of a Mak'a father and a Lengua mother who are raised in the Colonia Mak'a will almost certainly consider themselves Mak'a and will speak Mak'a as their first language. Similarly, the children of a Lengua father and a Toba mother raised in the Toba community of Cerrito will usually consider themselves to be Toba and will speak Toba as their first language.

The situation is not always even this clear, since a number of communities are distinctly multiethnic. The most complex situations—such as Puerto Casado, where the community is composed in almost equal proportions of Lengua, Guaná, Angaité, Sanapaná, and Toba-Maskoy— have arisen where the Indians are part of an urban labor force and live in segregated neighborhoods; but in certain areas, particularly in the Lower Chaco and along the Upper Pilcomayo, the Indian communities were traditionally characterized by considerable ethnic diversity. Sometimes women and children were captured in raids, but in other cases interethnic marriages provided a basis for political alliances between different ethnic groups. Here, as in the urban multiethnic communities, the repetition of interethnic marriages can, over the generations, give rise to a situation where some individuals are uncertain about their own ethnic identity. In Loma Alegre, for example, a number of people of mixed Nivaclé and Manjuy parentage who spoke both languages were unsure how they should describe themselves, and considered the issue to be of little or no importance (see chapter 6).

In this study, rather than focusing on a single community or ethnic group, I shall present an overview of the Indian societies of the Paraguayan Chaco. This approach, which reflects the circumstances of my fieldwork, can, I believe, be justified for reasons other than the difficulty of defining the community or ethnic group as such, or the seeming homogeneity of the Indian population in the context of the national society.

In the first place, despite their linguistic diversity, the Indian societies of the Chaco share many cultural features that distinguish them from the indigenous societies of neighboring regions. This is particularly true in the economic sphere, and I think it would be misleading to present the economy or the economic values of the Chaco societies as being peculiar to any one ethnic group, such as the Lengua or the Nivaclé. Rather, I shall present a general outline of the economy and economic values of these societies, against which the peculiarities of any community or ethnic group can be understood as variations on a general theme.

Second, the Chaco is a clearly bounded cultural area. In the east, the Paraguay River has traditionally formed a boundary between the societies of the Chaco and the Guaraní of Eastern Paraguay and Mato Grosso. Even today, apart from a few communities settled on the east bank of the river (discussed in the next chapter), the only exceptions to this are the Caduveo — a subgroup of the Guaicuruan-speaking Mbayá who have lived in Mato Grosso since the seventeenth century — and the Guaraní Occidentales (Guarayos). This latter group belongs to a Guaraní-speaking population whose ancestors occupied the sub-Andean region of what is now Bolivia in the fifteenth and sixteenth centuries, and who have been settled in the Paraguayan Chaco since the end of the Chaco War (1932–35).

In the north, the Chaco is largely uninhabited; the only Indians who live in the area are the Guaraní Ñandeva (Tapieté) and the Ayoreo, who are found on both sides of the frontier that divides Paraguay and Bolivia. To the south and west, the Pilcomayo forms the boundary of the Paraguayan Chaco. At present, the Pilcomayo coincides with the ethnic division of the Indian population. The Nivaclé, Mak'a, and Manjuy live on the Paraguayan side of the river, and the Mataco, Choroti, Toba, and Pilagá live on the Argentine side. However, the Pilcomayo is an area around which the Indian population has concentrated, rather than a boundary between two distinct cultural areas. On both sides of the river the Indian populations share similar cultures, and particularly on the upper reaches of the river, one finds people continually crossing from one side to the other.

Although the Chaco stretches well into Argentina and Bolivia, this study covers only the Indians living on Paraguayan territory. The main reason for this is that the Paraguayan Chaco, unlike the wider geographical region, is a single political and administrative unit. All the institutions, both governmental and private, with which the Indians come into contact are organized on a national basis, and the history of the region, certainly in the last century or so, has been largely determined by events that have occurred at the national level. There are two further reasons for limiting the scope of this study to the Paraguayan Chaco. The first is that my fieldwork was almost exclusively confined to Paraguay. The second is the importance to my study of the data provided by the 1981 Indian census of Paraguay (INDI 1982), which offer the opportunity to present a quantitative background to what is essentially an impressionistic account.

Fieldwork

Most of the fieldwork on which this study is based took place between 1975 and 1983. It was never entirely satisfactory as anthropological fieldwork. Indeed, it has taken me the best part of twenty years to come to terms with the sense of personal failure that I felt at never having spent a long period of time in any one community or having mastered any of the Chaco languages. I speak Spanish and Guaraní and eventually worked with a number of communities and ethnic groups, which has at least provided me with a useful overview of the region, but I have always felt that there are critical areas of cultural knowledge that remain outside the scope of my understanding.

Introduction

In retrospect, I can now appreciate that my failure reflected the real difficulties of working in the Chaco as much as any personal failings. The problem was not one of physical hardship or isolation, but rather the fact that at the time I started my fieldwork there were virtually no independent communities in the Chaco. Almost every community either belonged to a rancher or a missionary organization, or was controlled by a military garrison, and it was impossible to work as an anthropologist without the formal approval of the landowner, the missionaries, or the military authorities. As I shall explain, my initial experiences in Paraguay, my loyalties, and my sense of personal integrity made it very difficult for me to maintain good relations with the missionary organizations, the Mennonites, or the large landowners in the Chaco.

I first arrived in Paraguay in 1975. I had spent a few months traveling in South America, learning Spanish and looking for possible areas to carry out later fieldwork. I was interested in working with a development project and felt the need for a practical commitment that went beyond the simple collection of ethnographic information. Barbara Bentley at Survival International had suggested that I contact the Marandú Project. When I arrived in Asunción, I called on Miguel Chase Sardi, the project director, who invited me to join the Marandú team for a course they were giving in Puerto Casado in the Alto Paraguay. The Marandú courses were week- or two-week-long field trips designed to exchange information between an indigenous community and the Marandú team. The courses included surveys, household interviews, and group discussions, as well as lectures, film shows, and formal meetings that were usually held during the evenings.

Marandú was an innovative, participatory project, born in the spirit of optimism that characterized the early 1970s. It was supported by the Inter-American Foundation and was probably one of the foundation's first grassroots development projects. The stated aim of the Marandú Project was to provide Indian leaders and their communities with information about their legal rights. The reality of the project went beyond this, to helping the indigenous communities achieve an understanding of their situation and thus establish their own priorities and develop solutions to the problems that affected them. The philosophy of the project undoubtedly owed much to Paulo Freire's (1970, 1973) ideas of critical consciousness, but it was explicitly founded on Chase Sardi's concept of *autogestión,* probably best translated as "self-determination," which emphasized the right of indigenous cultures to choose and take responsibility for their own development.

This was a radical departure from the ongoing debate on whether indigenous peoples should be protected to preserve their culture or encouraged to integrate into the national society. Instead, the Marandú Project tried to present a culturally appropriate path to development and emphasized the need for indigenous people to understand their situation and to develop the capacity to resolve the issues that affected them. It did not offer any solutions to problems involving land, employment, health, or education, and it was often criticized for its lack of attention to the Indians' immediate needs. Rather the project sought—and in the Chaco I believe it was remarkably successful in achieving this aim— to transform indigenous people's self-perception and to convince them that they had the inherent capacity to improve their situation. The rhetoric was reinforced by the structure of the project. Not only did indigenous people work on the project team on equal terms with the non-Indian technical staff, but the management of the project was handed over to a council of Indian leaders (Consejo Indígena del Paraguay) that later developed into the Paraguayan Indian Association (Asociación de Parcialidades Indígenas—API). Today API has become the national association that formally represents the indigenous people of Paraguay.

In August 1975 I spent two weeks in Puerto Casado with the Marandú team, working as a photographer and carrying out a simple survey of the families living around the Salesian mission.[9] The experience provided me with an introduction to the world of indigenous wage laborers, second-class citizens who provided cheap labor for Carlos Casado SA's tannin factory, logging camps, and ranches. Most of the Indians were paid half wages, as if they were minors, and the payment often took the form of *vales,* credit notes that had to be exchanged at the company store for poor quality goods provided at exorbitant prices. The Indians were caught between the Casado company and the Salesian mission. The mission was the only place where Indians were allowed to live, and the missionaries ran a school, an orphanage, a clinic, and a carpenter's shop that specialized in the production of coffins. They demanded, and usually received, almost total obedience. They taught the Indians that their culture was backward, and strictly prohibited any form of cultural expression, shamanism, singing, or what they referred to as "savage dancing."

The impact of the Marandú Project was dramatic. I can remember Chase Sardi standing in a packed hall before a mixed audience of Indians and Paraguayans, explaining that there are no superior and no inferior races and that the Indians of the Chaco are just as capable as any other race. We showed films about indigenous culture and asked about the Indians' situation, their hopes and aspirations. We listened late into the night as the Indians debated. They talked about labor issues, the company store, alcoholism, tuberculosis, education, and their hopes of one day having land of their own. Toward the end of the course, the Casado company and the missionaries were drawn into the discussion. There was a sense of expectation, and talk that the company would be willing to sell a large area of land for the Indians. Even the missionaries seemed to show some willingness to rethink their attitudes to indigenous culture.

From Puerto Casado we made a brief trip to the Colonia Maria Auxiliadora. This was a Salesian mission for the Ayoreo, who at that time were still effectively cut off from contact with outside influences. We spent one evening under the stars, listening as Eroi, leader of the Garaigosode, performed a shamanic séance. I was enthralled and decided I wanted to work among the Ayoreo. In September I returned to England to start a postgraduate course at the LSE.

The great failing of the Marandú Project was the team's inability to fully comprehend the political power of the different interest groups that were involved with Paraguay's indigenous peoples. Rather than building alliances, the project began to alienate first the landowners, then the Mennonites, the military, and finally the Catholic Church. This came to a head on December 1, 1975, when the police raided the offices of the Marandú Project at the Catholic University of Asunción. Miguel Chase Sardi, Marilyn Rehnfeldt, and two of their colleagues were arrested, accused of being subversives, and held incommunicado and tortured. Chase Sardi was held until July 1976, and was only released as the result of a campaign organized by the Inter-American Foundation, Survival International, and Amnesty International, among others. By the time I returned to Paraguay, in December 1976, the project had left the Catholic University and had asked the Inter-American Foundation to support an ambitious, but in many ways more conventional, project involving land acquisition, economic development, and rural credit.

In the meantime I had spent a few weeks with the Ayoreo in Bolivia. At one time I thought I might not be able to return to Paraguay, and I looked on eastern Bolivia as a possible alternative. I visited the headquarters of the New Tribes Mission in Cochabamba, where I managed to copy the mission's "Ayoreo Pedagogical Grammar," and then traveled to Puesto Paz, in the department of Santa Cruz, where I stayed as a guest of the missionary, Paul Wyma, and his family. The Wymas were friendly and made every effort to help me. I copied all the information they had on the Ayoreo language, and I went through Paul Wyma's ethnographic notes. I felt ill at ease, however. Other anthropologists had visited Puesto Paz (Bórmida and Califano had carried out much of their research there), but none had stayed more than a few days. I felt I was imposing on the Wymas' hospitality, and the idea of living with the Ayoreo in the missionary's backyard hardly seemed a realistic alternative. I took the train to Puerto Suarez, crossed into Brazil, and took the bus to Asunción.

My intention was to return to the Colonia Maria Auxiliadora and work there until I had a good command of the Ayoreo language. In fact, I spent over two months in Asunción, trying to convince the bishop of the Alto Paraguay, Monseñor Alejo Obelar, to allow me to visit the mission. He was unwilling to give me permission because of my association with the Marandú Project, but eventually he relented, on condition that I not discuss the mission's cattle-raising project, which was financed by the Catholic agency Misereor.

In February 1977 I finally arrived back in Maria Auxiliadora and was lodged in the mission guesthouse. I spent about six weeks there, working with a paid informant, Santiago Pucherai, and Lázaro (Ajñui) — an old shaman who had a scar in the shape of a half-moon burned into his chest — recording myths and above all trying to learn the Ayoreo language.

I felt dissatisfied at the mission. It was a difficult moment for the Ayoreo. Eroi had been forced out a few months before, and the Ayoreo, under the leadership of Amadeo (Ijiñoi), had accepted a mass conversion to Christianity and were consciously rejecting much of their traditional culture. Padre Luis, the priest in charge of the mission, showed little interest in either the Ayoreo or their culture. He insisted that they attend mass if they wanted to receive their weekly wages and rations, and spent most of the service berating them for their laziness. I wanted to have a more direct, day-to-day contact with the Ayoreo, and I hired Santiago, Amadeo, and two of their close relatives to help me build a house in the Ayoreo village, which was about half a mile from the mission compound. We spent a couple of weeks cutting caranday palms, splitting the trunks, and hollowing them out for the roof, and were nearly ready to put the house up. I am not sure whether this house building was the cause, but one evening when I returned to the mission I was handed a letter from Padre Luis telling me that I had to leave Maria Auxiliadora on the next available boat.

I returned to Asunción and spent a month with API, just as the new project was getting underway. I also went to Filadelfia to discuss how the project would coordinate with the Asociación de Servicios de Cooperación Indígena y Mennonita (ASCIM), the Mennonite organization that works with indigenous peoples. I mentioned my interest in working with the Ayoreo, but saw little real possibility that I would be able to coordinate with either the Mennonites or the New Tribes Mission.

In the middle of May, I flew back to Maria Auxiliadora. The bishop was there and refused to let me stay in the mission, apparently because I had told a visiting priest that I did not think the cattle-raising project was of much interest to the Ayoreo. The bishop did, however, give me permission to go on to Fuerte Olimpo to work with the Chamococo, who I think he felt were already a lost cause. I loaded my things on the *Olimpeña,* the riverboat that plied a weekly service between Concepción and Fuerte Olimpo, and late the following evening arrived to find Fuerte Olimpo ablaze with colored lights for the *fiesta patronal,* the town's patron saint's day.

I enjoyed Fuerte Olimpo and the *fiesta patronal* but had difficulties with Sister Angela, the elderly Uruguayan nun who ran the mission. A year or two before I arrived, a few rebellious Chamococo families had abandoned the mission and were living in Cerro Kupé, a piece of waste ground belonging to the municipality, situated on the margin of the town beyond the brothel and the town cemetery. When I arrived in

Olimpo, the sister gave me permission to carry out a survey among the Chamococo on the condition that she accompany me at all times. For three days, covering part of the mission, we visited house to house, collecting information on household composition, work, and income. We then moved on to Cerro Kupé, where we were received reasonably well, even though—or perhaps because—the missionaries had put around a rumor that I was a communist. By the third day the sister and I were almost friends.

One afternoon I returned to the mission after the siesta and found that Sister Angela was nowhere to be seen. I asked the teacher at the mission school if she had seen her. "Don't worry," she said. "She probably won't come here this afternoon. We know you by now, go ahead, carry on with your work." I visited a couple more houses and then found myself in a house on the edge of the mission. The woman I was interviewing began her story: "That nun is really unpleasant. She stole three goats from me . . ." Without thinking, I automatically continued taking notes as I had for the previous few days, writing, "Señora D—— . . . says the nun is unpleasant and that she stole three goats." It transpired that the missionaries had given three goats to every family in the mission, with the idea that the Chamococo would breed them to provide meat and some cash income. But this particular woman had nothing to eat, so she slaughtered one of the goats. When the sister found out, she was furious. She stormed into the house, took away the two remaining goats, and sold the meat of the goat that had been slaughtered, leaving the woman with only the head.

As darkness was falling, I came back past the mission school. The sister was standing there with her arms folded, waiting for me. "Where do you think you have been? Don't you know that you can only come to the mission if I'm here?" "I'm sorry," I replied. "The teacher said it would be all right. You know what I have been doing by now. If you really want to, you can look at my notes." I handed her my notebook, and only then realized I had made a mistake. She went through the book page by page and then started to shake. She turned. "Señor Anthropologist," she said, "there are two things you should know. First, the Chamococo are lazy and never want to work. Second, they are inveterate liars." She then pulled the pages from the notebook, tore them up, and threw the pieces on the ground. From then on, she never accompanied me again, although I continued to visit the mission whenever I needed to.

I spent the remainder of 1977 and part of 1978 working in the Alto Paraguay, making regular trips back to Asunción for the meetings of API. I divided my time between Bahía Negra, Fuerte Olimpo, and later Buena Vista, a colony that API established thirty kilometers (eighteen miles) inland from Fuerte Olimpo. Bahía Negra is a naval garrison town, and my activities there were closely scrutinized by the military police. I managed to maintain reasonable relations with the navy but had to live in Bahía Negra itself, rather than in Puerto Diana, the Chamococo settlement, which is located about a mile to the south of the town. Puerto Diana was titled to the New Tribes Mission, but the missionaries, two elderly ladies, no longer lived there, and I saw very little of them. Indeed, the only formal permission I needed to work there was provided by Petty Officer Cleto López, a Chamococo veteran of the Chaco War, who had been given authority over the community by the navy (see chapter 7).

I still had hopes of working with the Ayoreo. In July 1977 I managed to make a brief visit to a small, isolated group of Ayoreo who were living in Potrero Para Todo, about seventy miles inland from Bahía Negra. I tried to return in October 1977, just as the summer rains were starting, but was unable to get back to the site. Finally, in May and June 1978 my wife and I spent a few weeks in the Mennonite Colonies, visiting some of the Ayoreo from the Colonia Maria Auxiliadora who were living and working on Mennonite farms.

From July to September 1978 we worked on an evaluation of API for the Inter-American Foundation. This work took me all over the Chaco, as well as to parts of Eastern Paraguay, and helped focus my attention on some of the themes considered in this study.

We then left for England, where I spent a year organizing the material I had collected and trying to draft my thesis. We returned to Paraguay in 1979, and I worked for few months on the evaluation of a program for small farmers in the departments of Guairá and Caazapá, in Eastern Paraguay.

In 1980 Colonel Oscar Centurion, director of the Instituto Nacional del Indígena (National Indian Institute—INDI), which was then still a dependency of the Ministry of Defense, offered me a position as consultant anthropologist. In retrospect, this was a wonderful opportunity to understand the inner workings of the Paraguayan government, even though I was paid only a minimal salary. At least I did not have to join the Colorado Party, which created confusion, however, since Colorado Party affiliation was obligatory for Paraguayan civil servants. At one point General Marcial Samaniego, the minister of defense, who had occupied the post for thirty years, demanded that the colonel who was the ministry's chief of personnel prepare my nomination as a full-time employee. The colonel took me aside. "Your papers," he said, "let me see your papers." "I only have my *cédula* [identity card], *mi Coronel*," I replied. He took my identity card and shook his head. "Born on the 18th of October [the day of the opposition Liberal Party]. Blue eyes [blue is the color of the Liberal Party]. No. You must be a communist." I never did get a formal contract with the ministry, and I had to be paid out of petty cash—nominally for renting a house "to be used as a lodging for Indians."

At INDI I was engaged in the preparation of various projects and was marginally involved in drafting the law on indigenous peoples (Law 904/ 81). Looking back, I feel I should have paid more attention to this law, but at the time I thought it was unlikely to have a significant impact. In this I was completely mistaken, and the law, for better or worse, has come to dominate every issue affecting indigenous people in Paraguay.

Over the next two years one project, the national Indian census, began to occupy most of my time. The census was carried out in collaboration with the census office (Dirección General de Estadística y Censos) and was supported by the United Nations Fund for Population Activities (UNFPA). I was initially responsible for supervising the Chaco and was involved in the preliminary phases: defining the concepts, designing and testing the questionnaire, coordinating the institutions that took part, and training the supervisors and enumerators.

In the last months of 1980 we were confronted with a major crisis. INDI had been supporting the expropriation of ten thousand hectares in Fortín Casanillo to be given to the Toba-Maskoy Indians who were living in the "worker villages" of Loma Plata. The land belonged to the Casado company, which was still powerful, but President Alfredo Stroessner had signed the decree for the expropriation, which, if it had gone ahead, would have been the first expropriation for an indigenous community in the Chaco. Colonel Centurion was at the gate of the ranch with the Toba-Maskoy, waiting for a justice of the peace to allow them onto the property, when the procedure was suddenly overturned. Apparently, the Casado family had managed to convince three of Paraguay's most influential military commanders that the expropriation was a communist plot, and they in turn persuaded Stroessner to rescind the order. The Toba-Maskoy were loaded onto military trucks and taken north, where they were left by the roadside in what later came to be known as the Colonia Santo Domingo (see chapter 1). Colonel Centurion was forced to take early retirement and was replaced by a colonel from Military Intelligence who had little or no sympathy for indigenous peoples.

I was about to resign from INDI, but colleagues in the census office convinced me to keep the Indian census alive. One of my colleagues from INDI, Graciela Ocariz, persuaded the minister of defense to allow us to set up an office for the Indian census in the Ministry of Defense, and once we had the general's support, the census went ahead. We divided the Chaco into different regions to be supervised by local indigenous leaders or missionary organizations. The census was designed to enumerate the Indians in their place of habitual residence, since the logistics would have made it impossible to carry out the census in only one or two days. We started by holding a course for the supervisors and enumerators from the Alto Paraguay, the Lower Chaco, and the High Chaco, and then worked together in the Colonia Mak'a, across the river from the Botanical Gardens.

In the Alto Paraguay the census was supervised by Bruno Barra, a Chamococo from Puerto Diana, working with enumerators from Diana, Olimpo, and Puerto Casado. At one point, Bruno and Guillermo Mallero had to walk in to the logging camps of the Casado company in Toro Pampa, a distance of over a hundred miles. There they made contact with the Tomaraha Chamococo, who had split from the Ebidoso over a century before. Later, after the census, the Tomaraha left the Casado logging camps and settled with the Ebidoso in the communities of Puerto Esperanza and Potrerito (see chapter 1).

In the Lower Chaco, Damian García and Marcelino Coronel carried out the census in their own community of Cerrito and then spent three weeks on horseback visiting the ranches up to the Montelindo River. They found over five hundred people, mostly Lengua, living dispersed throughout the area. Many of these families later settled with the Toba in San José and now have land of their own in La Esperanza (Angulo-kué).

The High Chaco was covered by Severo Flores, a Guaraní who at the time was president of API, and Pablo Flores, a Nivaclé, who had earlier worked with the Marandú Project. They started in Mariscal Estigarribia, then covered the Manjuy of Santa Rosa, the settlements in Pedro P. Peña, and the Guaraní communities situated up to the Bolivian frontier.

Alejandro López, a Nivaclé who had previously been the treasurer of API, supervised the Middle Pilcomayo, working with a team of enumerators from Pablo Stahl (Misión Esteros). Before the enumeration took place, Alejandro spent a few weeks exploring the ranches along the road from Chaco-í to Esteban Martínez, but did not find any Indians in the area. It is an area that may once have been inhabited by the Mak'a, but I suspect they were forced out after the Chaco War.

The Anglican missionaries supervised their own area of influence. José Cattaneo from the census department trained the Indian enumerators from the Anglican Mission, and then drove with them to all the ranches that were accessible from the Trans-Chaco Highway and the road from Pozo Colorado to Concepción. The Indian enumerators then traveled on horseback to the more remote ranches. The New Tribes missionaries carried out the enumeration of Riacho San Carlos, and the ranches between San Carlos and the southern boundary of the Casado company's property.

Wilmar Stahl, of ASCIM, supervised the census in the area of the Mennonite Colonies. Most of the enumerators were teachers and community leaders who had an intimate knowledge of the communities they were working in. Wilmar later carried out a detailed evaluation of the census results. He concluded that the census coverage in the agricultural colonies of the Central Chaco was reasonably accurate, with a 5–7 percent margin of error, due principally to the unwillingness of some families to declare the very young children of unmarried mothers.

The enumeration was virtually completed by May 1981, but there were one or two gaps, particularly in the area around the Mennonite Colonies. In the following weeks I worked with a team of enumerators, covering the Colonia Santo Domingo, Diez Leguas, and the ranches to the northeast of 25 Leguas. Once the enumeration was finished, I continued as adviser to the project, evaluating the results, designing the tables, and writing up part of the final report (INDI 1982). During 1982 I also worked as the regional supervisor of the Chaco for the Paraguayan national census.

Later in 1982 and 1983 I worked on the preparation of a rural development project for two localities in the northwest Chaco. The work was carried out for INDI and was financed by the Inter-American Indigenist Institute. I spent about three months in the field, dividing the time between the Nivaclé settlement of Mistolar and Pedro P. Peña, where I worked with the Nivaclé, the Manjuy, and the Guaraní Occidentales.

Although this fieldwork was relatively brief—and for my work with the Nivaclé and Manjuy I relied on an interpreter—the study was of great value in helping determine the content of my doctoral thesis. I spent much of the time working on genealogies and personal life histories, trying to build up a picture of the dynamics of the residential groups and factions, and I amassed a lot of the data on Nivaclé social organization that appear in the following chapters.

In Mistolar I stayed with Siriaco Pérez and his family—Siriaco was the leader of the community (see chapter 7)—and I was accompanied by Cirilo Pinto, an old friend from Filadelfia, who worked as my assistant and interpreter. There were no outsiders in any position of power, only two young Mormon missionaries who did not speak any Spanish and only appeared in the church on Sundays. It was early summer, and the community was enjoying the pleasant climate and an abundance of food. Visiting from house to house, Cirilo and I would be offered *tereré* (yerba maté with cold water) and something to eat: roast corn, squash, sweet potatoes, or fish. By midday we had usually worked our way back to Siriaco's house, and would find him waiting with smoked fish, bread, or cheese, which the *criollo* neighbors would exchange for yerba. This was an appetizer, and a little while later his wife would appear and ask us to come for lunch, a stew or a *locro,* with rice and lots of squash or sweet potatoes. Siriaco would say that he wanted me to "fatten up" while I was in Mistolar. My own supplies were soon used up, and to help out, Cirilo and I spent nights fishing in the Pilcomayo, and on the weekends we went hunting for charata, ducks, and rabbits around the lakes and *cañadas* near the village.

24

Pedro P. Peña was a bit more difficult. It is a dispersed settlement, strung out over twenty miles along the Pilcomayo. More or less in the middle were an army barracks; a mission, run by the Oblates of Maria; and the Government Delegation (Delegación de Gobierno) for the department of Boquerón, which was essentially a police garrison. There was also a small, poorly stocked store, owned by a Bolivian, which would regularly run out of the items most in demand: yerba maté, *caña*—indeed any kind of alcohol—and cigarettes.

When I arrived in Pedro P. Peña, I intended to set up in an abandoned cooperative store near the center of the settlement. However, the government delegate and the police chief, Pedro Ignacio Moran, insisted that we stay in the delegation, and I eventually relented. They were very hospitable, and we ate well, drank a lot, and spent the evenings listening to one of the conscripts playing the guitar and discussing geopolitics. The delegate and his police chief were enthusiastic supporters of Adolf Hitler, and we emptied many bottles of whisky, Aristócrata, and Argentine gin arguing about fascism and the Second World War. Cirilo Pinto was working with me, and during the day we would walk to the Nivaclé and Manjuy settlements, first to the nearby settlement in Campamento, and then to Loma Alegre, about ten miles downriver. Later Cirilo took advantage of a visit from the bishop of the Chaco and drove back with him to Filadelfia. I stayed on and visited the Guaraní settlements, most of which were situated upriver opposite the Argentine Mataco community of La Paz.

In June 1983 I returned to England and started to write my doctoral thesis. In August that year General Samaniego was removed from the Ministry of Defense, and the presidency of INDI was handed over to General Germán Martínez. Since then the institution has had its ups and downs, but it has never functioned efficiently, despite the personal commitment of some of the institute's staff, who have had to put up with low wages, little or no resources, and endless criticism from NGOs and the press.

In recent years I have made a few brief trips back to the Chaco. The last was in 1995, when I was helping to prepare a rural investment project for the World Bank. I visited Filadelfia, where I stayed in the Barrio Obrero with Cirilo Pinto. The Barrio Obrero is less strictly controlled by the

Mennonites than it used to be, and the fiestas on Friday and Saturday nights have become a magnet for all kinds of undesirables. There are German fugitives and Bolivian smugglers, Ayoreo girls in hot pants and Guaraní conscript soldiers, Lengua ranch hands with cowboy hats and dark glasses, and effeminate Mennonite boys with Mohican hairstyles and studs in their ears. The loudspeakers in the bars drown out the conversation—heavy metal competes with *chamamé*—and the beer flows. At the time, a Canadian brand was in vogue, since the cans were Liberal blue. At about four in the morning, the police came around in a pickup truck and threw some of the drunks in the back. One tried to slip out, got caught by his shirt, and, to everybody's amusement, was dragged for about a hundred yards before the truck stopped again. He picked himself up, shook off the dirt, and staggered off into the darkness. By normal standards, though, it was a quiet night, and unlike the previous week—when an Argentine *criollo* had killed a Paraguayan—no one was shot, stabbed, or seriously wounded.

From Filadelfia I traveled to the Angaité community of La Patria, where Marcelino Coronel, a Toba from Cerrito, is director of the school. La Patria, one the colonies acquired by the Anglican Church as part of the La Herencia project, comprises nine small villages, scattered across 30,000 hectares (75,000 acres). It is probably fairly typical of the Indian colonies that have been established in the Lower Chaco. The Indians have land of their own, but since the Anglicans withdrew from the community, they have received virtually no support from outside and endure subsistence-level poverty, combining minor agriculture with hunting, the sale of fence posts, and sporadic wage labor on the neighboring ranches. The Angaité seemed embittered. They had expected that their lives would improve when they were given land of their own. But isolation, lack of any real economic opportunities, and bad luck—they lost most of their cattle in an epidemic of bovine rabies—had left them with little or no income, and they often went hungry during the winter months.

The last trip I made was to Karcha Bahlut (Puerto 14 de Mayo), a Chamococo settlement on the Paraguay River between Bahía Negra and Fuerte Olimpo, which had been reoccupied only a few years before (it had been a ranch when I worked in the Alto Paraguay). I flew to Bahía

Negra with Bruno Barra—Bruno carrying a twenty-liter can of gasoline as hand luggage. A group of men from the community were waiting for us, but without the outboard motor, and from Bahía Negra we rowed down through vast, silent lagoons full of water hyacinth, avoiding the main channel of the Paraguay River. It was winter, and the river was in flood. Puerto 14 is one of the most important landmarks in Chamococo topography. It is the site where the *Anabsonro*—the mythical beings who taught the Chamococo how to initiate their young men—first came out of the earth, and where the Chamococo fought the Caduveo for control of the riverbank. It is really an island, built up on shell middens, and is the only place on the river that always remains above flood level. I spent a few days there, enjoying the warmth of the afternoon sun, drinking *tereré*, and talking with old friends and with a new generation that had grown up since I worked in Bahía Negra.

The Chamococo no longer worked on the ranches. When the Paraguay River was low, they could make good money fishing with drift nets, and the men had also learned to make beautiful, lifelike carvings of animals and birds from *palo santo*, "holy wood." We lived on a diet of capybara. I had brought a bag full of provisions and hung it from the beams of the house, but the dogs managed to reach it, tore it open, and ate everything, including two large bars of soap. At night the men would slip away quietly in their canoes to hunt by flashlight. There was no firm ground anywhere along the riverbank, and the capybara would come out onto the beds of floating reeds, where they could be easily shot. I walked to Potrerito, and made a quick trip to Puerto Esperanza, where I met many old friends from my days in Olimpo and Buena Vista.

Finally, I took a riverboat, the *Reina Isabel*, back to Vallemí. The trip was the same as always. The passengers were crowded onto the decks, between stacks of merchandise, crates of empty bottles, rolls of wire, and bundles of hides. We stopped at every ranch and port. At some places the women and children came on board to buy supplies: a few kilos of rice and flour, a liter or two of oil. At others a ranch owner would come aboard to unload a generator or some other piece of machinery. We passed two new floating hotels for eco-tourists on the Brazilian side of the river, but our Paraguayan crew was less ecologically minded and stopped to take shots with a .22 rifle at every capybara we passed. At

Puerto Mihanovich we waited while two Indian peons loaded a couple of hundred quebracho fence posts. The sun set over the river, and I lay back in a borrowed hammock. We stopped briefly at Olimpo and Maria Auxiliadora during the night. By mid-morning we reached Vallemí. I took the first plane and by early afternoon was back in Asunción, in the world of deadlines and appointments.

Literature on the Chaco

Throughout this study I have relied as far as possible on my own notes and observations, and I have tried to avoid undue reference to the fairly extensive literature on the Chaco. Some of this literature is, I feel, of rather doubtful value, since it tends to be based on the transcripts of interviews with selected, often aged informants whose observations, on what are at times rather general themes, seem to express ideals rather than historical fact. They often give what may be a false impression of the "traditional" culture of the Chaco societies. Two studies—both dating from the beginning of the twentieth century—do provide a useful historical perspective and a wealth of ethnographic detail and are referred to throughout this study. The first is W. Barbrooke Grubb's *An Unknown People in an Unknown Land* (1911) and the second a work by Erland Nordenskiöld that was published in French as *La vie des Indiens dans le Chaco* (1912).

W. Barbrooke Grubb, founder of the mission of Makthlawaiya, was the first Anglican missionary to work in the Chaco, and his books, of which *An Unknown People* is the most comprehensive, reflect the experiences of almost thirty years of living and working among the Lengua. Although his Victorian attitudes are often rather irritating, Grubb's ethnographic observations are detailed and accurate and provide what is probably the most reliable historical source on any of the societies of the Lower Chaco.

Nordenskiöld's work, originally published a year before Grubb's, belongs to a more modern genre and is essentially an ethnography of the Indians of the Upper Pilcomayo and the sub-Andean region of Bolivia. Nordenskiöld provides a description of the Guaraní and the Indians from various Chaco societies who were working in the cane fields and sugar mill at La Esperanza, Argentina. In 1908 and 1909 he traveled down the Pilcomayo from Fortín Guachalla (Pedro P. Peña) to the area of

Estero Patiño. His study contains a wealth of historical and ethnographic detail on the Mataco, Choroti, and Nivaclé (Ashluslay) and has been an important source of information for later writers, including Alfred Metraux, whose "Ethnography of the Chaco" (1963) is the most comprehensive account of the Chaco societies to have been published.

Two other writers, whose works have been published since I wrote my thesis, also deserve to be mentioned. Elmer Miller's *Nurturing Doubt* (1995) is an intimate personal account of his intellectual development and fieldwork among the Argentine Toba and brings into question the validity of the ethnographic enterprise. It is not, however, intended as a description of the Toba. I had read Miller's 1967 doctoral thesis while I was living in Paraguay but did not consciously refer to it, even though in retrospect it certainly helped inform my understanding of social change and religious conversion among the Chaco societies. Miller takes a phenomenological approach and argues that indigenous peoples' understanding of the national society is mediated by their own cultural perceptions and categories. With religious conversion, for example, rather than one belief system replacing another, the process can best be described as one in which a new system of values is comprehended through the conceptual categories of the old.

The other study is Jan-Åke Alvarsson's *The Mataco of the Gran Chaco* (1988), which is the only modern ethnography of a Chaco society to have been published in English.[10] It is not particularly light reading, but in a number of areas the conclusions support the hypotheses put forward in this study. Alvarsson's description of Mataco social and territorial organization is similar to the model I propose in chapter 6, and his observations on the Mataco economic system parallel many of the ideas put forward in chapter 5.

CHAPTER ONE

The Environment and Population
of the Paraguayan Chaco

T HE CHACO, the area of Paraguayan territory that lies to the west of the Paraguay River, constitutes 60 percent of the land surface of Paraguay, but owing to a combination of historical and environmental factors, it has always been the most marginal region of the country (see map 1). The present population of the Chaco—a total of around a hundred thousand people, including Indians, Mennonites, and ethnic Paraguayans—represents less than 3 percent of Paraguay's population, and in none of the region's departments does the density of population reach one person per square kilometer (DGEC 1992).[1]

Until the end of the nineteenth century, when the sale of state lands and the pioneering activities of the Anglican missionaries opened the Lower Chaco to international ranching and lumber companies, the only Paraguayan settlements were found on the western bank of the Paraguay River. The forest and swamps of the interior remained unexplored owing to the lack of any economic incentives and the hostility of the Indians. Since independence, Paraguay has disputed sovereignty of the region, first with Argentina and then with Bolivia. It was not until 1938 that the frontier with Bolivia was finally delimited, bringing to an end a conflict that, during the years of the Chaco War (1932–35), had cost an estimated seventy thousand lives. Even today, despite the improvements that have been made to the region's infrastructure, most of the population is to be found in the Mennonite Colonies of the Central Chaco and in the area immediately opposite Asunción.

The Environment

The Chaco is a great alluvial plain that stretches from the Paraguay-Paraná River in the east to the foothills of the Andes in the west. Geologically it is a uniform area, comprising silt deposits of immense thickness, built up on the bed of an ancient lake that once divided the Andes from the Brazilian Shield. In one or two places, isolated summits such as Cerro León and Cerro Chovoreca rise above the surrounding area, but for the most part the Chaco is almost completely flat, rising only a couple of hundred meters as one goes from southeast to northwest. In the north, the Bolivian Chaco reaches to the foot of the escarpment of the Cordillera de Santiago, where the arid plains and stunted bushes typical of the far north of the region are replaced by a higher, denser vegetation more akin to that of the tropical forest. In the south, the Chaco extends well beyond the Pilcomayo, and the palm swamps and islands of forest characteristic of the Lower Chaco only begin to give way to the open grasslands of the Pampas at around twenty-seven degrees south.

Lying on the Tropic of Capricorn, at no point less than six hundred miles from the ocean, the Chaco has a tropical continental climate, characterized by extremes of temperature and rainfall. Average annual temperatures are around 25 degrees Centigrade (78 degrees Fahrenheit), but both the seasonal and diurnal variations are marked. In the Central Chaco summer temperatures are often over 40 degrees Centigrade (105 degrees Fahrenheit), while in June and July the temperature can fall below freezing. Weather stations in Mariscal Estigarribia and Fortín Pratt Gill, in the center and northwest of the Paraguayan Chaco, have recorded summer temperatures of up to 46 degrees Centigrade (113 degrees Fahrenheit), while in winter these same stations have recorded temperatures as low as minus 7 (19 degrees Fahrenheit). The diurnal range of temperature can be as much as 20 degrees Centigrade (68 degrees Fahrenheit) and can fall this much in a few minutes with the appearance of a cold front driving up, unbroken by any natural obstacles, from as far south as Patagonia. At any time of the year a south wind can bring violent storms, followed by overcast, often bitterly cold days and nights. The hot dry weather in the Chaco is frequently accompanied by a strong north wind that dries up the landscape and raises the dust in clouds.

The rainfall in the Chaco is relatively low, sporadic, and often localized. In the southeast, close to the Paraguay River, the average annual rainfall reaches 1,300 millimeters (50 inches), but this decreases as one moves northwest. In the Central Chaco the average annual rainfall is

Map 1. The Paraguayan Chaco: Settlement and communication

BOLIVIA

BRAZIL

ARGENTINA

Cerro Chovoreca

Lagerenza

Río Timanes

Cerro Leon

Bahía Negra

Gral. E. A. Garay

Nueva Asuncion

Fuerte Olimpo

Mortinho

Vallemí

Mcal. Estigarribia

Loma Plata

Río Apa

Filadelfia

Pto. Casado

edro P. Peña

Pto. Pinasco

Río Paraguay

Neuland

Río Pilcomayo

Paratodo

Río Verde

Campo Aceval

Pozo Colorado

Concepcíon

Gral. Díaz

Río Siete Puntas

Río Montelindo

S. Pedro

Esteban Martínez

Río Negro

Rosario

Riacho He'é

Río Pilcomayo

Río Confuso

B. Aceval

Villa Hayes

Chaco-í

Asunción

tarmac
dirt roads
railways
frontiers
rivers
watercourses
swamps
mountains

around 700 millimeters (28 inches), and in the far northwest, on the frontier with Bolivia, it is only 350 millimeters (14 inches). There is a fairly well marked rainy season, but it begins at different times in different parts of the Chaco, and its onset can vary considerably from year to year. Typically, in the southeast the rains begin in September, but farther to the north and west they come rather later. In the Alto Paraguay the first heavy rains usually fall in October, and on the Upper Pilcomayo, even though some rain may fall in October, the rainy season rarely begins before the beginning of December. During the beginning of the wet season the rainfall can be very heavy, with up to 100 millimeters (4 inches) falling in a single day.

The rains mark the onset of the summer, a period of heat and high humidity when the dormant vegetation springs to life. The forest hums with insects: mosquitoes, horseflies, and the tiny *polverín,* a sand fly so small that its swarms resemble clouds of smoke hanging above the pools of water that form on the forest floor. In the following months the rains gradually decrease. By March, although banks of cloud build up on the horizon and the humidity remains high, the rainfall is much less and is localized—often nothing more than a brief shower that brings a respite from the heat and helps to settle the dust. By April or May the temperatures begin to drop and the nights are cooler. From now on, the only rain that falls, apart from the occasional thunderstorm, is brought by the south wind. Once an initial storm has passed, the cold weather can last for up to two or three weeks. The sky remains gray and overcast, the temperature below 10 degrees Centigrade (50 degrees Fahrenheit), and although the rainfall is light there is often a mist or continuous drizzle.

By the end of May the dry season has begun. Most of the trees have shed their leaves, and the grasslands are parched. By July they are as dry as tinder, and fires start spontaneously. Fanned by the driving north wind, flames may set large areas ablaze; in the daytime palls of thick black smoke rise in the distance, and at night the horizon is illuminated by the glow from the burning grasslands.

The sporadic rainfall and the flatness of the region combine to give the Chaco little permanent drainage. The Pilcomayo is the only river to cross the Paraguayan Chaco, carrying the runoff water from the eastern slopes of the Andes; the other rivers that rise in the Bolivian Andes, such

34

as the Parapití, run only a short distance into the Chaco before disappearing into swamps or salt lakes. The Pilcomayo is a powerful, dirty-brown, silt-laden river when it emerges from the foothills of the Andes around Villamontes, but it gradually diminishes in volume and eventually loses itself in the immense swamp of Estero Patiño. From here, the floodwater drains into a number of channels: the main ones being the Brazo Norte and the Brazo Sur of the Pilcomayo, which rejoin further downstream before discharging into the Paraguay River opposite Asunción. The floodwater also drains into the Montelindo, the Montelindo-í, and the Río Negro, which flow east and join the Paraguay River well to the north of Asunción. These, and the other permanent rivers of the Lower Chaco, such as the Confuso and Riacho He'e (Aguaray-guazú), follow erratic courses; they twist and turn through a maze of sandbanks, swamps, and lagoons, and after heavy rain they burst their banks, flooding large areas of grassland. In the dry season, when these rivers reach their lowest levels, the flow is hardly perceptible, although in June and July, when the Paraguay River is at its highest levels, their lower reaches may be flooded by water flowing back from the main river.

The other rivers of the Chaco are semipermanent. The Timanes, in the extreme north, carries a considerable volume of water in the rainy season but never reaches the Paraguay River and disappears completely during the winter. In the eastern Chaco, rivers such as the Siete Puntas, Río Verde, and Riacho Gonzalez drain large areas of swampland in the summer, but in the winter they are reduced to little more than pools of stagnant water. Similarly, in the western Chaco the *cañadas,* such as Cañada Mil, Cañada Milico, and Cañada Strongest, are dry for most of the year, except for a few pools where rainwater has collected. The water flows in these channels only after heavy rains, or when the Pilcomayo overflows its main channel during the floods that usually occur in February or March.

The combination of rainfall, drainage, soil types, and minor differences in elevation determines the ecological zones into which the Chaco can be divided. These zones tend to merge into one another, but it is possible to distinguish three major ecotypes, which I shall call the Lower, the Central, and the High Chaco.

The Lower Chaco coincides approximately with the area to the south and east of the 900-millimeter (35-inch) isohyet, a line running roughly from General Díaz in the west to Pozo Colorado, and from there to Bahía Negra in the extreme northeast (see map 2). The region is one of relatively high rainfall and heavy impermeable soils. The vegetation is typically grassland interspersed with stands of *caranday* palms (*Copernicia alba*).[2] Much of this grassland remains under water after a heavy rainfall and in some parts dries out only during the winter months. Scattered throughout the grassland are slightly elevated islands of denser vegetation, or *monte,* that include hardwood trees, some palms and cactus, and often a dense undergrowth of *caraguatá* or *chuza,* both spiny-leafed bromeliads. The soils of the *monte* are generally lighter and more permeable than those of the surrounding grasslands and allow a greater variety of vegetation. The predominant species of trees include the *quebracho colorado* (*Schinopsis balansae*), the *quebracho blanco* (*Aspidosperma quebracho-blanco*), various species of *algarrobo* (including *Prosopis alba* and *P. nigra*), *aromita* (*Acacia sp.*), *guaimí piré* (*Rupretchia triflora*), and *palo blanco* (*Calycophyllum multiflorum*), as well as palms, including the *carandilla* (*Trithninax bizlabellata*) and, in the extreme southeast of the region, *pindó* (*Syagrus romanzoffiana*). Unlike the caranday palm, most of these species are unable to survive prolonged periods of flooding and are restricted to those areas that remain above flood level. Even so, in the last few decades there has been a tendency for the grasslands, particularly in the drier areas, to suffer colonization by thorny trees and bushes such as *viñal* (*Prosopis ruscifolia*) and algarrobo. This may be due to overgrazing and to the custom, common on nearly all the ranches, of burning the pastures in the winter months to promote a new growth of more tender grass.

Moving toward the Central Chaco, the area around the Mennonite Colonies coinciding more or less with the 700-millimeter (28-inch) isohyet, one finds less grassland, and the wet grassland with caranday palms is almost entirely absent. Here the grass grows on light sandy soils left from ancient riverbeds, and *espartilla* grass (*Elyonurus adustus*) predominates under natural conditions. In the Mennonite Colonies most of these areas have been plowed up, since the soils of the *espartillares* are the only ones permeable enough to retain sufficient moisture for crops to be grown.

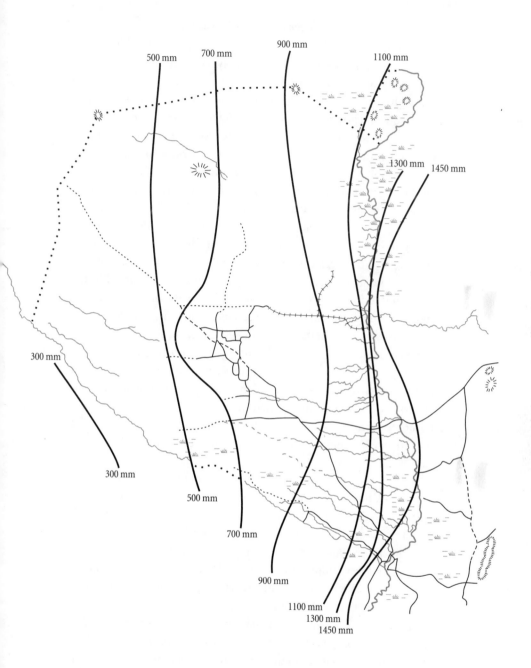

500 mm

700 mm

900 mm

1100 mm

1300 mm

1450 mm

300 mm

300 mm

500 mm

700 mm

900 mm

1100 mm

1300 mm

1450 mm

Map 2. The Paraguayan Chaco: Rainfall

Although the grasslands have been of importance for the development of agriculture in the region, they probably cover only about a quarter of the surface of the Central Chaco. The rest of the area is *monte* similar to the High Chaco. On the more permeable soils one finds large trees, principally quebracho blanco, *coronillo* (*Schinopsis quebracho-colorado*), and *para todo* (*Tabebuia caraiba*), while in the low-lying waterlogged areas the predominant species are *palo santo* (*Bulnesia sarmientoi*), the *samuhú* or bottle tree (*Chorisia insignis*), and a variety of cacti.

The High Chaco is an arid region, much of which has an average annual rainfall of less than 400 millimeters (16 inches). The area is covered in thorny scrub forest, although there are patches of espartilla grass on the lightest soils. The vegetation varies considerably from area to area according to the permeability and the salinity of the soils. The poorest, most saline soils are covered by a dense growth of stunted bushes, sometimes only just over a meter in height, or by salt-resistant plants such as the *sachasandia* (*Capparis salicifolia*) and the *payagua naranja* (*Capparis speciosa*). In the better drained areas, one finds widely spaced stands of large trees, usually coronillo, quebracho blanco, or *guayacán* (*Caesalpina paraquariensis*), often covering a dense undergrowth of spiny bromeliads. In some of the damper areas, most notably in the region of the Upper Pilcomayo, there are also stands of algarrobo, *chañar* (*Geoffroea decorticans*), and *mistol* (*Ziziphus mistol*), fruit-bearing trees that are of considerable importance for the Indians of the region.

The Population and Economy

The population of the Chaco is concentrated in three main areas: the area around the towns of Villa Hayes and Benjamín Aceval in the southeast, the Mennonite Colonies of the Central Chaco, and the industrial and ranching towns of the Alto Paraguay. In the rest of the Chaco the population is very thinly distributed, and to the north of the Mennonite Colonies virtually the only settlements are the military garrisons that guard the frontiers with Bolivia and Argentina.

The area of Villa Hayes and Benjamín Aceval is more akin to the Eastern Region of Paraguay than to the rest of the Chaco. The area is suitable for agriculture, and much of the land is given over to sugarcane, which is processed at a mill in Benjamín Aceval. Since 1979 a bridge over the Paraguay River has linked the area to Asunción. Villa Hayes, which was traditionally an entrepôt for the Chaco, has now become part of the industrial belt of Asunción, and is the site of Paraguay's only steelworks — a project responsible for about half of the country's national debt. The towns of Villa Hayes and Benjamín Aceval are also the main service centers for the southern Chaco and are the focus for transport, commerce, and craft industries, especially leatherworking. Between them, these two towns account for nearly a quarter of the total population of the Chaco.

The two towns serve much of the Lower Chaco. They are linked to the region by two roads. The Trans-Chaco Highway is a paved road that runs northwest from Villa Hayes to Mariscal Estigarribia and then continues as a dirt road to the Bolivian border. The other is the poorly maintained dirt road that runs parallel to the Pilcomayo from Chaco-í to Esteban Martínez. The pastures of this region are some of the finest in the Chaco, and the entire area is given over almost exclusively to extensive cattle ranching. The size of the ranches varies greatly: some of the largest, such as La Concepción and Pozo Azul, cover over 140,000 hectares (345,000 acres), while at the lower end of the scale, usually in the less accessible areas, one can find small ranches of only 1,500 hectares (3,700 acres).

The traditional methods of beef cattle production practiced in the Lower Chaco require relatively little in the way of manpower or investment; most ranches employ only a few hands, and the main expenses are limited to the construction and maintenance of the boundary fences, drinking ponds, and corrals. Whenever extra labor is needed, for branding, vaccinating, or driving the cattle, the ranch owner usually hires extra hands on a temporary basis and pays them a daily rate that varies according to whether or not they bring their own horses. The workers employed for the construction of fencing and for clearing overgrown pasture, the *contratistas,* are also contracted on a daily or piecework basis. The permanent employees, the *estancieros,* live on the ranches, although their families may live in town, but the temporary ranch hands and *contratistas* are brought in from outside. They are usually either Indians from the missions or landless Paraguayans from towns such as Villa Hayes, Benjamín Aceval, and Concepción, or from the precarious settlements strung out along the right-of-way of the Trans-Chaco Highway, such as Río Negro, Montelindo, and Kilometer 190.

The more highly capitalized ranches have invested in improving pastures and have become major employers of casual labor. *Contratistas* are employed to clear the areas that have become overgrown with thorn scrub, and bulldozers are used to clear the stands of caranday palms. This is intended to increase the area available for grazing, because the cattle have difficulty feeding if fallen palm leaves cover the pasture. Once the palms have been cleared, the grasslands are plowed up, and more nutritive pastures such as *pangola* and *estrella* are planted by hand. Although the weight and the quality of beef cattle have probably been improved by the introduction of artificial pastures, it is doubtful, given the present market for beef, whether the returns really justify the expenses involved. At least one of the larger ranching concerns is reputed to have had difficulty repaying the loans, figured in millions of U.S. dollars, which were taken out for improving pastures and stock. Furthermore, there are doubts about the long-term ecological effects of clearing large areas of palm swamp, and many of the larger ranches are having difficulty controlling the growth of viñal and other scrub plants that rapidly colonize the newly plowed areas.

The Central Chaco is the only region where agriculture is practiced on a commercial scale, and here one finds the second major concentration of population. This population is mainly Indian and Mennonite, in about equal proportions, and the only ethnically Paraguayan population is found in a few small settlements such as San José Obrero, 25 Leguas, and Campo Aceval situated to the south of the Mennonite Colonies. In the last few years Paraguayan settlers have also been moving into the forested areas to the north of the Mennonite Colonies, mainly into the area accessible from the road that runs north from Teniente Montania.

The Mennonites, named after their founder Menno Simons, are members of a nonconformist church that broke away from Calvin and Zwingli in the sixteenth century. Persecuted in Russia and facing problems with the education board in Canada, they sent expeditions to the Chaco in the 1920s to look for lands that would be suitable for colonization and sufficiently isolated to allow them to practice their religion unmolested by outside interference. In 1921 they signed an agreement with the Paraguayan government that allowed them the benefits of the Law of Colonization, freedom from military service, and the right to educate their children in their own Low German dialect. In 1928 the first settlers from Russia founded the Menno Colony on lands purchased from the Casado company, and two years later a second colony, Fernheim, was founded by Mennonites from Canada. The third and smallest of the colonies, Neuland, was founded in 1947 by a group of Mennonites who had managed to escape from Russia at the end of the Second World War.

The Mennonites were essentially subsistence farmers until the mid-1950s, when they began to mechanize their agriculture and develop cash crops. Commercial production was facilitated by the construction in the early 1960s of the Trans-Chaco Highway, which, although still a dirt road, provided direct access to Asunción. In the following years the Mennonites expanded into agricultural processing industries, with cotton, peanuts, and castor beans becoming the main crops. Ginneries in Filadelfia and Loma Plata, the main urban centers of the Mennonite Colonies, process the seed cotton, and the lint is then exported through Asunción, while the cotton seed and peanuts are processed into edible oils for sale on the national market.

Cultivation in the Mennonite Colonies is carried out on the sandy soils of the *espartillares*. These soils are light and subject to erosion, but they are the only soils that retain enough moisture to allow crops to be grown. Plowing starts as soon as the summer rains begin and has to be completed before the topsoil dries out or the furrows will collapse. Large areas can only be planted using tractors, and once the rains fall, the Mennonite farmers work day and night to prepare their fields for planting. Even when the seeds have germinated, there is no guarantee of a successful harvest: rainfall is uncertain, and it is not uncommon for a Mennonite farmer to replant an entire crop if early rains are followed by a period of drought. Prolonged periods of drought can be disastrous, and overall it is likely that the Mennonite farmers achieve good yields only about three years out of five.

The Mennonite farmers use the heavy soils of the *monte* for intensive cattle raising. They clear the forest cover using bulldozers and then plow the soil up and plant artificial pastures, the most widely used being buffel grass (*Pennisetum ciliare*). On these pastures the Mennonites raise both beef and dairy cattle, and the milk production provides the basis for a flourishing dairy industry. The cheese, butter, and milk, which is processed in Filadelfia and Loma Plata, is sold on the national market and is almost the only commercial dairy produce available in Paraguay. The timber from the forest clearance is used by other industries: carpenters' shops in Loma Plata manufacture high quality furniture, and there is a factory that produces tannin and essence of palo santo from low-grade timber. The smaller hardwood trees are used for fence posts, and until the Colonies were connected to the national electric grid in 1997, the firewood was used to generate electricity.

Since the late 1980s the Mennonites have become increasingly dependent on their dairy production, and the area under cultivation appears to have declined significantly. The Mennonites have had difficulties controlling pests in their cotton—although the Central Chaco is still the only area of Paraguay that remains free of boll weevil—and prices for cotton have been unstable. Cotton is still the main cash crop for the Indian and Paraguayan smallholders, who rely on family labor and use lower inputs of agrochemicals, but is no longer viable as a mechanized, capital-intensive cash crop. Another factor that accounts for the decline in agriculture is the need to control wind erosion, which by the early 1980s was turning parts of the Mennonite Colonies into a dustbowl.

Industrialization and the increasing prosperity of the Mennonite Colonies have begun to alter the orientation of the Mennonite communities. The administrative and commercial sectors have expanded rapidly, and today half the Mennonite population is concentrated in the four towns of Loma Plata, Filadelfia, Neu-Halbstadt (Neuland), and Hochstadt (Para Todo). Many of the younger generation are no longer content with the prospect of a future dedicated to farming and bound by the traditional values of the Mennonite Church, and are eager to emigrate to Asunción or to the Mennonite colonies of Canada. Since completion of the paved Trans-Chaco Highway, the Mennonite Colonies are only a few hours' drive from Asunción, and the increased contact with the outside world has accentuated the pressures for change. In recent years the Mennonites have become involved in local and regional politics, providing candidates for all three parties. Indeed, the first elected governor of the department of Boquerón was a Mennonite candidate from the Encuentro

Nacional Party who had previously been the administrator of one of the Mennonite cooperatives.

During the first half of the twentieth century the most prosperous region of the Chaco was the Alto Paraguay. This region is now one of the most economically depressed and backward in the whole of Paraguay. The collapse of the region's industries and a series of disastrous floods have forced much of the population to emigrate to Asunción or to the cities of Brazil and Argentina, and the once populous industrial towns along the Paraguay River are now little more than ghost towns.

The prosperity of the Alto Paraguay was based on the production of tannin and on ranching. The forests of the region provided the quebracho colorado for the tannin industry, the natural pastures were well suited for extensive ranching, and the Paraguay River afforded easy communication with Asunción and Buenos Aires. The region was developed in the late nineteenth century after various governments, bankrupted by a legacy of debts from the War of the Triple Alliance, raised funds through the sale of large areas of state-owned land. In spite of efforts to limit the size of individual holdings, a small number of companies managed to acquire enormous tracts of land in the Chaco: the largest, the Casado company, at one time owned over 5.5 million hectares (13.5 million acres) (Laino 1989:151). Four major tannin factories were established along the Paraguay River—at Puerto Pinasco, Puerto Casado, Puerto Sastre, and Puerto Guaraní—and two companies, Casado and the International Products Corporation (the owners of Pinasco), built narrow-gauge railways to transport the quebracho from the logging camps to their factories. Indeed, until the Trans-Chaco Highway was completed in the 1960s, the railway line from Puerto Casado to Kilometer 160 provided the only link with the Central Chaco. It was along this line that the Mennonites traveled to found their colonies, and when the Chaco War broke out, it was the Casado railway that carried the Paraguayan troops to the front.

By the 1960s the tannin industry had fallen into decline owing to the shortage of quebracho, obsolete plants, poor management, and competition from synthetic tannin. The factories at Pinasco, Sastre, and Guaraní were declared bankrupt, leaving thousands out of work, many of whom were unable even to draw the wages that were owed to them.

Some families moved to Puerto Casado, where, in spite of stoppages and part-time hours, the last of the tannin factories continued in operation until the mid-1990s, and others found employment with the National Cement Industry in Vallemí, just across the river from Casado. The majority, however, left for Asunción or crossed to Brazil, settling in Porto Mortinho, Campo Grande, and São Paulo.

Today ranching is virtually the only source of employment in the Alto Paraguay, although that industry also is in a state of decline. The large international concerns that used to combine ranching with the exploitation of quebracho in the area to the south of Fuerte Olimpo have largely been abandoned and their holdings broken up and offered for sale. The decline of companies like the International Products Corporation, Liebigs, and Colón was due to the collapse of the traditional export markets—the result of European and U.S. import quotas, increased competition from Brazil and a number of African countries, and a reduced demand for tinned beef. Another major problem on all the large ranches of the region is the degeneration of the grasslands, which are being colonized by thorn scrub. As the scrub has spread—covering up to 30 percent of the pasture on some ranches—it has become increasingly difficult to control the cattle, and in many areas they have run wild and can only be caught using traps.

In the area of Fuerte Olimpo and Bahía Negra the ranches are generally smaller and have fared better. Some of the cattle are shipped downriver for sale on the national market, but with the high cost of transport to Asunción, they are also sold in Brazil. The exchange rates have sometimes been unfavorable, but the main difficulty facing these ranches in recent years has been the flooding caused by the exceptionally high levels of the Paraguay River. The floods, which reached their highest recorded levels in 1979, 1981, and 1982, completely inundated Fuerte Olimpo and Bahía Negra and have since become a regular phenomenon, repeated every two to three years. Initially, most of the population moved to higher ground or lived on the roofs of their houses until the floods subsided, but in subsequent years families began to abandon the region, and many are unlikely to return. Some of the ranches, particularly along the Río Negro, the border between Paraguay and Bolivia, have been wiped

44

out by the floods, but others have kept going, moving their cattle to inland pastures every time the river levels start to rise.

The High Chaco has also suffered from depopulation. This is a direct consequence of the decline in trapping, which in the early 1970s was supporting a population of over six hundred in the region to the west of Fuerte Olimpo (Chase Sardi 1971:15). The trapping of ocelot, jaguar, and margay was made illegal in 1975, but it continued for some years on a reduced scale. The prices paid for pelts, however, have dropped dramatically as a result of the import controls imposed by most of the world's developed countries, and since jaguar and ocelot have become rare in even the most isolated parts of the Chaco, trapping is now no longer a viable activity.

In the western part of the High Chaco, particularly along the Upper Pilcomayo, the non-Indian population is composed mainly of Argentine *criollos,* who over the years have moved into the Paraguayan Chaco from the provinces of Salta and Formosa. The *criollo* families live by raising goats, sheep, and small herds of cattle, which graze freely in the forest and are kept under control through regular rounding up, as well by as their dependence on the few waterholes that are found in the beds of the *cañadas.* Until 1983 none of the *criollo* families owned the land on which they were settled, and none had attempted to put up fences or make any but the most rudimentary improvements to the areas they occupied. Since then, some families have received title to small areas of land, of around 300 hectares (740 acres) apiece, from the Institute for Agrarian Reform (Instituto de Bienestar Rural—IBR). Those who are settled on privately owned land make payments, usually in kind, to the landowners or to the people who claim to represent them.

In one or two areas of the High Chaco, ranching companies, such as the Fiduciaria Transatlántica Alemana, have tried to develop a system of ranching based on the use of artificial pastures, similar to that of the Mennonites. So far, it seems the results have failed to justify the investments required: the costs of clearing the forest, planting, and managing the pastures are high, and at present the price of meat is low and export markets restricted. Moreover, the pastures are unsuitable for grazing during periods of drought. Even the Mennonites, who have the most experience with this kind of ranching, were, during a prolonged drought in 1981, forced to raise a loan of around a million U.S. dollars to buy and transport sugar cane from Benjamín Aceval just to keep their dairy herds alive. A more feasible alternative would be to combine the traditional methods of extensive ranching—allowing the cattle to graze freely in the forest—with the use of small areas of artificial pasture where the cattle could be fattened once they were ready for market. Even for this to succeed, however, the ranches would have to count on better access roads than the ones that exist at present. Indeed, it seems that some of the new ranches that have been established in the most remote areas of the Chaco are little more than covers for smuggling operations.

Ever since the Chaco War there has been a strong military presence in the region. In the Lower Chaco, the cavalry is responsible for the region along the frontier with Argentina. The First Cavalry Regiment has its headquarters in General Díaz. Until recently the Second Cavalry Regiment had its headquarters in Cerrito, but an attempted coup obliged the government to move the regiment farther from Asunción. In the Central Chaco, the Third Army Corps has its headquarters in Mariscal Estigarribia and covers the region of the Upper Pilcomayo and the frontier with Bolivia. The navy has bases on the Upper Pilcomayo at Pozo Hondo and on the Upper Paraguay River at Bahía Negra, while the air force has bases at Pratt Gill, Nueva Asunción, and Chovoreca. There are two battalions of engineers in the Chaco. The Fourth Battalion, based in Teniente Ochoa, has been employed in the construction of the Trans-Chaco Highway, and the Fifth Battalion, based near General Bruguez, is responsible for maintaining the road from Chaco-í to Esteban Martínez.

In addition to being responsible for defense, the military units usually police their respective areas of influence, although there are police garrisons in Villa Hayes, Benjamín Aceval, Filadelfia, and Fuerte Olimpo. The Ministry of Defense has also tried to organize colonization programs in some isolated frontier regions, including Lagerenza and Chovoreca. During the 1970s Japanese colonists were settled in Lagerenza, but the colony foundered because of poor communications, shortage of water, mismanagement, and corruption. Since 1989 Fortín Lagerenza has returned to its earlier use as a prison camp, housing members of the Stroessner regime, as well as drug traffickers and other common criminals.

One of the major changes that has taken place since the overthrow of General Stroessner's regime in 1989 has been the establishment of a system of elected local governments, *gobernaciones,* at the departmental level. These replaced the Government Delegations, which had previously been nominated by the president. In the Chaco, the administrative structure has been simplified, and the five original departments have been amalgamated into three—Presidente Hayes, Boquerón, and Alto Paraguay—which have their administrative centers in Villa Hayes, Filadelfia, and Fuerte Olimpo, respectively. Using funds from central government, the departmental governments are beginning to take some responsibility for the development of social infrastructure, such as access roads, schools, and health posts.

The Indian Population

The Indian population of the Paraguayan Chaco is largely concentrated in the regions of the Central and Lower Chaco. Of the 26,006 persons enumerated in the 1981 Indian census, almost half—12,382—were living in the Mennonite Colonies of the Central Chaco, and a further 9,451 were enumerated in the Lower Chaco. In contrast, the population of the High Chaco, a region that includes the relatively densely populated area of the Upper Pilcomayo, totaled only 4,173 persons (INDI 1982).

The Indian population is divided into thirteen distinct ethnic groups, which belong to five linguistic families. The Zamuco linguistic family includes the Ayoreo and the Chamococo. The Lengua-Maskoy linguistic family includes the Lengua, Guaná, Sanapaná, Angaité, and the Toba-Maskoy—so named as to avoid confusion with the Guaicuruan-speaking Toba—while the Mataco-Mataguayo linguistic family includes the Nivaclé, the Mak'a, and the Manjuy as well as the Choroti and Mataco of northwest Argentina. In Paraguay, the Toba (Qom) are the only ethnic group belonging to the Guaicurú linguistic family. A much more numerous population of Toba and of the closely related Pilagá is found in Argentina; in Brazil, the Caduveo, descendants of the Mbayá, also belong to this linguistic family. The only Tupi-Guaraní speakers found in the Paraguayan Chaco are the Guaraní Ñandeva (Tapieté), and the Guaraní Occidentales (Guarayos); this latter group, who have settled in the region only since the Chaco War, is a fraction of the much larger population settled in the sub-Andean regions of Bolivia and Argentina. The linguistic division, population, and other terms used for these ethnic groups are resumed in table 1.

These figures require some explanation. Population figures are sensitive, and there is a tendency to overestimate the Indian population in order to justify their importance in the national context. The figures also provide a basis for land claims, since the 1981 law on indigenous peoples determines that every indigenous family in the Chaco should have a minimum area of 100 hectares (247 acres).[3] In 1971 Chase Sardi estimated the total Indian population of Paraguay at over 100,000, and this figure is often quoted, even though it bears little relation to the figures that he cites for each ethnic group (Chase Sardi 1971; Dostal 1972).

In 1980 Maybury Lewis and Howe (1980:18) provided a useful summary of the estimates then available, most of which gave figures of around 25,000–30,000 for the Indian population of the Chaco. None of these estimates, however, offered much more than inspired guesswork about the size of the dispersed population that was living on the ranches of the Lower Chaco or in the logging camps of the Alto Paraguay. The 1981 Census and Study of the Indigenous Population of Paraguay, carried out by the Instituto Nacional del Indígena (INDI) and the Paraguayan census department (DGEC), made the first serious attempt to enumerate the entire Indian population, including the dispersed populations of the Chaco. Most of the enumerators and supervisors were Indians, although in the Mennonite Colonies and the area of influence of the Anglican Mission the census was coordinated, respectively, by the Mennonite-run Asociación de Cooperación Indígena y Mennonita (ASCIM) and by the Anglican Mission.

The coverage of the 1981 census was reasonably good in the Chaco, given the efforts made to locate even the smallest groups. Unlike the situation in Eastern Paraguay, where the Mbya Guaraní refused to cooperate, the Indians of the Chaco, and even the landowners, accepted the census and allowed the enumerators to work freely. The final estimates of the Indian population, shown in table 1, were derived by estimating different levels of error for the different types of population. In the more stable nucleated populations, such as the agricultural colonies of the Central Chaco, the population was unlikely to have been under-

Table 1: Indian population, by ethnic group and linguistic family

	Pop. enumerated 1981	Estimated pop. 1981	Population enumerated 1992	Projected population 1998*	Other cited names
Tupi-Guaraní					
Guaraní Occidentales	1,464	1,535	1,254	2,500	Guarayos (Chase Sardi 1971), Chriguanos (Susnik 1962)
Guaraní Ñandeva	1,024	1,125	1,827	1,800	Tapieté (Chase Sardi 1971), Ñanaigua (Nordenskiold 1912)
Lengua-Maskoy					
Lengua	8,121	8,770	9,501	14,200	Enxet
Angaité	2,060	2,370	1,647	3,800	Enxet
Guaná	383	440	84	700	Kaskihá (Susnik 1968)
Sanapaná	1,794	1,970	1,063	3,200	Kisapang (Grubb 1911)
Toba-Maskoy	1,280	1,395	2,057	2,200	
Guaicurú					
Toba (Qom)**	572	630	781	1,000	Emok (Susnik 1968)
Zamuco					
Ayoreo	1,120	1,225	814	2,000	Moro, Tsirakua (Nordenskiöld 1912)
Chamococo	963	1,000	908	1,600	
Mataco-Mataguayo					
Nivaclé	6,667	7,030	7,934	11,500	Chulupí (Chase Sardi 1971), Suhin (Grubb 1911), Ashluslay (Nordenskiöld 1912)
Mak'a**	608	640	1,061	1,000	Tóóthli (Grubb 1911)
Manjuy	319	370	229	600	Yobwjwa, Wikina Wos, Thlawaa Thlele (Siffredi 1973)
TOTAL	26,375	28,500	29,160	46,100	

Sources: INDI 1982; DGEC 1992.

* The projections are based on the 1981 estimates, projecting an annual growth rate of around 3.1 percent.

** Some communities are located in Eastern Paraguay.

estimated by much more than 5 percent; the main cause of error was the failure to record newborn children. In the less stable nucleated communities, such as the "worker villages" of the Mennonite Colonies or the missions of the Alto Paraguay, the level of error was estimated at 10 percent. Among the dispersed populations of the ranches and logging camps, the population may have been underestimated by as much as 20 percent. Although this was a rather crude rule of thumb, it offered a reasonable idea of the accuracy with which the different types of population were enumerated. The main weakness of the 1981 census was the lack of any systematic attempt to detect the indigenous population living in Asunción and other major cities.

The 1992 census figures cited in table 1 were reached by asking all the respondents of Paraguay's national census whether they belonged to an indigenous ethnic group. The census offered good coverage of Paraguay's urban indigenous population but seems to have significantly underestimated the more dispersed and isolated populations in the Chaco. For instance, the figure for the Sanapaná, many of whom live dispersed on the ranches of the Lower Chaco, is significantly lower than the figure provided by the 1981 census. In contrast, the Mak'a, most of whom live in Asunción, have a higher population than expected, suggesting that the 3.1 percent annual increase in population is an underestimate, at least for indigenous populations that have some access to primary health care.

Some of the differences between the census figures may be explained by changes in ethnic identity. In some cases this may have been the result of inconsistency in the way the enumerators assigned individuals to one group or another. Both Guaraní-speaking groups are likely to have identified themselves as "Guaraní," leaving it to the enumerator to decide whether they were "Guaraní Occidentales" or "Guaraní Ñandeva." In other cases individuals of mixed parentage may have responded in different ways in the 1981 and the 1992 census. This may help to account for the apparent decline in the number of Guaná, some of whom seem to have redefined themselves as Toba-Maskoy or Lengua. It is no coincidence that the number of individuals identifying themselves as Toba-Maskoy seems to have increased, because land was acquired for the Toba-Maskoy, first in Kilometer 220 and then in Fortín Casanillo.

The projections for 1998 are based on an estimated 3.1 percent annual increase since 1981. This is the average annual increase in the rural population of Paraguay between 1982 and 1992 and may be a slight underestimate for the indigenous population. In general, the indigenous population is characterized by higher fertility rates than the rest of the rural population, but these are likely to be offset by higher mortality rates, particularly among children. Infant mortality appears to have declined dramatically as a result of immunization programs but still remains high, owing to waterborne diseases and respiratory infections.

The Ayoreo, who use this name to refer to themselves, may number around 2,000 persons in Paraguay, although the total population, including those living in the Bolivian Chaco, is probably over 4,000. The Ayoreo in Paraguay are divided into two main groups: those associated with the Catholic mission of Maria Auxiliadora on the Paraguay River, and those associated with the evangelist mission of Campo Loro, most of whom work as casual laborers in the Mennonite Colonies.

In Bolivia the first groups of Ayoreo were pacified in the 1950s, but in Paraguay the Ayoreo remained hostile until the early 1960s when the Salesians made contact with a large group of Ayoreo that had appeared near Fortín Teniente Martínez. This group later split: One faction stayed with the Salesians and was settled for a time in Cauce Indio, near Kilometer 220, before being moved to the Colonia Maria Auxiliadora. The other faction disappeared into the Chaco but was contacted again in 1968 by evangelist missionaries belonging to the New Tribes Mission. This group was first settled in Cerro León and was then moved south to El Faro Moro, where they were employed by the missionaries in trapping ocelot and jaguar. By 1978 most of this group had taken to working in the Mennonite Colonies, and the missionaries decided to purchase Campo Loro, on the periphery of the Mennonite Colonies, in the hope that the Ayoreo would devote themselves to agriculture. So far, however, most Ayoreo have continued to work as casual laborers and live on their employers' property, returning to a hiring camp at Montecito, near the center of Filadelfia, when their contracts come to an end.

Since the late 1970s Ayoreo from the Colonia Maria Auxiliadora have also been traveling to the Mennonite Colonies to work as casual laborers; they tend to keep themselves apart from the evangelist Ayoreo, since the sectarian differences have aggravated the division between these two groups. A few families from the Colonia Maria Auxiliadora have returned to their traditional territory in the region of Chovoreca and with help from the Asociación Indigenista del Paraguay (AIP) have acquired title to 20,000 hectares (50,000 acres). Other families from the same group have also established an independent settlement, known as Jesuide, just to the north of Teniente Montania (Kilometer 220).

One small group of Ayoreo, the Totobiegosode, who probably number around fifty people, has managed to remain hidden in the northern Chaco. In 1981 and 1986 members of this group were contacted by Ayoreo from Campo Loro, five of whom were killed in the second encounter; both times the contacted Totobiegosode were eventually settled in the evangelist mission (Escobar 1988). In 1998 another family of seven Totobiegosode was contacted near the Estancia Nueva Berlin, situated some seventy-five kilometers north of Teniente Montania; they too decided to settle in Campo Loro. A few days later a group of Ayoreo was reported to have attacked the ranch and to have fled only after the ranch foreman fired a shot in the air.

The Chamococo, who call themselves Yshyr, are estimated to number about 1,600 persons. They are divided into two main groups: the descendants of the Ebidoso, Horio, and Jeiwo, who live on the western bank of the Upper Paraguay River, and the Tomaraha, a group of some thirty-five families, who used to live in the logging camps and ranches of the Casado company. In the mid-1980s the Tomaraha joined a group of Ebidoso from Bahía Negra to settle in Potrerito (Wututa), an inland settlement within the 21,300 hectares (52,600 acres) titled to the colony of Puerto Esperanza. The main settlements on the Paraguay River are Puerto Esperanza (Onchita), Puerto 14 de Mayo (Karcha Bahlut), Bahía Negra (Puerto Diana and Dos Estrellas), and the Catholic mission of Fuerte Olimpo. There are also a few families living in the colony of Buena Vista (Ilyhyrta), some twenty miles inland from Fuerte Olimpo, which was set up by the Asociación de Parcialidades Indígenas (API) in 1978, and others who live on some of the ranches situated on the Paraguay River.

Most of the Tomaraha have since left the Ebidoso. Initially they moved from Potrerito to a piece of land that INDI had acquired for them in Puerto Caballo, on the Río Negro, the frontier with Bolivia. The area is subject to continual flooding and was unsuitable for permanent settlement. INDI eventually acquired another property for the Tomaraha — Maria Elena (Pechunta), which is situated on the Paraguay River between Esperanza and Fuerto Olimpo.

In recent years there have been few opportunities for wage labor in the Alto Paraguay, because the tannin industry has collapsed and there is little demand for the caranday palms that used to be exported downriver to Argentina for use as telegraph poles. Ranching has suffered from the floods, and most Chamococo have had difficulty finding any employment. Many families have returned to a subsistence strategy, based on agriculture, hunting, and in some cases stock raising; others continue to hunt caiman, sometimes risking their lives by hunting illegally in the Brazilian Pantanal. Some families have emigrated to Puerto Casado and, increasingly, to Asunción and parts of Eastern Paraguay. A few Chamococo, originally from Fuerte Olimpo, live in the area of Curuguaty, and they have attracted others, who usually come to work there during the cotton harvest.

The Lengua, who along with the Angaité, Sanapaná, and Guaná call themselves Enxet or Enlhet, are the largest ethnic group in the Paraguayan Chaco, with a population of around 14,200. The area inhabited by the Lengua used to cover much of the Lower and Central Chaco, and extended from the Paraguay River to Fortín Nanawa in the west, and from Faro Moro in the north to the Río Negro in the south. Today more than half the Lengua population is found in the Mennonite Colonies. In the agricultural colonies run by ASCIM, the Lengua live in the settlements of Yalve Sanga, Paz del Chaco, La Esperanza, Pozo Amarillo, Campo Largo, and Colonia Armonía Laguna. They also live in the worker villages of Loma Plata, Nueva Vida, Filadelfia, Para Todo, and Colonia 14 of Fernheim.

In the Lower Chaco, most of the Lengua live dispersed on the ranches. The main nucleated settlements are the Anglican mission of Makthlawaiya and the agricultural colonies of Sombrero Pirí and El Estribo, which were established in the 1980s by the Anglican Mission's La Heren-

53

cia settlement program. A further group of about forty families are settled in Angulo-kué, a ranch acquired by the Catholic Church which has
been renamed La Esperanza. On a few ranches, such as Santa Gabriela,
Alborada, Loma Porã, and Loma Verde, there are quite large populations of Lengua. In most cases, however, they live in small groups of
two or three families, since the ranch owners are unwilling to allow anyone other than permanently employed ranch hands to settle on their
property.

The Anglican missionaries of the South American Missionary Society
began working among the Lengua in 1889, and eight years later founded
Makthlawaiya, the first mission to be established in the Paraguayan
Chaco. In the following decades, as the Lower Chaco was surveyed and
divided up among the international ranching and tannin companies, the
Lengua were forced to settle on the ranches or in the tannin ports. By
the 1960s the tannin industry had virtually collapsed, and the Lengua
began to migrate to the Mennonite Colonies and to the ranches situated
along the Trans-Chaco Highway; however, there are still some Lengua
in Puerto Casado, Carayá Vuelta, Colón, and in a marginal *barrio* on the
outskirts of Concepción.

The Angaité, who may number as many as 3,800 persons, are closely
related to the Lengua. Many live on the ranches of the Lower Chaco,
particularly the ranches that used to belong to the International Products Corporation and the Casado company. In the Central Chaco, a large
group is settled in Diez Leguas, a colony on the southern fringes of Neuland, originally established by API. This first inhabitants of this colony
came from Cora'í, one of the ranches of the Estancia Zalazar, but they
were later joined by Angaité who had been evicted from the Estancia
Tuparendá and other ranches to the northeast of the Estancia Zalazar.
Some Angaité can still be found along the Paraguay River, in the Salesian
mission of Puerto Casado and in the New Tribes mission station at San
Carlos. At one time there was a large population of Angaité living in the
towns along the river, but with the collapse of the tannin industry many
moved away to seek work in the interior of the Chaco, in the Mennonite
Colonies, and even in Asunción. Some have since settled in Casanillo
and the Colonia Santo Domingo, while others live in temporary camps
wherever they can find work.

As a result of their long association with the ranches and the tannin industry, the Angaité are often considered to be one of the most deculturated Indian groups in the Chaco (e.g., Chase Sardi 1971, 1990). More than half the Angaité no longer speak their own language and have adopted the Jopará Guaraní of the Paraguayan population; the proportion of Guaraní speakers is, moreover, similar among both sexes and all age groups, which suggests that this is not a recent phenomenon (INDI 1982:table 13).

Many of the people who were identified as Angaité in the 1981 census are likely to have mixed parentage and, as I mentioned earlier, may have identified themselves as belonging to a different ethnic group in the 1992 census. In the towns and logging camps of the Alto Paraguay and, perhaps to a lesser extent, on the ranches of the interior, there has been an unusually high proportion of mixed marriages among the Angaité, Sanapaná, Guaná, Toba-Maskoy, and Lengua. This intermarriage is obviously due to the mixing of different ethnic and residential groups in the context of the tannin industry, but it also, I believe, reflects the widespread prohibition on marriage with all kin, which often limits the range of potential marriage partners within the same ethnic group.

The situation of the Sanapaná, who call themselves Enxet or San'am, is similar to that of the Angaité and Lengua. Of a population that may reach 3,200, just under half live in the Mennonite Colonies, mainly in La Esperanza, an agricultural colony established by ASCIM. Another large group is settled in La Patria, a colony established as part of the Anglican colonization program (Chase Sardi 1990). Some families also live on the ranches of the Lower Chaco: on the Estancia Zalazar, on the ranches of the Casado company, and in the area around Makthlawaiya. There used to be a large population of Sanapaná in Puerto Pinasco, but at present the only settlement on the Paraguay River is the mission of Puerto Casado, where many of the Sanapaná have intermarried with the Lengua, Angaité, Guaná, and Toba-Maskoy.

The Guaná are referred to by Susnik as the Kashkiha-Maskoy and are classified by Klein and Stark as members of the Lengua-Maskoy linguistic family (INDI 1982:9; Klein and Stark 1977). Their origins are obscure:

55

the name Guaná suggests a Chané origin, and Susnik considers them to have been vassals of the Chané (INDI 1982). She remarks that the Guaná, unlike the other Lengua-Maskoy speakers, at one time practiced stock raising and intensive agriculture, features that she regards as more typical of the Chané-Arawak cultures.

The Guaná, who may number some 700 persons, used to inhabit the area around Puerto Sastre and were employed in the tannin factory and logging camps of the Sastre family. When the company went bankrupt in 1963, one group of Guaná moved to the Salesian mission of Puerto Casado and another to Maria Casilda, a ranch belonging to the Casado company. Most of this latter group were evicted from the ranch in 1977 and were forced to move to Vallemí, on the other side of the river, where they are now employed by the National Cement Industry as stevedores. The shortage of opportunities for work has led many Guaná to emigrate from the Alto Paraguay. A few families moved to the Mennonite Colonies and later settled in the Colonia Santo Domingo. Others moved to Asunción, and some even settled for a short time in a colony intended for Paraguayan *campesinos* in Itapua, Eastern Paraguay.

The Toba-Maskoy, who call themselves Enenlhit, were first identified as members of the Lengua-Maskoy linguistic family by Klein and Stark (1977), who coined the term Toba-Maskoy to avoid confusing this group with the Toba (Qom) of Cerrito, who speak a Guaicuruan language. Although the word list presented by Klein and Stark provides clear evidence of the linguistic affiliation of the Toba-Maskoy, there is doubt about their origin. Susnik (1961) identifies the Toba of the Alto Paraguay with a group of Toba-Takshik who emigrated from the province of Formosa, Argentina, in 1870, and who later settled in the area of Puerto Sastre. Conceivably this group could, in subsequent years, have been assimilated into the surrounding Lengua-Maskoy–speaking population. The Toba-Maskoy insist on calling themselves Toba when speaking Spanish or Jopará Guaraní and claim to have come from the area around Fortín Casanillo.

Of a population estimated at around 2,200, some two-thirds are settled in the Mennonite Colonies: in the agricultural colony of Pozo Amarillo, in the worker villages of Laguna Porã and Loma Plata, and dispersed in small groups on the property of their Mennonite employers. Other Toba-Maskoy are settled in Fortín Casanillo, a colony established in 1986 by the Catholic Equipo Nacional de Misiones (ENM), and there are a few families in the Colonia Santo Domingo. This colony originated in 1980 when the Casado company managed to persuade President Alfredo Stroessner to overturn a presidential decree intended to expropriate 10,000 hectares (25,000 acres) in the area of Fortín Casanillo. A large group of Toba-Maskoy had been waiting at the entrance to Casanillo when the decree was annulled; they were ordered onto military trucks and taken to a site in the middle of an area of low-lying forest, some ten miles to the north of Teniente Montania. For some months the Ministry of Defense provided rations and even opened areas for cultivation using bulldozers, but the area had little agricultural potential, and the most of the Toba-Maskoy eventually went back to working for their Mennonite employers. A couple of years later the ENM was able to negotiate the purchase of Casanillo from Casado. There are probably still some Toba-Maskoy living on the ranches that belonged to the Casado company and in the Catholic mission in Puerto Casado.

The Nivaclé, who also refer to themselves by this name, appear in the literature as Chulupí (Chase Sardi 1971), Suhin (Grubb 1911), and Ashluslay (Nordenskiöld 1912). In Paraguay their population can be estimated at around 11,500, to which can be added the population that lives in Argentina, in the missions of La Paz and La Bolsa, and in the Indian *barrios* of Tartagal.

The largest Nivaclé population is found in the Mennonite Colonies: in the agricultural colonies of Yalve Sanga, Campo Alegre, and Nich'a Toyish, and in the worker villages of Filadelfia, Colonia 8 of Fernheim, Cayin'o Clim, Cruce Filadelfia, and Sandhorst. Although some groups of Nivaclé have always inhabited the area around Mariscal Estigarribia, most of the Nivaclé who now live in the Central Chaco originally came from the area along the Pilcomayo and emigrated to the Mennonite Colonies in the 1950s.

The first Catholic missions were established on the Pilcomayo before the Chaco War, and during the war they provided a refuge for those

Nivaclé that remained on the Paraguayan side of the river. Today these missions, Laguna Escalante and San José de Esteros, are the largest Nivaclé settlements in the region. In the 1940s the Oblates of Maria established other missions in Pedro P. Peña and Mariscal Estigarribia. These were originally intended for the Guaraní, but in the 1950s the Nivaclé began returning from Argentina to Pedro P. Peña, and they are now largely intermarried with the Manjuy and Choroti. Another group of Nivaclé moved to Mariscal Estigarribia after an uprising in the Mennonite Colonies in 1962, and they are now settled in the mission of Santa Teresita.

Dissatisfaction with life in the Mennonite Colonies has led some groups of Nivaclé to return to their ancestral lands along the Pilcomayo. In 1976 Nivaclé from Filadelfia established the colony of Pablo Stahl, bordering on Misión Esteros, and in the same year a group from Cayin'o Clim settled in Yishinachat. Finally, in 1980 a number of families from Yalve Sanga and Sandhorst moved to Mistolar on the Upper Pilcomayo.

The southernmost groups of Nivaclé live on the ranches along the road from Pozo Colorado to General Díaz; the only large settlement in this area is in Loma Pytä, which is a mixed community of Nivaclé, Mak'a, and Lengua.

The Mak'a, who according to Klein and Stark (1977) call themselves and their language by this name, may number 1,000 persons, most of whom live in the Colonia Mak'a situated in Mariano Roque Alonso on the outskirts of Asunción near Puente Remanso, the bridge across the Paraguay River. Traditionally, the Mak'a inhabited the area to the south of the road from Pozo Colorado to General Díaz, and a few families still live in the Estancia Loma Pytä.

In the period before the Chaco War, the Mak'a were used as scouts by General Juan Belaieff, a White Russian who had been engaged to prepare the cartography of the Chaco for the Paraguayan army. General Belaieff was one of the founders of AIP, and he managed to acquire a 355-hectare (875-acre) island in the Paraguay River, opposite the Botanical Gardens of Asunción, for the Mak'a. In the years following the Chaco War, the Mak'a were forced off their lands by ranchers, and by the 1960s nearly all had settled on the island. In the late 1970s and early 1980s the island was subject to regular flooding, and the Mak'a had to camp in the Botanical Gardens. In 1984 INDI acquired a 3-hectare (7.5-acre) plot for the Mak'a in Mariano Roque Alonso. Most of the Mak'a now live there, although there are small groups who spend most of their time in Ciudad del Este and Encarnación (Chase Sardi 1990:133).

The Mak'a live mainly from the manufacture and sale of handicrafts and from showing tourists around their colony. These activities have provided a steady source of income for the Mak'a and have allowed them a greater degree of independence than that experienced by Indian communities forced to rely on wage labor. The New Tribes Mission and other missionaries, including a Korean evangelical mission, have attempted to work with the Mak'a, but their impact has been minimal, and the Mak'a have shown little interest in adopting the lifestyle of Paraguayan society. They do, however, devote a lot of time to soccer and have produced a number of professional players.

The Manjuy, who may number around 600 persons, are a subgroup of the Choroti. The name Manjuy is of Nivaclé origin; according to Siffredi (1973), this group calls itself Yobwjwa and corresponds to what Hunt (1915) terms the Choroti "*montaraces.*" Siffredi mentions that the Yobwjwa are divided into two groups—the Thlawaa Thlele or "east wind" and the Wikina Wos or "north wind"—both of which live to the east of the Pilcomayo. The Nivaclé refer to the Choroti who live on the western bank of the Pilcomayo as Eklenjuy; at one time this group also inhabited the area of Pozo Hondo, but they moved across to Argentina during the Chaco War and are now settled in Misión La Paz.

At present there are at least three distinct groups of Manjuy in the Paraguayan Chaco. The first group, now largely intermarried with the Nivaclé, originally lived in Cañada Milico but now moves between Pedro P. Peña, Mistolar, and Sandhorst. The second group is settled in the New Tribes mission station of Santa Rosa. The third group, originally from the area around Mariscal Estigarribia, is closely intermarried with the Nivaclé and is divided between the worker villages of Colonia 22 and Colonia 6 in the Mennonite Colony of Fernheim. There may also be another uncontacted group of Manjuy living in the area between the Estancia Safari and Fortín Pratt Gill.

The Guaicuruan-speaking Toba, who call themselves Qom, may have a population of around 1,000 persons in Paraguay. Linguistically they are affiliated to the more numerous Toba and Pilagá of northern Argentina, and some of the Toba in Paraguay have relatives in the province of Formosa. At present most of the Paraguayan Toba live in Cerrito (Colonia Qom) and Villa Rosario (Eastern Paraguay).

The population of the Franciscan mission of Cerrito is divided into three groups. The Cerriteños were the first group to settle there, having been evicted by the army from the Estancia Avanzada in 1970. A short time later they were joined by the Toba of Río Verde, who were expelled from Potrero Para Todo of the Estancia Villa Rey, a ranch belonging to the La Gauloise SA. Again the army intervened, and a number of Toba were killed when the soldiers opened fire, apparently without provocation. The Rosarinos joined the colony in 1972, this time at the invitation of the Franciscan missionaries. This group had been living in Puerto Rosario, and a few families remained behind when the rest of the group moved to Cerrito. In 1991 INDI acquired a plot of 154 hectares (380 acres) for the Toba at Palma near Villa Rosario and purchased an additional fraction in 1997. At present there are at least twenty families living in Rosario.

The colony of Cerrito is too small to support the families that live there. The men work on the sugarcane plantations of Benjamín Aceval or on the ranches situated along the Trans-Chaco Highway. In 1982 most of the Rosarinos, and a few families from Río Verde, moved to San José, a 7,500-hectare (18,500-acre) ranch that had been acquired by ENM and the Instituto de Bienestar Rural. This colony has now been all but abandoned, owing to its isolation, its lack of economic opportunities, and the continual threats from neighbors and rustlers. A few other families, most of which are mixed marriages with the Lengua, live in the new colony of La Esperanza (Angulo-kué).

The Guaraní Ñandeva or Tapieté, who have a population of around 1,800, nowadays refer to themselves as Guaraní, although Gonzalez (1968) notes that when they first appeared in Mariscal Estigarribia this term was unknown to them. Like the other Guaraní-speaking Indians of Paraguay and Bolivia, they also call themselves Ñandeva. They also appear in the literature as Yanaygua or Ñanaigua (Nordenskiöld 1912; Holmberg 1950; Gonzalez 1968). The name Tapieté, although widely used, is derisive and is probably derived from *tapy'yeté* meaning "servants"—a term used by the Guaraní Occidentales to describe their Chané vassals.

The ethnic origin of the Guaraní Ñandeva is unclear: culturally they appear to belong to the Chaco, but they speak the same dialect of Guaraní as the Guaraní Occidentales. They may be descendants of the Chané, vassals of the Guaraní, who at some stage migrated into the northern Chaco. Nordenskiöld (1912), on the other hand, has suggested that they may be of Mataco origin.

The Guaraní Ñandeva are found in the Mennonite Colonies—in the worker villages of Colonia 5, Colonia 3, and Colonia 11 of Fernheim, and in the colony of Laguna Negra. Another group is settled in Nueva Asunción, on the air force base and on the Estancia Co'e Pyahu; a small group is also settled in Mariscal Estigarribia.

The Guaraní Occidentales, who refer to themselves simply as Guaraní, are something of an anomaly in the Chaco. Descendants of the Itatines, a Guaraní population who migrated from Mato Grosso to the eastern foothills of the Andes during the fifteenth and sixteenth centuries, the Guaraní Occidentales have an agricultural tradition and a social organization that is distinct from that of the other Chaco societies. Indeed, the majority of these Indians, usually referred to as Chiriguanos in Bolivia and Argentina, continue to inhabit the sub-Andean region, and the population in Paraguay, which may reach around 2,500, probably represents less than 3 percent of the total population (Grunberg and Grunberg 1974).

The Guaraní Occidentales of Paraguay originally belonged to two separate groups, both of which settled in the Paraguayan Chaco during, or immediately after, the Chaco War. The Machareteños, nominally Christian, from the Franciscan mission of Machareti in the department of Chuquisaca, Bolivia, sided with the Paraguayan troops during the Chaco War and migrated to Paraguay after the cease-fire, lured by promises made by Paraguayan officers. The Izozeños, who came from the region of the Parapití River, were conscripted by the Bolivians and surrendered to the Paraguayan army. After the war most of the Guaraní settled in Pedro P. Peña, where there is still a sizable population. Many families eventually left, however, because of the isolation and the lack of opportunities for wage labor. Some of the Guaraní settled in Mariscal Estigarribia, where they now live in the town and in the mission of Santa Teresita. Others migrated to the Mennonite Colonies and live in the Catholic mission in Filadelfia and in the agricultural colony of Laguna Negra. Finally, there are still a few Guaraní families in Puerto Casado, living in a Paraguayan *barrio* rather than among the Indians in the Catholic mission.

Of all the Indians of the Chaco, the Guaraní Occidentales have shown the strongest desire to integrate themselves into Paraguayan society. This owes something to their Guaraní identity, which in the Chaco, where two-thirds of the population do not consider themselves to be ethnically Paraguayan, has allowed them to identify more closely with Paraguayans. In Filadelfia they tend to work in the better paid and more prestigious posts, in the factories or as builders and drivers, while in Mariscal Estigarribia quite a few are noncommissioned army officers, truck drivers, or members of the army band.

CHAPTER TWO

The Subsistence Economy

ALL THE INDIAN communities of the Paraguayan Chaco, with the exception of one or two bands of Ayoreo and Manjuy who have managed to remain isolated in the most inaccessible areas of the northern Chaco, are in some sense integrated into the national economy. The extent of their integration varies considerably, however. At one end of the scale are communities such as Pedro P. Peña and Mistolar, where most households live from hunting, fishing, and gathering, from cultivating small subsistence plots, and in some cases from stock raising. Here, the few necessities that have to be purchased are paid for by the sale of animal skins or items of handicraft, or by short periods spent working on the neighboring ranches. At the other end of the scale are urban communities, such as Puerto Casado or the Barrio Obrero of Filadelfia, where the population depends almost exclusively on wage labor and is employed in manufacturing, construction, and service industries.

Between these two extremes one finds a variety of situations. In most communities, subsistence activities, particularly hunting and fishing, continue to be important, even though they are usually combined with wage labor or production for the market. Indeed, the emphasis on subsistence activities is perhaps one of the main features distinguishing the Indians from the rest of the region's population. The subsistence economy is not simply a hand-to-mouth existence but involves cycles of exchange, within and between households, which operate independently of the market economy. These cycles of exchange are founded on different values from those of the market, making the subsistence economy a moral economy that contrasts sharply with what the Indians perceive as the market-oriented morality of the nonindigenous population of the Chaco (see Perafán 2000:4).

Unlike Paraguayan ranchers or Mennonite farmers, the Indians of the Chaco view the natural environment as a bountiful one and do not regard foraging as work comparable to agriculture or wage labor. This perception of the natural environment is manifest through an economic strategy that aims at satisfying basic needs through a reliance on immediately available resources, rather than through accumulation or the maximization of production (see Woodburn 1982). This reliance on foraging, not just as a means of subsistence but as a kind of economic rationality, dominates the Indians' attitudes toward all productive activities. Even in those communities that have to depend on wage labor, and where hunting, fishing, and gathering at best provide only a secondary means of subsistence, the values associated with foraging still tend to provide the model for the Indians' overall economic strategy.

The resources acquired through wage labor, stock raising, and even agriculture are treated in the same fashion as more immediately available resources, and are subject to the same kinds of obligations that operate in the subsistence economy. This may limit the potential of activities that involve delayed returns, which, when judged by the criteria proper to a market or agricultural economy, often appear to be characterized by a remarkably low level of production. But in the traditional context, this strategy was an effective response to the conditions imposed by the natural environment. The Chaco is characterized by alternating periods of drought and floods, and both season and climate are relatively unpredictable. Few resources are available all year round, and they vary considerably from year to year. This in part explains the highly opportunistic nature of foraging in the Chaco, with subsistence activities varying from season to season and from day to day.

The relation between subsistence and ethnic identity is often expressed in terms of diet or dietary preferences. In general, indigenous people are believed to prefer the produce of hunting and gathering, and they themselves may express preferences for particular kinds of game or fish. Typically, these preferences are associated with particular ethnic or territorial groups. For instance, the name Ashluslay, used by Nordenskiöld (1912), Metraux, and Clastres (1977) to refer to the Nivaclé, is taken from the Choroti term *alhuhlai,* which literally means "eaters of the iguana." There is also a generalized belief that indigenous people traditionally rejected many of the store-bought items that have now become a staple part of the diet. It is often claimed that the oldest, most traditional members of the community never ate sugar, salt, or cooking oil, although today it is unusual to find anyone who refuses these items when they are available.

In fact, store-bought items, such as rice, noodles, flour, and cooking oil, constitute the bulk of the diet for most Indian households, while the products of gathering and agriculture are usually little more than a supplement. The only exceptions are the most remote communities, such as Pedro P. Peña, where there are virtually no opportunities to acquire cash or to purchase foodstuffs. This is in marked contrast to Eastern Paraguay, where most indigenous households rely on agriculture for the bulk of their subsistence. In the Chaco, the relation between diet and dependence on the market economy is complex. The need for store-bought foodstuffs and manufactured items, such as clothing, steel tools, or cooking pots, obliges the Indians to engage in the market economy, usually on the most unfavorable terms. However, the dependence on these goods is itself a statement about how the Indians see themselves in relation to the rest of the national society. From a wider perspective, the level of the community's dependence on the market is determined by factors outside their control. Above all, these include land tenure or access to land, environmental factors, and the regional economy, as well as the presence or absence of aid and development programs.

Hunting

Of all foraging activities, hunting is perhaps the most varied in terms of the techniques and the resources exploited. Hunting is an almost exclusively male activity, and men hunt even when other activities, such as wage labor, can be practiced closer to home. Hunting can provide a source of cash comparable to wage labor, but the importance given to hunting reflects more than its potential for generating income.

There are times when one hears certain groups, such as the Ayoreo who have settled in the Mennonite Colonies, refer crudely to hunting as "looking for meat." But this expression, along with the attitude it implies, has been adopted from the Indians' employers or from missionaries, and it is used more as an ironic comment on an unsuccessful hunt than as a negation of the value of hunting. Even among the Ayoreo, who appear to be making a conscious effort to rid themselves of their identity as "wild" Indians, and indeed even among more acculturated populations, the importance of hunting is apparent from its dominance as a theme of conversation and narrative. Moreover, hunting knowledge and skills are still familiar to many of the younger generation, even in urban communities such as Puerto Casado and the Barrio Obrero of Filadelfia, where the Indians are employed as factory workers.

Large game animals appear to be more abundant in the Chaco than in the tropical forests of Eastern Paraguay. The Lower and the Central Chaco conform to the picture of tropical savanna, described by Foley (1982) as characterized by grass-dominated plant communities and a high large mammal biomass. The High Chaco—parts of which receive an average annual rainfall of less than 400 millimeters (16 inches)— is more akin to what he describes as thorn woodland. This ecotype, adapted to long periods of drought, is characterized by a flora in which highly nutritious storage adaptations are common, but by a lower large mammal biomass.

Nowadays, hunting and even gathering are restricted by the difficulty of gaining access to privately owned land. In most parts of the Chaco, including the whole of the Lower and Central Chaco, the land is privately owned and permission is granted only by some landowners. The missions and Indian colonies of the Lower and Central Chaco are too close to heavily populated areas or are too small to support their populations from hunting and gathering. In the Lower Chaco many ranches refuse access to Indians under any conditions. The Toba of Cerrito, for example, are not allowed to enter the 120,000-hectare (295,000-acre) property of the Estancia Villa Rey, which one group traditionally inhabited and which now belongs to La Gauloise SA, because they are accused of being cattle thieves. Nor are they allowed to enter the 140,000-hectare (345,000-acre) property of the Estancia Pozo Azul, because many years ago a Toba man killed the ranch foreman. On other ranches Indians are refused entry because they are believed to deplete the game, or because the ranch owner or the foreman dislikes them, or as one so often hears, because they believe the Indians should be made to work.

In the Mennonite Colonies hunting has been declared illegal. The Mennonites themselves can often be seen carrying rifles as they ride around the colonies on their motorbikes, but if an Indian is found hunting on a Mennonite's land, he is likely to have his firearms confiscated and may have to appear before the Mennonite *comisario*. Some Mennonite landowners do give Indians permission to hunt on their property, but they are often forbidden from killing certain animals, such as the rhea, which is believed to kill snakes. In other cases the landowner may even demand a portion of the game that is taken.

In the High Chaco there are large areas of unoccupied land. Most of the region has been sold to private landowners, but large parts remain unfenced and no permission is required to hunt there. The population is still very sparse, and most species are more abundant here than in other parts of the Chaco.

In recent years the depletion of large game has been due to overexploitation, by Indians as well as Paraguayans, and is most noticeable among species of commercial value. The jaguar (*Panthera onca*) and ocelot (*Felis pardalis*), at one time the most valuable animals, are rare in even the most isolated areas of the Chaco, although they are apparently beginning to reappear now that their pelts have no commercial value.[1] The jaguar, and to a lesser extent the puma (*Puma concolor*), have also been hunted to prevent them killing cattle. The caiman (*Caiman sp.*) has been massively depleted: at one time caiman abounded along all the major rivers, but they were slaughtered in huge numbers to satisfy the market for crocodile leather and today are found only in the lakes and rivers of the interior. The smaller species that are hunted for their pelts—the margay (*Felis wiedi* and *F. tigrina*), the fox (*Dusicyon sp.*), and the iguana (*Teuis teyou*) —have also been reduced in some areas but have reestablished themselves whenever market prices have fallen. The rhea is another species that has been hunted commercially and may have fallen in numbers, but it is protected on many ranches and is abundant in the area of the Mennonite Colonies.

The larger herbivores that are hunted for their meat seem to have declined less than the commercially valuable species. Deer are found throughout the Chaco, but in many parts their numbers have diminished owing to hunting and possibly to competition from cattle for the same pasture. They are most abundant in the wetter areas of the High Chaco, where there are few people or established ranches. Peccaries, particularly the white-lipped peccary (*Tayassu pecari*) and the recently discovered *taguá* (*Catagonus wagneri*), have obviously been depleted and are rarely found in the more densely populated areas of the Chaco. The Indians attribute this to the presence of cattle, but hunting has undoubtedly been another factor.

Most Indians use firearms for hunting, either .22 rifles or shotguns. These are usually old and badly maintained, sometimes held together with pieces of wire, and it is surprising that there are so few serious accidents. In the Lower Chaco, .22 rifles are preferred because they have a better range and the munitions are cheaper. The Manjuy of Pedro P. Peña and Santa Rosa have heavy caliber Mauser rifles from the Chaco War. These are apparently taken from a cache that was hidden during the war, and the munitions are still sufficient to keep the Manjuy supplied. The exact location of the cache is a well-kept secret, and the Manjuy have killed at least one Paraguayan who was intent on finding it.

In the Central and High Chaco, 16- or 20-bore shotguns are more popular. Here, animals are usually encountered in fairly dense forest, and there is little likelihood of having to fire at a range of over thirty yards. Most hunters buy caps, powder, and shot and refill their own cartridges, measuring the powder and shot according to the kind of game they intend to hunt. In the Mennonite Colonies, where large game is generally scarce, the hunters usually carry two kinds of cartridge: one with a small charge of powder and fine shot for killing birds and small animals, and another with more powder and heavier shot for large animals such as deer or peccaries. Shotguns are never fired at birds on the wing but are used to hit them when they are sitting. They are used to kill charata (*Ortalis canicollis* and *O. pantanalensis*) and pigeons (*Columba picazuro; Leptotila sp.*), which often congregate around waterholes, a single shot sometimes killing as many as fifteen birds.[2] In the more remote parts of the High Chaco, shotguns are only used for large game, and the cartridges are loaded with heavy shot. The Indians kill birds such as charata, pigeons, and even ducks with catapults made from strips of inner tube, which fire pellets of sunbaked clay because there are no stones in this part of the Chaco.

A number of traditional weapons are still in use. The *fija*, a harpoon or lance, today tipped with a steel point some fifty centimeters in length, is found in many parts of the Chaco. In the Lower Chaco, the Toba and

Lengua use a *fija* of up to three meters in length for hunting the nine-banded armadillo (*Dasypus novemcinctus*), a species found only in this region which is much appreciated for being one of the few animals with a lot of fat. One of the best times for hunting armadillo is after a period of heavy rain, when the grasslands are under water and the armadillos seek refuge in the islands of forest that remain above flood level. Here they build nests in the dense patches of *chuza* and *caraguatá* (*Bromeliaceae*) or in underground burrows and venture out only at night. The nests can be located using dogs or by looking for the trails the armadillos leave when they collect grass and leaves to line their nests. Once the nest or burrow has been found, the armadillos can be speared or dug out; hunters have to be careful, however, since they may find the old nests and burrows occupied by rattlesnakes (*Crotalus sp.*).

The Indians of the Lower Chaco also use the *fija* to kill collared peccary (*Tayassu tajacu*). This animal, the smallest of the three species of peccary found in the Chaco, lives singly or in pairs and when disturbed sometimes goes to ground in a burrow or hollow log where it can easily be speared. In the High Chaco the Ayoreo hunt white-lipped peccary and taguá with clubs and lances. The Ayoreo use two types of lance: *guebe,* literally "iron," a lance of about two meters (six feet) in length, tipped with a machete blade; and *ojnai,* literally "needle," a throwing spear of about a meter and a half (four–five feet) in length tipped with a long steel point. The longer lance doubles as a machete and is used to hack through dense undergrowth, while the shorter lance, which was also a weapon of war, is used in combination with a short club or machete and has even been used to kill jaguars.

Some animals are taken by hand. The Ayoreo spend a lot of time looking for tortoises (*Testudo denticulata*), which they collect and keep until they are needed. The tortoises have a large liver, which the Ayoreo consider a delicacy. The Ayoreo are not sentimental and simply throw the tortoises onto the fire; when they stop kicking, they are turned over and chopped open with a machete. The three-banded armadillo (*Tolypeutes matacus*) is the smallest of the armadillos that are hunted. It has little meat but is eaten by most Indians, although the Nivaclé regard it as unsuitable for children and young adults, possibly because it has a lot of fat. The three-banded armadillo is found throughout the Chaco but is particularly abundant in certain areas of the High Chaco. When disturbed it rolls itself into a ball and can easily be picked up.

The iguana is another species that can be taken by hand. It appears only during the summer months and hibernates in the winter. During the middle of the day iguanas sun themselves on open ground and when disturbed retreat into their burrows, from which they can be pulled or dug out. This has to be done carefully because the iguana can bite if it is not grasped firmly by the head. The iguana is mainly hunted for its skin and is eaten only by some groups, such as the Nivaclé.

The iguana is also taken using dogs. In the dense thorny undergrowth typical of the islands of forest of the Lower Chaco this is the easiest way of finding small game, and trained hunting dogs are regarded as a valuable asset. Metraux (1963:265) mentions that dogs may have been domesticated by the Chaco societies in aboriginal times, and they are mentioned in the ethnographies of Grubb (1911) and Nordenskiöld (1912). The Ayoreo, however, claim to have acquired dogs only in recent years, and they prefer to hunt without them. In nearly all communities one finds a large number of fierce, half-starved dogs, most of which are used only as watchdogs.

The short bow and arrow, typical of the Chaco, is no longer used for hunting, although it is still widely used for fishing in shallow water. One of the techniques originally used when hunting with the bow in areas of open grassland has been adapted for use with firearms. This is the camouflage referred to as a *poncho*. The *poncho* is made from vines and from the leaves of the caranday or pindó palm tied together to cover the hunter's head and chest so that from a distance he looks like a small tree. This technique is used for hunting rhea, and the Toba also use it when hunting feral pigs (*Sus scrofa*), which are found in some of the more remote ranches of the Lower Chaco.

The rhea is the main quarry in the areas of open grassland. It is hunted both for its meat, which has a rather strong oily flavor but which is appreciated by the Toba and the Nivaclé, and for its feathers and hide, which sometimes fetch good prices. The rhea move in small flocks, comprising an elder male and a harem of some three to fifteen females, and are shy birds with sharp eyes and keen hearing. When a hunter sights a flock of rhea, he closes in as far as cover permits, prepares his *poncho*, and then begins to work his way slowly toward the flock, walking upwind to prevent the rhea from hearing him. This is easiest when there is a strong north wind, rustling the leaves of the caranday palms. As he gets closer, the hunter waits for the rhea to turn. He moves forward, then waits again. Eventually the rhea may even get curious. Once the flock is close enough—with a .22 rifle the hunter has to be fairly sure of hitting the rhea in the head or thigh—he fires. Sometimes the rhea get confused and rather than running become aggressive. This gives the chance of another shot, and with luck the hunter can kill three or four before the rest finally turn and run off.

There are at least three species of deer in the Chaco, but of these the largest, the *ciervo* (probably the marsh deer, *Blastocerus dichotomus*), is extremely rare and is confined to the eastern side of the High Chaco and to the swamplands along the course of the Riacho He'e. The other species, the *guazú virá* (the grey brocket deer, *Mazama gouazoubira*) and the *guazú pytā* (*Mazama americana*), seem to inhabit the same environments and are distributed throughout the Chaco.

In the Lower Chaco, deer generally spend the daylight hours in the thicker areas of forest and only venture out to graze at dawn and dusk. At these times of day a hunter can work his way around the edge of the forest in the hope of catching a deer grazing. Deer are wary, and they often see or hear the hunter first and crash off into the undergrowth. Once the deer reaches cover, however, it may wait and turn to see if it is being pursued; if a hunter is quiet, he can go into the forest and work his way close enough to get in a shot. In the forested areas of the Chaco, especially during hot weather, deer sometimes come out into the clearings to take a respite from the heat and the mosquitoes.

In periods of drought, deer and other species are found in the vicinity of watercourses or drinking ponds, particularly at dawn and dusk. In the High Chaco, the watercourses are usually the best areas for hunting. Large animals such as tapir (*Tapirus terrestris*) and peccaries come to drink. The waterholes also support aquatic animals, including caiman and capybara (*Hydrochaeris hydrochaeris*), as well as ducks and other waterfowl.

The Chamococo like to hunt in the watercourses at night, using flashlights to illuminate and dazzle the animals. Capybara can be found grazing along the water's edge; when illuminated, they sometimes freeze rather than take to the water. Caiman are also taken at night; their eyes show red when illuminated by flashlight, and they can be shot or harpooned. Caiman are hunted mainly for their skins. Although the sale of caiman skins is illegal, they can easily be sold in Paraguay; indeed, the Chamococo occasionally risk crossing into the Brazilian Pantanal to hunt caiman, even though some hunters are known to have been murdered by the Brazilian forestry police.

On the Upper Pilcomayo, the Nivaclé and the Guaraní hunt charata at night. The birds roost together, often near water, and give themselves away when they call. On windy nights, when there is no moon, a hunter can approach the roost without disturbing the charata, which can be picked off with a catapult or knocked off the lower branches with a long pole.

Hunters tend to set off in search of a particular kind of game, and the choice of the area to be hunted is largely determined by the climatic conditions and the kind of animals the hunter hopes to find. In the Lower Chaco, a critical factor is the degree of flooding or drought. After heavy rain, when the rivers burst their banks and the grasslands are under water, animals congregate in the islands of forest that remain above flood level. These are good conditions for hunting armadillos and any other animals that find themselves trapped in the patches of grassland that are left above water. When the grasslands dry out, and the weather is clear with a strong north wind, rhea can be stalked using a *poncho*. During times of drought, when the rivers are reduced to little more than stagnant pools, the hunters are more likely to work along the watercourses looking for caiman, capybara, or other animals that come to drink in the remaining pools of water. In the dry winter months, hunting is best when the weather is dull and overcast with a south wind blowing; deer and other large animals stay in the open, and armadillos can be found hiding in their nests or burrows.

The people of the Lower Chaco who live some distance from areas good for hunting, such as the Toba of Cerrito and the Mak'a, sometimes organize hunting trips that last three or four weeks. They usually leave with the intention of hunting a commercial species: rhea, iguana, and, in recent years, live rattlesnakes, which are sold for good prices to Chinese and Korean merchants in Asunción's main market, apparently for use as folk medicine. The hunting trips are also opportunities to "fatten up," and in addition to eating large amounts of meat, the men bring home dried meat (*cecina*) for their families.

In the Central and High Chaco, most hunting trips are of fairly short duration, and the distances covered are usually less than in the Lower Chaco. In the agricultural colonies of the Central Chaco, men often spend a few hours looking for small game—charata, pigeons, or rabbits—with the chance of perhaps finding a deer. They usually hunt alone and are likely to return home if they make a kill. In the more marginal "worker villages" such as Sandhorst and Colonia 22, the Indians make trips to the less populated areas on the edge of the Mennonite Colonies. The men go is search of larger game and are sometimes accompanied by the women and children, who spend their time gathering wild fruits. Hunting and gathering expeditions of this type are again seen as opportunities to "fatten up," and most of the game is consumed immediately. The hunting parties tend to return to their traditional areas: the Nivaclé and Manjuy of Sandhorst go to the west of Cruce de Mattei, while the Ayoreo of Campo Loro travel north to hunt along the road from Kilometer 220 to Teniente Martínez.

Along the Upper Pilcomayo, the Nivaclé and the Manjuy, and even the occasional family of Guaraní from Pedro P. Peña, travel inland, usually about a day's walk, to hunt in areas where game is more abundant. These trips rarely last for more than three or four days and are mainly intended to provide a good supply of meat, although in the summer the men may hunt iguana, using dogs, and in the winter set traps for fox, ocelot, and margay. The hunters travel in small parties, usually of close kin or affines, and in summer they may be accompanied by the women of the household, especially if they travel to sites with an abundance of algarrobo or chañar.

For much of the year the High Chaco is dry, and the animals congregate in the vicinity of the waterholes and cañadas. The Indians work along the beds of the cañadas looking for the tracks of peccary. The white-lipped peccary and the taguá move in herds. When the hunters come across their tracks, they follow them at a run. Once they can hear them—the peccaries make a great deal of noise as they crash through the undergrowth—the hunters split up and try to surround the herd, then close in, killing as many as they can. White-lipped peccaries are vicious and may attack, circling the hunters and slashing at them with their razor-sharp tusks. Among the Ayoreo, who used to hunt peccary with clubs and lances, many hunters have been savagely scarred in encounters with white-lipped peccary. Nowadays most Indians hunt peccary with guns, and if the herd does become aggressive, the hunters climb out of reach. Even so, they may have to wait, quiet and perfectly still, for a couple of hours before the herd finally leaves them and moves off.

After a heavy rain has fallen, the larger animals disperse through the forest. Traveling becomes difficult because the floor of the forest turns to mud, and in these conditions hunters prefer to work along open paths or boundary lines in the hope of finding deer or collared peccary. In early summer they try the stands of algarrobo and chañar, where the peccaries come to feed on the fallen fruits; later on, in March and April, they may hunt in the stands of mistol, which also attract animals of various kinds. The areas of open grassland can also be good for hunting. Walking is easy, even after a heavy rain, and the hunters can work along the edge of the forest, looking for rhea, deer, and, if there is nothing else, rabbits, pigeons, and charata.

Honey Collecting

Hunting is often combined with the search for honey. Like hunting, honey collecting is almost exclusively a male activity, and hunting parties often include men who bring no weapons but only axes and pots for carrying honey.

Honey is highly appreciated by all the Indians of the Chaco; indeed, the Ayoreo regard honey as a staple and complain of hunger if it runs out, even though other kinds of food may be available. Honey is found all year round, but its abundance varies from season to season. In spring and early summer, when most of the trees come into flower, honey is at its most plentiful, and the bees' nests are full of new combs. Later in the year there are other periods, coinciding with the flowering of particular trees, such as the coronillo in March, when the bees again build new combs. During the winter, however, the bees are dormant and sustain themselves from the honey produced earlier in the year.

Nearly all the honey that is collected belongs to three species of bee. By far the most prolific is *la reina* (*Apis mellifica*), the domestic bee, which has colonized the region after being introduced from Europe. This bee produces much more honey than any of the native species, and the largest hives—those that are at least two or three years old—can contain twenty-five to thirty liters of honey. The honey of la reina is the same as that of any domestic bee, although the flavor, color, and density will vary according to the age of the combs and the type of vegetation in the area. The hives are found in hollow trees, although occasionally they are built in the open, hanging from the branches of trees or even fence posts.

The other two species, which belong to the Meliponidae family, are the *tapesu'a* (*Trigona bipunctata*) and the *rubito* or *jate'i*. The tapesu'a is a black bee about the size of a housefly; it has no sting, but when disturbed it defends itself by crawling into the hair, ears, eyes, and nostrils and biting. The bite itself is painless, but within a few minutes an irritating blister develops that can last for a couple of days. The tapesu'a builds its nest in hollow trees, and the combs, which look like little pots, about a centimeter in diameter, are made of a mixture of clay and wax. At best, the nest contains only a liter or two of honey, which is darker than that of la reina and has a distinct, rather piquant taste. The rubito, as its name suggests, is a tiny yellow bee. It does not sting and again usually nests in hollow trees. The entrance to the nest is easily recognized from the wax spout through which the bees enter the nest; it is sometimes possible to push a straw down the spout to see whether there is any honey inside. The combs of rubito are similar to those of tapesu'a, but the nest is smaller and rarely contains more than half a liter of a liquid, rather dark honey with a delicate flavor.

Another kind of honey that can sometimes be found is a variety of *lecheguana,* or wasp honey, produced by a small black-and-white stingless wasp. The nest of this wasp contains a small quantity of honey and is apparently only worth collecting when the caranday palm is in flower.

Hunters usually check any hollow trees or fallen logs, and if they come across a large beehive, they leave it, taking care to remember its precise location and return later. Honey is sometimes found by observing the bees when they come to drink and following the line they take as they return to the nest. Apparently, after drinking, the bees return to the nest in a straight line, and even if the hunters lose sight of them, the nest can be found by continuing in the same direction and examining all the larger trees and fallen trunks. Some people are supposed to be capable of following the path of the bees' flight by eye, and indeed the Ayoreo say they pluck the hair from their eyebrows for precisely this reason.

Once a hive has been found, the Indians fell the tree, and if the nest is small, they split the trunk open to expose the combs. The larger nests of la reina and tapesu'a have to be smoked out to stupefy the bees and prevent them from becoming aggressive: the area around the base of the tree is cleared of undergrowth and a fire is lit. Handfuls of leaves or grass are thrown onto the fire to produce a thick smoke, and the smoking grass is pushed into the entrance to the nest. The men then begin to cut the trunk open, taking care not to damage the combs, and they keep blowing more smoke into the nest. Once the combs are exposed or can be reached by hand, they are prized apart and gently lifted out. The men then usually sit down to eat some of the honey and the bee larvae, which have a sweet, rather milky taste. The honey is consumed in its pure form, rather than being diluted with water as in other parts of South America, and the men chew the combs, spitting out the wax and pollen. Honey induces thirst and has a soporific effect, and the men usually rest and drink water or *tereré* (yerba maté with cold water) before moving on. The honey that remains is put into cooking pots or plastic bags; traditionally, special bags were made from whole goat, rabbit, or rhea skins. The honey is often separated from the combs, strained, and stored in bottles. It will keep for a long time and is one of the few products that can always be sold to Paraguayans.

Some Ayoreo, Nivaclé, and Manjuy climb trees to collect honey, using a technique that was probably more widespread before steel axes became available. They climb using a rope tied around the trunk of the tree, and once they reach the bees' nest, they lean back and support themselves on the rope. This leaves their hands free, allowing them to cut a small opening in the trunk, just large enough to reach into the hive. They do not use fire, and the honey is placed in bags or pots tied around the waist.

Honey is used for some fermented drinks. The Nivaclé prepare a potent kind of mead by diluting honey with water and leaving it to ferment in large gourds. The mead is ready in a few days, as soon as the fermentation ceases. Only the mature men drink. They sit in a circle, drinking and singing until the mead is finished or until they have all passed out. The Mak'a also use bee larvae to prepare a type of *chicha*.

Fishing

Fishing is important for many Indian communities, and along the Paraguay and Pilcomayo rivers it is the Indians' principal source of subsistence during certain periods of the year. The traditional techniques—nets, harpoons, and arrows—are still widely used, but fish hooks and lines have also been generally adopted and allow the Indians to fish when the conditions would otherwise be unsuitable.

Nets are used by the Indians of the Upper Pilcomayo—by the Nivaclé on the Paraguayan side of the river, and by the Mataco, Choroti, Toba, and Pilagá on the Argentine side. Net fishing is most effective during the period from April to July, when the Pilcomayo falls to its lowest levels and huge shoals of fish ascend the river. The most abundant species of fish is the *carimbatá* or *sávalo* (*Prochilodus sp.*), a kind of carp, which is much appreciated by the Nivaclé. The other species that are taken include *surubí* (*Pimelodus tigrinus*), *dorado* (*Salminus maxillosus*), and catfish or *mandi'i* (*Pimelodus charias, P. albicans,* and *P. ornatus*). At this time of year a single man can catch sixty to eighty carimbatá, with a total weight of over a hundred kilos, in just one day's or night's fishing.

There are two kinds of nets. The first is a dip net, triangular in shape, tied to the lower ends of two crossed poles, each about two meters in length, that are worked like scissors to open and close the mouth of the net. The other is smaller and is attached to two flexible rods, a meter to a meter and a half in length, which are tied together at both ends. The rods are pulled apart to open the net; when released they spring closed.

The dip nets are used by a group of eight to ten men who fish together in a line, forming a barrier across the shallow river. They choose a site where there are no holes on the bed of the river and wade in up to their waists or chests; then they wait, facing upstream. In the meantime, one or two other men, carrying the smaller nets or long poles, walk upstream five hundred to a thousand meters, plunge into the river, and then work their way down toward the men who form the barrier. They swim, wade, and dive into the deeper pools and beat the surface of the water with their poles to disturb the fish and drive them downstream.

When one of the waiting men feels a fish enter his net, he closes it and lifts it out of the water. He stuns the fish with a blow from a short club, picks it out of the net, and threads it onto a rope, using a large wooden needle that he passes through the fish's gills and out its mouth. As soon as this is done, the fisherman lowers his net into the water again.

Meanwhile the fisherman with the smaller net dives under water, and when he feels the vibrations made by a fish pulls the mouth of the net open and tries to trap the fish inside. When he surfaces, he stuns the fish, threads it onto a rope tied around his waist, and dives again. A large fish can drag a fisherman under the water. Apparently a large surubí can run up to three hundred meters before it tires enough for the fisherman to pull it to the surface; even then it may dive a number of times before it can finally be pulled out onto the bank. Fishing with the smaller net requires considerable skill and endurance, and it is noticeable that today it is usually the older, more experienced men who use this method.

Once the men with the poles and the smaller nets reach the line of fishermen who form the barrier, everyone leaves the water. The men clean and gut the fish and give some of the catch to the men with the poles. Then they move off to another site and start again.

The Nivaclé often fish at night, and since the fishing season is the coldest time of the year, they prepare great bonfires on the beach. They cook the entrails and the fat from the fish with hot peppers and herbs, and eat the stew as they rest and warm themselves by the fires. Meanwhile the women cut the fish open lengthwise, place them in cleft sticks, and leave them to smoke at the side of the fires. The smoked fish can be kept for some time, and once completely dried it can be crushed in a mortar to make a fish meal that will last for months.

The turbid, silt-laden waters of the Upper Pilcomayo can only be fished using nets or lines, but in other waters fish can be taken with arrows or harpoons. The typical bow, used by the Toba, Mak'a, and Lengua on the rivers of the Lower Chaco, and by the Chamococo who fish in the swampy areas that fringe the Paraguay River, is about a meter in length. It is used with a wooden arrow, of about the same length, tipped with a wire point to which a nail or another piece of wire has been bound to form a barb. The arrows are not flighted, and the shaft is sometimes tied to a line, with the other end attached to the fisherman's wrist or the middle of the bow. When the arrow is fired, it lodges in the fish and can be hauled in even if the fish tries to dive into deeper water. The Nivaclé who fish the lower reaches of the Pilcomayo around Estero Patiño use a longer bow about a meter and a half in length and flighted arrows about the same length made from *caña de castilla* (*Arundo donax*). The Nivaclé arrows are not attached with line and once fired have to be retrieved by hand.

Harpoons vary in size and are often prepared on the spot. Some are tipped with the same wire point as the arrows and are barbed, while others have a heavier steel point and are similar to those used for hunting armadillos. In shallow water, fish can also be shot with .22 rifles, but this is less effective, since the fish are often just wounded and dive out of reach into deeper water.

The main species taken in shallow water is the carimbatá, a plankton feeder that in times of flood leaves the main rivers to feed in the surrounding swamps. Other species, including dorado and surubí, also move into shallow water during the floods and are sometimes taken with bow and arrow. At the height of the flood the fish are not that abundant, or are not easily seen, but as the waters begin to recede, the fish are left trapped in shallow pools where they can easily be taken. When the conditions are right, a skilled fisherman can take as many as twenty carimbatá, weighing from twenty to thirty kilos, in only a few hours.

When using the bow and arrow or harpoon, the fishermen wade cautiously through the shallows, taking care to avoid any sudden movement that could disturb the fish. They look for telltale movements of the grass and reeds where the carimbatá are feeding, and listen for the sucking sound of the fish feeding on the surface. During the middle of the day, when there are fewer reflections on the water, the fish can be seen swimming around just below the surface, and their tails and fins sometimes break the surface. In these conditions the fishermen wait—perfectly still, standing under a tree or in front of a steep bank to avoid being silhouetted against the sky—until the fish swim into range.

Fish hooks and nylon lines are also widely used. On the Upper Pilcomayo the Nivaclé still regard the use of hooks and lines as something of a novelty, and it is the younger men who use this method while the older men rely on their nets. When the Pilcomayo is in flood, the Nivaclé use lines to fish in the deep pools and eddies, using a single hook and weighted line, baited with cactus fruit, frogs, or bee larvae. The fishing is best at night, and in a single night a fisherman can take up to twenty kilos of fish. The main species taken when the Pilcomayo is in flood are catfish (*mandi'i*) and the armored fishes known as *armados* or *viejas* (*Dores armatus, D. weddellii,* and *D. maculatus*).

Lines are also used in the Lower Chaco and along the Paraguay River. The lines are weighted with a lead sinker and carry a single, usually fairly large, hook, often tied with a length of wire to prevent it being bitten off by *pirañas* (*Serrasalmo sp.*). The baits include worms, small fish, meat, frogs, and freshwater mussels. On the Paraguay River fishing is best when the river reaches its lowest levels, in January and February, but most species are taken throughout the year. On the tributaries that flow across the Lower Chaco, the fishing is not very good when the rivers are low; during the daylight hours the pirañas are a nuisance, snatching the bait and often biting off the hooks, and other species seem unwilling to feed. Once a heavy rain has fallen and the rivers begin to rise, the fishing improves: shoals of small catfish feed voraciously, snatching the bait as soon as it hits the bottom, and there is always a chance of other, larger species including armados, surubí, dorado, *pacú* (*Colossoma sp.*), and *boga.* By the time the rivers reach flood level and burst their banks, the fishing slackens off, and the main channels are often difficult to reach on foot.

The lakes, drinking ponds, and flooded grasslands of the Lower Chaco support large numbers of small fish such as *tare'ýi* (*Hoplias malabaricus*), *pira-mbocayá* (*Hoplosternum littorale*), and *pastel,* a small brown catfish. They are taken on small hooks, usually tied to a couple of meters of line attached to a pole; the hooks are baited with small pieces of meat and dropped in among the reeds and lilies. This type of fishing is not taken very seriously. A group of women may go to the pond to fish and to wash clothes, and the children fish and bathe. These small fish do, however, provide a supplement to the household's supply of food and in the interior of the Chaco are the only fish that are readily available.

During periods of drought, when the ponds and watercourses dry out, large numbers of small fish are trapped in the remaining pools of mud and stagnant water and can be scooped up in nets or buckets. Two species, the eel-like *mbusú* (*Symbranchus marmoratus*) and the larger *mbusú-capitán* (South American lungfish: *Lepidosiren paradoxa*), are adapted to survive long periods of drought by burying themselves in galleries under the mud, where they secrete a jellylike substance that keeps them moist until the rains fall again. The Lengua dig them out of the mud, and the Chamococo and the Mak'a take them with harpoons (Miraglia 1975:42).

Wild Fruits and Vegetables

Most wild fruits and vegetable products are gathered and processed by women. Men do collect small quantities of fruits or palm hearts while out hunting, but these are usually eaten on the spot. Although women are usually less directly involved in wage labor than men, the importance of gathering appears to have declined markedly in the communities that are more integrated into the market economy.

Today the diet of most Indian households is based on purchased foodstuffs, principally rice, noodles, flour, *fariña* (coarse manioc flour), and *locro* (dried white maize), and it is only when these items are unavailable that gathering takes on any importance as a means of subsistence. This suggests that gathering is something of a marginal activity, providing little more than a supplement to a diet based on the products of hunting, fishing, and wage labor. In the Lower Chaco gathering plays an insignificant role in the Indians' subsistence strategy, although in other areas, such as the Upper Pilcomayo, where there are very few opportunities for acquiring a cash income, it provides a more substantial part of the household's diet.

The importance of gathering also varies between ethnic groups: Nivaclé women, even in urban communities such as the Barrio Obrero of Filadelfia, spend the summer months gathering and processing algarrobo, while the Lengua and Guaraní ignore gathering as a potential means of subsistence. In more isolated communities, such as Pedro P. Peña, the importance of gathering reflects the different subsistence strategies of particular groups. The Guaraní, who rely on a double cycle of agriculture and in some cases stock raising, gather very little in the way of forest products, whereas the Nivaclé and Manjuy give more emphasis to hunting and fishing and rely on gathering for most of the year.

The importance of gathering may also vary between the different eco-

logical regions of the Chaco. The most nutritious fruits—algarrobo, chañar, and mistol—are more abundant in the dry forest of the Central and
High Chaco than in the Lower Chaco. Both kinds of algarrobo (*Prosopis
alba* and *P. nigra*) are found in the islands of forest characteristic of the
Lower Chaco, but they rarely occur in dense stands of the kind found in
the drier regions, while chañar and mistol are rare or nonexistent in the
Lower Chaco. These differences, rather than the degree of integration
into the market economy, may in fact explain the relatively insignificant role of gathering in the subsistence strategy of almost all the Indian
societies of the Lower Chaco.

In the Lower Chaco the principal vegetable products consumed by
the Indians are palm hearts and the fleshy bulbs of certain species of
caraguatá. The palm hearts are taken from the caranday palm and sometimes from the carandilla, a smaller palm found in forested areas. They
are usually consumed raw, although the pithy, rather bitter base is sometimes boiled. Palm hearts are at their best during the winter months,
when they are large and tender, but they can be gathered at any time of
the year.

Some edible species of caraguatá (*Bromelia sp.*) are found in the forested areas of the Chaco. They are gathered during the winter months,
when the outer leaves have dried up and the inner bulb is swollen with
starch. The plants are rooted out with a forked stick, heaped into a pile,
and burned to remove the thorny leaves. Once the fire has died down,
the bulbs are removed from the ashes and can be cut open and eaten.
They can also be boiled and have a taste similar to that of potatoes.

In the Central and High Chaco most fruits come into season during
the summer, from October to March. The first to ripen is the algarrobo,
which is gathered from October until the middle of December. There are
a number of edible varieties of algarrobo (see Stahl 1982:38), but of these,
two—the white algarrobo (*Prosopis alba*) and the black algarrobo (*P.
nigra*)—are the most important. During early summer, Nivaclé women
in communities such as Mistolar and Pedro P. Peña leave their villages almost daily to harvest algarrobo. They leave in small family groups, with
their caraguatá fiber bags strapped across their foreheads, carrying long
poles hooked at the far end that are used to pull the pods of algarrobo
from the higher branches. After a few hours the women return laden with

great quantities of algarrobo, which they spread out on mats or animal skins to dry in the sun.

Of the two varieties, the white algarrobo is less abundant than the black, but it has a softer, fleshy pod and can be consumed raw. Both varieties are made into flour and paste. The pods are ground with a hardwood pestle until the seeds are separated from the fleshy material, which, if the pods have been dried thoroughly, is reduced to flour. This is sieved through a bag or a finely woven mesh of caraguatá fibers to separate it from the remaining seeds and fiber. The flour is stored in skins, or now in plastic bags, and the seeds and fiber are mixed with water to make a paste that can be chewed to extract the sweet-tasting flour that remains. The flour will keep for some time and can be consumed raw or mixed with water or stews. Traditionally, it was also used for making *chicha,* a fermented drink that was consumed in large quantities during feasts that could attract visitors from great distances and could last five or six weeks.

From the beginning of November onward, the fruits of the chañar start to ripen. The fruits are collected along with those of the algarrobo, although in smaller quantities, and continue to be harvested until the middle of January, unless the Pilcomayo floods early and inundates the stands of chañar. The fruit can be consumed raw, and when dried in the sun for a few days will keep for long periods. The pulp tastes something like dates and is made into small cakes or cooked with fish oil.

The other wild fruits that are gathered during the early summer include the *sachasandia,* the *payagua naranja* or *bola verde,* and cactus fruit or *tuna* (*Harrisia sp.*). The fruits of both the sachasandia and the payagua naranja are poisonous and require considerable preparation before they can be consumed. Nivaclé women regard the sachasandia as the more poisonous of the two and handle the fruits with great caution. The fruits are pulled from the plant using a long pole, hooked at the end; most of the poisonous white powder that covers the fruits is knocked off when they hit the ground. Even so, the women take care when filling their bags to ensure that none of the powder touches their lips or gets in their eyes. They boil the fruits to remove the poison, and since the poison dissolves slowly, they change the water a number of times. The mature fruits are less toxic than the unripe ones, but even these may have to be boiled as many as six times before they can be eaten.

The sachasandia can be stored until winter. The fruits are cooked overnight in a tunnel-like oven dug in the ground; they are placed in the hot ashes, and the tunnel is closed off. After cooking, they are left in the sun for a few days until partially dehydrated and then stored in bags until needed. Even after this treatment, they have to be boiled about four times before they can be eaten, and they are usually added to stews of fish or meat.

The mature fruits of the payagua naranja are collected where they have fallen to the ground. They are peeled, the seeds and pulp are boiled for three days and nights to remove all the poison, and they are then left in the sun to dry. Once dry, the seeds are cracked open and the kernels eaten. After being boiled, the seeds can be preserved for storage by being cooked overnight in an oven of the kind described above; they will keep until winter but have to be boiled again before they can be eaten.

The fruits of tuna are also picked off the ground. The most commonly consumed variety has no spines and can be eaten raw. The pulp containing the seeds is soft and jellylike and has a sharp taste, something like a kiwi fruit. The fruits can be preserved if they are cooked overnight in hot ashes; once dried they are threaded onto a string and hung inside the house. Dried tuna is used as a condiment—often mixed with herbs or hot peppers—and an infusion of the dried fruits is used as a remedy for diarrhea.

During March and April the mistol and the *poroto del monte* (*Capparis retusa*) come into season. The Indians of the Upper Pilcomayo disregard the mistol today, perhaps because it ripens at the same time that their gardens are at their most productive. The small berries of the mistol can be eaten raw, and they also provide a nourishing fodder for sheep and goats. The poroto del monte is a more important resource, since it can be dried in the sun and stored for the winter months. Like the sachasandia and the payagua naranja, it is poisonous and has to be boiled as many as six times to render it edible.

The winter is a difficult time for nearly all the Indians of the Chaco. There is no agricultural production, and if there are no opportunities for wage labor, they have to resort to gathering the meager resources that are available, since even the most frugal households will have exhausted their stores of algarrobo, poroto del monte, and sachasandia. In the area of the Upper Pilcomayo, the Manjuy, and occasionally some of the Nivaclé, travel inland to search for caraguatá, for a species of liana (possibly *Phaseolus caracalla*), and for a wild variety of bitter manioc. The wild manioc has to be crushed and treated in the same way as the poroto del monte or the sachasandia and is not very effective in satisfying the Indians' hunger. In other areas caraguatá is virtually the only vegetable product available.

The Indians of the Chaco gather other vegetable products, including condiments—particularly a small wild variety of hot pepper—and a variety of herbal remedies and stimulants. Certain species of caraguatá are also gathered to make thread. The women strip the leaves of their flesh, using the back of a knife or a piece of iron, and hang the fibers up to dry. They roll the dried fibers on their thighs to produce a fine thread, which is then plaited into whatever thickness of string is required. The thread is used for a range of items. Nearly all the Indians use caraguatá string bags: women use large bags for carrying wild fruits, garden produce, and firewood; men use a different style of bag to carry their hunting equipment, and small bags for carrying personal items such as pipes, documents, cartridges, and so on. The Chamococo and some of the Lengua-Maskoy–speaking groups manufacture string hammocks, which are used mainly for infants, and the Indians of the Upper Pilcomayo use caraguatá string for their fishing nets. Traditionally, caraguatá thread was also used for certain items of clothing, such as women's skirts and the leggings worn by men as protection for walking in dense thorny undergrowth.

The caranday palm is another important source of raw material. In the Lower Chaco women gather and dry the leaves for use in weaving fans, baskets, and straw hats. Although these skills may originally have been acquired from Paraguayans, the items manufactured by some Indian women, especially among the Chamococo, are far more carefully made than those produced by Paraguayan artisans. The Chamococo decorate their fans and baskets with intricate symmetrical designs, which are achieved by interweaving the palm leaves with lengths of black and brown *guembe-pí* (the outer skin of a liana). The flowering stems of the caranday palm are used for making brooms, which along with the fans and basketry can provide the women with some cash income.

Other plants are used as a source of water. Permanent settlements are always sited close to a source of drinking water, but hunters and small nomadic bands, like the Manjuy, sometimes have to rely on the water that remains trapped between the leaves of the *chuza* (a broad-leaved bromeliad). The water can be sipped from the chuza by inserting a hollow straw between the leaves, or the plants can be uprooted and tipped into a cooking pot. In times of severe drought, even the water in the chuza dries up, and the Indians may be forced to drink the water contained in the large underground tuber of the *sipoi* or *yvy'á* (*Jacaratia hassleriana*). This liquid quenches the thirst but has a high mineral content and causes stomach cramps if relied on for more than a couple of days.

This chapter has tried to illustrate the diversity of the foraging economy, in terms of the resources exploited and the techniques utilized. I have shown how this diversity responds to the variations in season, climate, and the regional ecology of the Chaco.

Moreover, although foraging activities are today almost invariably combined with wage labor, agriculture, or stock raising, I have suggested that it is the rationality of the foraging economy that dominates the Indians' perception of all productive activities. This is a theme to which I return in the next two chapters, where I examine agriculture and stock raising and production for the market. I shall describe how the potential of these activities is constrained, not only by the environment, but also by an economic strategy that is oriented to the exploitation of more immediately available resources. This in turn is founded on a perception of the natural resources of the Chaco as bountiful and potentially unlimited.

A further point that merits comment is that the activities considered in this chapter demand very little in the way of cooperation. Within the limits imposed by the sexual division of labor, there is little or no specialization of tasks, and most activities can be carried out, if absolutely necessary, by a single man or woman. Even in the case of fishing with nets—

the one technique that does demand some cooperation — the groups that participate can be, and indeed are, formed on an informal, day-to-day basis. Social relations, at least above the level of the household, are thus in no sense dependent on relations of production. This has allowed the indigenous societies of the Chaco the possibility of a social organization characterized by great flexibility and by a strong emphasis on indepen-dence and personal autonomy. These again are themes to which I return later in this book.

CHAPTER THREE

Agriculture and Livestock

Agriculture

AGRICULTURE APPEARS never to have been of as much importance for the Chaco societies as it is for most of the societies of the tropical forest regions of Lowland South America. This is due both to the ecology of the Chaco—poor soils and drainage, unfavorable and unpredictable climate—and, in the modern context, to the lack of legal access to land, as well as to the emphasis that the Indians give to the exploitation of more immediately available resources.

In historical times almost all the Indian societies of the Chaco practiced some form of agriculture. The accounts of the early Spanish explorers mention groups that cultivated large areas (Susnik 1971), as do the accounts of the Jesuit missionaries who worked among the Zamuco-speaking tribes in the eighteenth century (Lussagnet 1961–62). The ethnographers from the beginning of the twentieth century also provide brief accounts of the agriculture practiced by the Choroti, Lengua, Nivaclé, and Mataco (Rosen 1904; Grubb 1911; Nordenskiöld 1912). Some of the Guaicuruan tribes are reputed to have abandoned agriculture when they adopted the horse, but they continued to exact produce from their Arawak vassals (Metraux 1963:250). Only the Chamococo claim to have lived exclusively from hunting and gathering some two hundred years ago, when the Horio and Ebidoso inhabited the interior of the Chaco (Susnik 1969).

Table 2 provides some idea of the present-day importance of agriculture. The regions shown in this and the following tables are shown in map 3. The figures refer to subsistence production—there were virtually no cash crops except in the Central Chaco—during the 1980–81 agricultural year. The table shows that, despite the Indians' agricultural tradition, some 52 percent (2,116) of households cultivated nothing during the 1980–81

Table 2: Households cultivating land, by region and type of settlement

	0 ha	<0.5 ha	0.5–2.9 ha	3.0–4.9 ha	>4.9 ha	Total no. of house-holds
Lower Chaco	993	333	214	0	3	1,543
Missions	210	169	159	0	3	541
Assisted communities	62	0	0	0	0	62
Others	721	164	55	0	0	940
Central Chaco	852	545	412	64	91	1,964
Missions	15	32	40	2	3	92
Assisted communities	703	491	368	62	88	1,712
Others	134	22	4	0	0	160
High Chaco	271	152	158	6	4	591
Missions	139	95	100	4	3	341
Assisted communities	32	42	24	0	0	98
Others	100	15	34	2	1	152
Total	2,116	1,030	784	70	98	4,098
Missions	364	296	299	6	9	974
Assisted communities	797	533	392	62	88	1,872
Others	955	201	93	2	1	1,252

Source: INDI 1982.

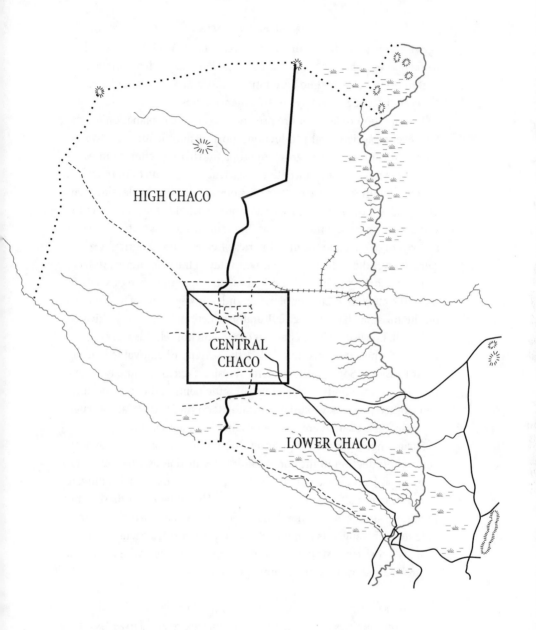

Map 3. The Paraguayan Chaco: Census regions

agricultural year, while a further 25 percent (1,030) cultivated less than half a hectare. This contrasts with Eastern Paraguay, where only 9 percent of households had no agriculture, and 72 percent planted areas of between 0.5 and 2.9 hectares of subsistence crops.

The situation of land tenure provides part of the explanation for the low level of agricultural production: most of the Indians that live on ranches are not allowed to grow any crops, and in other communities insecurity of tenure is a disincentive to agricultural production. In table 2 the communities that are neither missions nor assisted by development projects have the highest proportion of households that do not cultivate (76 percent). On the missions, the Indians enjoy a certain de facto security of tenure, and the missionaries often encourage agriculture because it gives the Indians an incentive to stay in the community. Indeed, some missions even provide limited assistance in the form of seeds or use of the mission tractor for plowing, and only 37 percent of households on the missions have no agricultural production. The areas cultivated are small, however, with 49 percent of mission households working less than half a hectare. This may reflect the scarcity of cultivable land on most missions. Some, such as Santa Teresita, Puerto Casado, and Cerrito, are situated on the edge of urban settlements and have little land, while others, such as Makthlawaiya and Maria Auxiliadora, are situated in low-lying areas that are largely unsuitable for agriculture.

Surprisingly, there is a high proportion of households without agricultural production in the communities classified as assisted by development projects (43 percent overall), and most of those that do cultivate have less than half a hectare (28 percent). The situation of these communities varies, but in general they enjoy greater support and security of tenure. This suggests that the relative importance of agriculture in the Indians' subsistence strategy is the result of other factors, which can best be understood by looking at some specific cases.

AGRICULTURAL COLONIES IN THE CENTRAL CHACO

Those communities in the Central Chaco that are referred to as "assisted communities" consisted of seven agricultural colonies at the time the 1981 census was carried out.[1] The first of these colonies, Yalve Sanga, was founded in 1955, while Nich'a Toyish and Paz del Chaco had been settled only a year or two before the census was taken. In all these colonies, the intention was to provide the Indians with an independent economic base so as to reduce the social pressures caused by the chronic under- and unemployment that has existed in the Mennonite Colonies since mechanization was introduced in the 1960s. The program is also genuinely seen by the Mennonite advisers as one of "guided social change" (Stahl 1974), aimed at raising the Indians' standard of living.

Stahl (1974) describes the colonies as being organized along "traditional lines." In fact, the organization, at the level of both the village and the colony, is more akin to that of the Mennonites than to anything the Indians would have known before. Title to the land is vested with ASCIM, the Mennonite agency responsible for the settlement program, and the Indians enjoy the use of their plots under conditions of usufruct. If they abandon their plots, or are expelled from the colony (among other things, alcohol is forbidden), they lose all rights to the land.

Each colony is divided into villages of ten to thirty households settled along the access roads that cut across the areas of open grassland. Most dwellings are located on the roadside, and each household has rights to an area of at least five hectares of grassland and about twenty hectares of forest. The sandy soils of the grasslands are used for agriculture, while the heavier soils of the forest can be cleared and put into pasture. Each household is expected to cultivate both food staples (sweet potato, squash, maize, beans, and watermelon) and cash crops (usually peanuts, cotton, or castor beans). Each village is also expected to cultivate a communal plot of up to fifty hectares of cash crops. ASCIM has provided the Indian cooperatives with tractors for plowing, with priority given to the communal plots, and in the most recently established colonies the Indians receive shares in other items of equipment such as plows, horse-drawn carts, and seed drills. Small amounts of credit are also available to cover the costs of seed and insecticides (for cotton), and to provide for the basic needs of the household in the period between planting and harvest. Technical assistance is provided by Mennonite agronomists and by village leaders who have attended elementary courses in agriculture or veterinary medicine.

In spite of the efforts of the Mennonite advisers and the village leaders, it is apparent that these colonies do not even achieve a level of self-subsistence. Some 41 percent of the households cultivated no food staples during the 1980–81 agricultural year, and of those that did cultivate, 49 percent worked less than half a hectare. In contrast, however, 5 percent of the population claimed to have cultivated more than five hectares of food staples, an amount that would appear to be surplus to any household's requirements.

The Indians themselves usually explain the low level of agricultural production in terms of their dependence on wage labor. They claim that the credit they receive is insufficient to cover their needs, and that they are obliged to work outside the colonies at critical moments in the agricultural year when they should be planting or weeding their own crops. This argument has some truth to it, but there are certain assumptions underlying it that reflect the role of agriculture in the traditional subsistence strategy of the Chaco societies.

Cultivation on the grasslands of the Central Chaco involves less effort than cultivation in the tropical forests of Eastern Paraguay. There is no forest cover to clear, and the staple crops—sweet potato, maize, beans, watermelons, and several varieties of squash and pumpkin—demand little in the way of attention. Once the land has been cleared, the seeds can be planted with a manual seed drill or by hand, and the soil needs no other preparation. Sweet potato is usually weeded twice to allow the tubers space in which to develop; other crops are weeded only when the first shoots begin to appear, and if necessary can be left untended. If there is sufficient rainfall, crops are planted at the end of October and are harvested from December through to March or April. Only sweet potato can be harvested all year round, and from April onward the gardens are otherwise unproductive.

In principle, the Indians could cover their annual needs through storage—maize, beans, and the smaller varieties of pumpkin (*anco* and *anda'i*) can be sun-dried or roasted and will last almost indefinitely—or through the sale of cash crops, which are harvested from February onward. In reality, by March or April, when the Indians have harvested their cotton, and sometimes before then, the Indians abandon their own plantations to work for the Mennonites, harvesting cotton and castor beans. Even the Indian schools close for the cotton harvest to allow the children to join their parents in the fields. By May the cotton harvest

94

is finished, and the opportunities for wage labor become much scarcer; some families are employed harvesting grass seed, while the men work clearing pasture or cutting fence posts and firewood.

The middle of the winter, from May to September, is the hardest time of the year. Any crops that have been stored rarely last beyond May, and the earnings from cash crops are used to pay off the loans that were contracted during the previous year. The small scale of storage may also be due to social pressures—this is a theme to which I shall return later—but above all it is a reflection of traditional attitudes to agriculture, which is seen as a marginal enterprise that compares unfavorably with foraging and wage labor.

In spite of the relative ease with which gardens can be cultivated, one of the reasons why agriculture is not perceived as a vital activity is that the results are uncertain. Climatic conditions in the Central Chaco are such that the rains that fall in September or October, at the beginning of the summer, may be followed by a drought lasting well into the middle of December. Moreover, the rain that does fall during this critical period is often sporadic and very localized. In November 1979, for example, rain fell on only two of the villages in Yalve Sanga; others, only two or three kilometers away, received no rainfall from early October onward. Where the rain had fallen, the maize and watermelons were almost ripe, while in the other villages the crops had been scorched and the harvest appeared to be lost. Those households that still had seed intended to plant again as soon as a heavy rain fell, but others were desperate and were looking for work with Mennonite employers.

Rainfall is vital in determining the success of agriculture in the Chaco, and it is precisely in the critical month of November that rainfall is at its least predictable (Gorham 1973). Heavy or continuous rain can be just as disastrous as drought: the seeds and shoots can be washed away, and later in the season the root crops, squash and pumpkins, will rot in the ground. Birds, particularly parakeets (*Nandayus nenday*), and insect pests can also damage or completely destroy an otherwise successful crop.

Small-scale farming in the Central Chaco, without the organization, self-discipline, and technology of the Mennonite farmer, is at best difficult. The Mennonites themselves expect to make a reasonable profit about three years in every five, and they plan their expenditure accordingly: the years of bonanza are the years in which capital investments are made and any luxuries purchased, while the bad years are years of belt tightening. For the Indians, practicing agriculture at subsistence level, there is no chance of tightening their belts any further. The drought that destroys a Mennonite's crop may force him to put off the purchase of a new car or tractor for another year, but the Mennonite, unless he overextends his credit, in the long run still expects to make a reasonable living from agriculture. In this respect the drought that destroys an Indian's crop is different. At best it will force him to abandon agriculture for some other activity that can offer immediate returns—hunting or working for a *patrón*. At worst it can mean starvation.

Under these circumstances, it is hardly surprising that after one or two bad years the Indians lose heart. This is perhaps the most striking contrast between Indian and Mennonite attitudes to agriculture. In the years following a bad harvest, the Mennonites continue to cultivate according to plan and select their crops, mainly cash crops, by balancing the expectation of prices, production costs, and relative risk. The Indians, on the other hand, reduce the scale of their cultivation; and the expectation of success, the optimism that follows a good year, is almost completely absent. The low level of production is not simply the result of a shortage of seed, difficulties in obtaining credit, or the need to work outside— although all of these factors play a part—but at a more general level it is a denial that agriculture can provide the basis for subsistence. However, after a good year, or a particularly hard year of unemployment, low wages, or payment in credit notes (*vales*), these expectations can be reversed, with wage labor becoming the less favored alternative: "working to make the Mennonites rich" or "working to get enough to eat."

TRADITIONAL SYSTEMS OF CULTIVATION

Since agriculture is so uncertain, it is worth considering why the Indians bother to cultivate at all. To answer this question, it is useful to examine the systems of agricultural production among the more traditional groups who live in the most isolated areas of the Chaco.

The Ayoreo belonging to Menuane's group, who inhabited an area some seventy kilometers (forty-five miles) to the west of Bahía Negra, were a small band, totaling only nineteen people, and were part of a larger group known as the Garaigosode, "people of the grasslands." The area they inhabited, on the margins of the High Chaco, was mostly forest: the better drained areas included stands of quebracho colorado, *lapacho* (*Tabebuia impetiginosa*), and *trébol* (*Amburana cearensis*), while the wetter areas were dominated by palo santo and guaimí piré. The forest floor was covered with a dense undergrowth of caraguatá and chuza, which provided the Ayoreo with food, fiber for making string, and water, and was a good area for hunting the tortoises and armadillos that made up the bulk of their diet. There were also small patches of open grassland, with a shallow sandy soil underlain by layers of clay, as evidenced by the presence of a few caranday palms.

Menuane's band never moved far from the grasslands. They usually camped on the edge of the forest, in places slightly elevated above the surrounding area. These sites were above the level of the floods and were shaded by large trees; the breeze from the grasslands also offered a break from the heat and mosquitoes of the forest. At the time I visited the area, in the winter of 1977, the Ayoreo were living near the few Paraguayans, ocelot hunters and small ranchers, who had moved into the area during the previous five years. The movements of the band followed no particular pattern. They had remained for months at some sites, usually where they could acquire yerba maté, tobacco, or sugar from a Paraguayan. Other sites had been occupied for only a few days, for example, when they had been gathering the fruit of the *mbocayá* palm (*Acrocomia totai*), which grew in a few places in this area.

Although none of the camps were permanent, Menuane's band had planted small patches of crops wherever they stayed any length of time and, having abandoned the site, would later return to harvest the crops that were left. Few of the abandoned gardens were more than a day's walk from any other camp, and visits to the abandoned gardens were inevitably combined with hunting or honey collecting.

The crops were planted near the camp, on the edge of the forest, or in the grassland. The men and women cooperated in clearing the undergrowth and planting. Although the Ayoreo had steel axes, they left the larger trees standing; as well as reducing the work, this may have helped by providing shade and shelter from the north wind. The band planted

97

a limited range of crops: squash, beans, maize, watermelon, and gourds (used as containers). At some of the garden sites they planted only squash and watermelon, the crops that require least attention. All the crops they planted have a short growing season, are relatively hardy, and are able to tolerate poor soils. Indeed, these are the specific qualities described in the myths that explain how the original people (*Jnani Bajade*) became the plants and animals that they are today.

This choice of crops allows the Ayoreo to practice a form of agriculture that requires a minimum of effort and leaves them free to move from site to site. As well as providing the opportunity to combine agriculture with a seminomadic existence as hunters and gatherers, the strategy of maintaining a number of small gardens scattered over a wide area has the advantage of spreading the risks. The average annual rainfall in the area I have described is probably around 900 millimeters (35 inches)— higher than in the Central Chaco, but equally unpredictable and often very localized. The rainfall, particularly in the summer and early autumn, may vary greatly: one garden may receive little or no rain, while another only a few kilometers away may receive adequate rainfall or even be flooded out.

The Ayoreo spread their risks temporally as well as spatially. Since no two gardens are planted at the same time, the crops continue to ripen at staggered intervals. A month or two's drought may destroy any crops planted after the October rains, but gardens that are planted later may be more successful. The Ayoreo continue to plant well into the new year in order to take advantage of the sporadic and usually very localized rains that fall between March and May. Since some of the crops, particularly squash, produce over quite a long period, the Ayoreo, in a good year, may be harvesting well into the winter months. Indeed, in July 1977, after some months without any heavy rainfall, the Ayoreo were still harvesting enough squash to support not only themselves but also a couple of Paraguayan hunters who were living at their camp site.

This strategy appears to have been common among the Chaco societies. Even in the Lower Chaco, where rainfall is higher and the soils poorer and less permeable, this would be the only way of combining cultivation with a seminomadic existence. Only along the Upper Pilco-mayo do any communities appear to have led a more sedentary existence. Here, the conditions for agriculture were better, with opportunities for fishing as well as an abundance of algarrobo and chañar. Even so, in the area bordering the Upper Pilcomayo, subsistence strategies vary considerably across ethnic groups and between communities of the same ethnic group, although this appears to be less marked than in the period before the Chaco War.

The Manjuy of Loma Alegre, who are now largely intermarried with the Nivaclé, live on a bluff overlooking the Pilcomayo, some fifteen kilometers (nine miles) downriver from the Catholic mission of Pedro P. Peña. The composition of the group varies from day to day, as the families move between Loma Alegre, the mission in Pedro P. Peña, Misión La Paz (Argentina), Mistolar, the neighboring ranches, and Sandhorst in the Mennonite Colonies. This traveling is due to various factors: pressure from the mission sisters, who want the children living close to the mission school; the need to earn money; and at times nothing more than the desire for a change of scenery or diet.

In spite of the continual movement, the Manjuy of Loma Alegre grow some crops, although by the standards of their Nivaclé and Guaraní neighbors their gardens seem almost totally unkept. The brushwood enclosures, built to keep out the neighbors' pigs and cattle, are in a state of disrepair, and some of the gardens are not enclosed at all but have been planted in the middle of the settlement. The houses, surrounded by squash plants and with their roofs buried under the runners of gourds, seem almost hidden among the foliage, and to reach the houses one has to walk through a tangle of vines—squash, watermelon, and gourds, all intermixed one with another. The trees around the settlement have been felled, but this was done some years before, when the Manjuy were given rations by API to encourage them to develop the gardens in Loma Alegre. Since then little has been done: much of the area that was cleared is now not even cultivated, no time has been spent preparing the soil, and none of the gardens have been weeded. The crops—squash, watermelon, gourds, and a few maize plants—are those that require the least attention and can be grown from small amounts of seed.

The other Indians of the region believe that the Manjuy were originally hunters and gatherers who knew nothing of agriculture, but the Manjuy claim to have always cultivated in much the same way they do at present. The families in Loma Alegre originally came from Cañada Milico, a riverbed that runs parallel to the Pilcomayo some fifty kilometers (thirty miles) inland. There they moved between two sites, Anacché and Juansocín, where they cultivated small plots. According to one of the older men, the group would abandon one site as soon as the crops were finished and then move on to harvest at the other. This account may exaggerate the importance of agriculture, but it does suggest that the Manjuy abandoned their gardens between planting and harvest and that they expected to harvest at various times during the year.

For much of the year no water flows in Cañada Milico, but there are pools of water in the bed of the cañada during the driest months. In the winter this is the only source of water in the interior of the Chaco, and large animals come here to drink. The Manjuy probably spent much of their time hunting in the cañada and never camped more than a day or two from their gardens.

The gardens were planted in the bed of the cañada, where the soils retain some moisture throughout the year; there were no trees or dense undergrowth because floods, which occur after a period of heavy rain, would wash out the bottom of the cañada. The seeds were planted and the crops left until they ripened. The gardens would have survived all but the severest droughts, and the main problems would have been flooding and the damage caused by wild animals, particularly the white-lipped peccary, which abound in this area. Unlike some of the other cañadas, Cañada Milico only rarely carries floodwater from the Pilcomayo, but the floods caused by heavy rain would wash away any crops planted in the riverbed. This makes it unlikely that the Manjuy could ever have depended on agriculture as a subsistence activity; rather, as in the case of the Ayoreo, agriculture seems to have provided a useful supplement to a diet that was based mainly on hunting and gathering.

THE NIVACLÉ

The importance of agriculture varied between the different groups of Nivaclé. The Jotoi Lhavos, "people of the grasslands," and the Yitá Lhavos, "people of the thorn forest," appear to have cultivated in the same way as the Manjuy and the Ayoreo. The Towok Lhavos, "people of the river," were more sedentary and cultivated on a larger scale.

Most of the Nivaclé of Mistolar and Pedro P. Peña have spent many years working in the Mennonite Colonies, but they practice a type of agriculture similar to that from the period before the Chaco War. The soils along the Pilcomayo are different from those of the Central Chaco: wooded areas rather than grasslands are cultivated, and there are no cash crops because the markets are too distant. They prepare their gardens on the high banks of the Pilcomayo, which remain above the usual flood level, and choose areas of lighter, sandy soil that are indicated by a fairly dense growth of herbaceous plants. They clear most of the trees as well as the undergrowth; the tree trunks and the larger branches are used to construct the enclosures (*cercos*) needed to keep cattle, pigs, and goats out of the gardens, and the rest of the undergrowth is left to dry and is then piled up and burned. The ashes are scattered over the gardens, and after the first summer rains have fallen, the garden is dug over, nowadays with a spade or a hoe. If the early rains are sufficient, part of the garden will be planted in September, first with maize and then, if the soils are still moist, with squash, pumpkins, and watermelon. A period of drought often follows, and planting may be delayed until December or January.

The planting of maize, and sometimes of other crops, is staggered to extend the period of harvest and limit the risk of drought. Nowadays the maize tends to be sown in straight lines, often interplanted with beans, squash, or sweet potato, while the other crops are planted in irregular patches in different parts of the garden. The Nivaclé expect a low rate of generation from their seed; they dig a shallow hole with a machete and sow five or six different seeds at a time. Sweet potato is grown from runners, transplanted singly, and manioc from cuttings, also planted singly.

The staple crops are squash, pumpkins, beans, maize, sweet potato, melon, watermelon, and some sweet manioc. Apparently the Nivaclé also used to plant a variety of bitter manioc (a crop virtually unknown in other parts of Paraguay), but this crop, which requires more care in processing, has since been abandoned. Some of the varieties of pumpkin, maize, and watermelon are peculiar to the Nivaclé and are unknown in other parts of the Chaco. The Nivaclé take a certain pride in these crops; they appear to yield less than other varieties but may be hardier. The small varieties of pumpkin can also be dried or roasted for storage. In addition to these food staples, the Nivaclé also plant tobacco, hot peppers, and *c'uvaitsi,* a yellow flowering plant that looks similar to a daisy and is used as a condiment or masticated to relieve fatigue and hunger.

The crops are weeded only if the growth of weeds is intense. Otherwise the garden receives little attention, although at the beginning of the winter the surviving runners of squash and sweet potato are covered with dry grass or weeds to prevent frost damage.

In a good year the harvest can extend from November until May, and most of the crops are consumed as soon as they are harvested. Beans, maize, and pumpkins are sometimes dried for storage, and the seed is kept in bags or gourds hanging from the roof of the house.

The main effort demanded by this kind of cultivation is the construction of the enclosures (*cercos*), a task in which men and women both participate. The enclosures are necessary because the sheep and goats of the Nivaclé, and the pigs and cattle of their *criollo* neighbors, graze freely around the settlements. In some areas, particularly around Pedro P. Peña, the viscacha (*Lagostomus maximus*) is a menace. These large rodents live in underground colonies and come out to forage at night, and they can quickly strip any gardens that have not been properly fenced in.

A number of techniques are used for building the enclosures: The simplest is to pile up branches at the edge of the garden, but these piles usually collapse after a couple of years and are insufficient to keep the viscachas out. Another is to erect forked posts along the perimeter of the garden and to lay tree trunks along the forks; smaller trunks and branches are then leaned along both sides, forming a fairly compact wall. The most effective, but also the most time-consuming, technique is to build a solid wall of upright posts around the edge of the garden. A height of about one and a half meters is sufficient to keep most animals out, but even a wall of only a meter in height can be built up by laying thorny branches against it.

Neighboring families often work together to construct the *cercos,* and either plant their own gardens within the same enclosure or share a common dividing wall. Once constructed, the enclosure can continue in use, with only minor repairs, for a number of years. The Nivaclé cultivate the same patch of ground for longer than is usual in Eastern Paraguay, and there appear to be no problems of soil exhaustion. Indeed, the Nivaclé believe that crop yields improve as a result of continued cultivation, and they continue to plant the same crops in the same places within the garden. The heavy Chaco soils have high levels of nutrients and may well produce better after a number of years in cultivation, since the successive planting and turning help to aerate the soil and improve its capacity for retaining moisture.

This type of agriculture is part of a relatively sedentary subsistence strategy, which combines agriculture with fishing, gathering, raising sheep and goats, and, since the turn of the twentieth century, migrant wage labor. Hunting is of less importance than fishing: the Pilcomayo abounds in fish, particularly during the winter months, but large game animals appear to have always been scarce in the area close to the river (Nordenskiöld 1912). During the summer, from October to April, agricultural produce is supplemented with wild fruits, especially algarrobo, chañar, and later the poroto del monte. The most difficult months are August and September, which the Nivaclé traditionally survived by gathering sachasandia, caraguatá, and a liana that Metraux (1963:247) identifies as *Phaseolus caracalla,* and if necessary by slaughtering the sheep and goats, which would be short of pasture. For many years now, the winter months have also been a period of migrant wage labor, in the cane fields of northern Argentina and more recently in the Mennonite Colonies.

Not all the Nivaclé led such a sedentary life; indeed, some of the communities that considered themselves Towok Lhavos, "people of the river" spent part of the year living away from the Pilcomayo.

The Votsopú Lhavos, a group of some ten to twelve households, moved between four sites: Votsopú, a hunting camp, noted for an abundance of rhea and wasp honey (from which the site took its name); Toyshivoyish, another hunting camp, located near a permanent waterhole; Campo Ampú, a garden site situated in an area of grassland and located near a large stand of algarrobo; and Tinayfas, a fishing camp on the Pilcomayo that was shared with another group from the interior, the Yitauyis Lhavos. The Votsopú Lhavos did not own any livestock, and the gardens at Campo Ampú were left without enclosures. Agriculture here was probably fairly rudimentary, something like that described for the Ayoreo, and the people who lived in Campo Ampú remember the site more for its abundant algarrobo than for its gardens.

While Campo Ampú was clearly a summer site and Tinayfas a fishing site, occupied from May to July, the other two sites were less obviously seasonal in character. Toyshivoyish, with its waterhole, was probably occupied during periods of drought—the waterhole would have attracted game as well as providing a permanent source of water—but the community seems to have moved between this site and Votsopú whenever game became scarce or the families wanted a change.

The transhumant strategy of groups like the Votsopú Lhavos offered the possibility of exploiting some of the best sites for hunting, gathering, and fishing at the appropriate times of the year, but at the cost of a less sophisticated agriculture and little or no stock raising. The strategy depended on the goodwill of the riverine Nivaclé; indeed, the Votsopú Lhavos were closely intermarried with the Nivaclé who lived at the original site of Mistolar. The Nivaclé of the interior, such as the Yitá Lhavos, were, on the other hand, regarded as inferior, or even as potentially hostile (Chase Sardi 1981:19). In this sense the Towok Lhavos were as much a political as an ecological unit, encompassing two different populations: the sedentary groups settled on the river and the groups, such as the Votsopú Lhavos, that moved to the river only for the fishing season.

Most of the sites in the interior were abandoned after the Chaco War. The inhabitants eventually settled in the Mennonite Colonies, but before the migrations of the 1950s the Nivaclé moved to sites along the river. Some elderly men claim they moved to Mistolar or Pedro P. Peña because the conditions were better for agriculture, but two other factors also appear to have underlain the increasingly sedentary pattern of settlement. The first was a dramatic decline in the population brought about by the epidemics that followed the Chaco War, which left many small groups unable to continue as viable hunter-gatherer bands. The other was the encroachment of Argentine and Paraguayan settlers into areas that had previously been occupied only by the Nivaclé. Indeed, often the mere presence of settlers was sufficient to force small groups to abandon their traditional sites in the interior and seek refuge among the larger communities on the river.

The subsistence strategies considered so far can be conceived of as different points on a continuum. At one end are the seminomadic bands of hunters and gatherers, like the Ayoreo, and at the other are the Guaraní Occidentales, who have a true agricultural tradition, although they have only been settled in the Chaco for the last sixty years.

The Guaraní of Pedro P. Peña practice a subsistence strategy that is based almost entirely on agriculture and stock raising. They cultivate throughout the year, alternating between the bed of the Pilcomayo and the high banks that remain above flood level. Their summer gardens, situated above flood level, are similar to those already described for the Nivaclé, although they are usually larger — sometimes covering up to two hectares (five acres) — and better cared for, and the enclosures are more substantial. The staple crops are the same as those of the Nivaclé, although maize is of more importance, part of the harvest being stored in specially constructed shelters (*trojas*). The maize is consumed during the period between the end of the summer harvest and the beginning of the winter harvest, and it is also fed to pigs and chickens.

When the Pilcomayo reaches its lowest level, in the months of May or June, the Guaraní build new enclosures on the exposed bed of the river. Every year the river washes the bed clear of any vegetation, and they have to rebuild the *cercos* that have been carried away during the previous year. The *cercos* are built using the stems of the *palo bobo*, a tall plant found growing at the edge of the river, and are not very substantial.

These winter gardens are small, rarely covering more than half a hectare (one and a quarter acres). The crops are planted closer together than in the summer gardens, and although the crops are essentially the same as in summer, they tend to be planted in reverse order. The first crops to be planted, as soon as the winter frosts are over, are melon, watermelon, squash, and pumpkins, which are followed by the faster growing crops, principally sweet potato, maize, and beans. This order allows all the different crops to be harvested before December or early January, when the river usually rises again and floods the gardens.

The silt soils are fertile and retain moisture throughout the winter, even though the rainfall is scanty. The gardens are weeded about two months after the last crops have been sown, and the first maize and beans can usually be harvested in September; the sweet potato, squash, and pumpkins produce from October until January, by which time the summer gardens are starting to produce.

The most difficult months for the Guaraní are from July to September. Some households work in their gardens and hunt or look for wage labor; some even participate in the fishing expeditions organized by the Nivaclé. But fishing and hunting are not the focus of interest that they are among the other Chaco societies, and if possible the Guaraní prefer to combine work in the gardens with stock raising. This is in marked contrast to the other societies of the region, and I shall return to this issue later. First, however, it will be useful to look more closely at the importance of livestock in the rest of the Chaco.

Livestock

The 1981 census data on livestock are summarized in table 3. This shows that livestock is of limited importance: 66 percent of households had none at all; only 18 percent owned any cattle, 18 percent owned sheep or goats, and 8 percent owned pigs. Moreover, the majority of the households that kept livestock had only a small number of animals. Only 2 percent had more than ten head of cattle, only 5 percent had more than ten sheep or goats, and less than 1 percent had more than ten pigs.

There is some variation between the regions. In the Lower Chaco 77 percent of households had no livestock at all, since they lived on ranches, where they were not allowed to keep livestock of their own, or on missions, where there is insufficient grazing land. In the Central Chaco, where over half the households live in agricultural colonies, 68 percent of households had no livestock, but 25 percent had some cattle, acquired through projects promoted by the Mennonites. The holdings were generally small, however, and of the households that owned cattle, 62 percent had only one or two head, and only 3 percent had herds of ten or more. Only 12 percent of the households in the Central Chaco had any sheep or goats, and of these only 14 percent had ten or more animals. This is probably because the Mennonites used not to allow the Indians to bring their flocks with them to the Mennonite Colonies for fear they would damage the crops. This would also account for the limited distri-

Table 3: Households owning livestock, by region

Region	Total no. of households	Cattle				Sheep and goats				Pigs				Families without livestock
		1–2	3–9	10+	None	1–2	3–9	10+	None	1–2	3–9	10+	None	
Lower Chaco	1,543	46	29	12	1,456	103	63	31	1,346	120	38	7	1,378	1,181
Central Chaco	1,964	311	169	15	1,469	80	116	33	1,735	23	11	1	1,929	1,334
High Chaco	591	53	61	37	440	60	134	129	268	49	62	19	461	201
TOTAL	4,098	410	259	64	3,365	243	313	193	3,349	192	111	27	3,768	2,716

Note: Based on INDI 1982: table 32. The Lower Chaco corresponds to the regions termed Bajo Chaco, Anglicana, and Alto Paraguay in INDI 1982, while the High Chaco corresponds to the regions termed Pilcomayo Medio and Chaco Norte. The Central Chaco is the same as in INDI 1982. See map 3.

bution of pigs, which were owned by less than 2 percent of the households in the Central Chaco.

In the High Chaco a higher proportion of households possessed livestock: 26 percent owned cattle, 54 percent had sheep or goats, and 22 percent had pigs, and only 34 percent were without any livestock. The holdings were also larger than in the other regions: 25 percent of the households with cattle had ten or more head, and 40 percent of the households with sheep or goats had flocks of ten or more. This reflects the availability of grazing land and the lack of restrictions, and indeed it is perhaps surprising that stock raising is so limited in this region.

Metraux mentions that the Chaco tribes probably began to herd sheep, which they had acquired through raiding, at the end of the seventeenth century. The Guaicuruan peoples also appear to have adopted horses and cattle. However, Metraux does not consider them to have been herdsmen, since the cattle they took in raids were slaughtered to provide for their needs and replenished through further raiding (Metraux 1963:265; Dobrizhoffer 1822; Sanchez Labrador 1910–17).

By the turn of the twentieth century, stock raising was well established among most of the Chaco societies. Nordenskiöld, who visited the Pilcomayo in 1908–9, notes that the Choroti and the Nivaclé owned large flocks of sheep and goats, and that some Nivaclé had horses and cattle. He estimated that in one Nivaclé village, near Estero Patiño, the four hundred inhabitants between them owned two hundred cattle, two hundred horses, and over five hundred sheep and goats (1912:50). Nordenskiöld seems to have assumed that stock raising played a significant part in the subsistence economy of all the Indians of the Pilcomayo, and he explains the absence of livestock in some communities as being due to their dependence on whites. He asserts: "The positive influence of White culture is, generally speaking, greater in those parts where the Indians live far away from Whites, than in those where they live in direct dependence under the White man. Thus the Ashluslay [Nivaclé], who have preserved their independence, carry on ranching on a large scale, whilst some Mataco tribes, almost entirely dependent, have no cattle at all. Up to quite recent times, the Ashluslay were in the happy position of being able to derive advantages from the Whites without falling into irretrievable poverty" (1919:232, quoted in Metraux 1963:212).

This view is similar to that of Belaieff, who describes the tribes of the Pilcomayo as owning herds of sheep, goats, and cattle but continues: "The floods of the previous years and the extraordinary dryness of 1941 caused *mal de cadera,* which first destroyed the horses and then reduced the sheep. Today the Indians find it difficult to restore their earlier economy" (1963:374).

Metraux cites Nordenskiöld's observations, noting that "goats are fairly common in the native villages of the Pilcomayo" (1963:265), while the only mention of livestock in the Lower Chaco comes from Grubb, who writes: "Sheep are scarce and of poor quality, owing to the flat and swampy nature of the country, and as the Indian is not given to thrift, he often falls back on his small flock to supply any shortage of rations" (Grubb 1911:66).

All these authors mention weaving, which implies that sheep must have been of importance as a source of wool. But even if one accepts Nordenskiöld's and Belaieff's accounts of the decline of stock raising, there is no firm evidence to suggest that livestock ever played a major role in the subsistence economy of the Chaco societies. Rather, stock raising, like agriculture, seems to have been a supplementary activity within an economy that was based primarily on hunting, gathering, and in some cases fishing.

For the Guaicuruan tribes such as the Abipón and the Mbayá, herding, or rather cattle raiding, was more akin to hunting than to the stock raising practiced in the Chaco today. Indeed, Metraux remarks that "the Mbayá hunted the wild cattle roaming in their territory exactly as they did deer" (1963:265). Even the herds and flocks mentioned by Nordenskiöld would have been insufficient to provide a regular supply of meat for the inhabitants of the village mentioned above. Each household would on average have owned eight to ten sheep or goats, and it must be remembered that Nordenskiöld chose to describe this particular village precisely because he regarded it as one of the most prosperous in the region.

Grubb's comments quoted above are perhaps the most pertinent. In particular he notes that the environment is not particularly suited to stock raising. Even today, ranching is a fairly risky undertaking. The more successful ranchers are those who adopt a strategy, like that of the Mennonite farmers, of spreading their risks over a number of years, making capital investments in times of bonanza and keeping their costs to a minimum in the years of drought, flood, or low prices. Lacking the resources available to modern ranchers, the Indians appear to have deliberately limited their dependence on livestock by keeping their holdings at a level that allowed them to maintain enough mobility to pursue other, more reliable activities.

To Grubb, the Indians' attitude to livestock may have seemed surprising, if not irrational. In the context of a hunting and gathering economy, however, such an attitude is quite reasonable. Livestock was never the Indians' principal resource but rather was used as a reserve, meat on the hoof, that could be called on in times of shortage. Indeed the Indian who fell "back on his small flock to supply any shortage of rations," far from acting in an irrational manner, seems to have been using his livestock in precisely the manner for which it was intended.

The one exception to the situation outlined above is that of the Guaraní. Indeed, if one looks at Pedro P. Peña, where land is available to all, it is apparent that there is a significant difference in the distribution of livestock among the Guaraní, the Nivaclé, and the Manjuy. The Guaraní are the only Indians in Pedro P. Peña who keep cattle, and they also have larger flocks of goats and sheep than the Nivaclé and the Manjuy.

Table 4 shows that only 5 percent of the Guaraní households have no livestock, as against 28 percent of the Nivaclé and Manjuy. Their flocks are larger: 56 percent of Guaraní households have more than ten goats, as compared to only 16 percent of the Nivaclé and Manjuy households. Flocks of less that ten goats would be insufficient to provide a regular supply of meat, and the figures suggest that the Nivaclé and Manjuy are not relying on goats, or any other livestock, to provide a regular supply of food or cash income.

While the Nivaclé and Manjuy rely on hunting and fishing for the protein in their diet, the Guaraní, because of their emphasis on agricul-

Table 4: Ownership of livestock in Pedro P. Peña, 1981

	Guaraní	Nivaclé and Manjuy
Sheep		
1–3	3	4
4–9	13	2
10+	11	1
Goats		
1–3	5	8
4–9	7	5
10+	23	4
Pigs		
1–3	7	1
4–9	8	1
10+	6	0
No livestock	2	7
Total no. of households	41	25

tural production, are more dependent on their livestock. The families that have reasonably large flocks of sheep and goats slaughter their animals throughout the year, providing most of the meat consumed by the household. If the flocks are insufficient to provide a continual supply of meat, the Guaraní supplement their diet with the small game that can be found in the vicinity of their gardens, such as charata, rabbits, and even parrots.

In contrast, among the Nivaclé and the Manjuy livestock are usually reserved for times of need. Animals are slaughtered on special occasions, such as visits from outsiders, but the place of livestock in the subsistence strategy is to supply meat at the times when hunting and fishing fail to provide an adequate supply of food, especially during the difficult months of August and September. The Nivaclé and the Manjuy are less concerned about depleting their flocks, and they slaughter their animals whenever they want to eat meat.

The management of sheep and goats is essentially the same among the Guaraní and the Nivaclé. The women are responsible for most tasks, except constructing the pens where the livestock are kept at night. Sheep and goats are penned at night to prevent them getting lost or eaten by wild animals; at daybreak they are let loose to wander freely. The young lambs and kids are kept penned throughout the day or are tied up close to the house. The sheep and goats fatten rapidly during the summer months, when there is an abundance of algarrobo, chañar, and mistol. During the winter, pasture is scarce, and the goats strip all the accessible leaves off the trees, leaving large areas bare and eroded.

The sheep and goats require little attention: their owners mark them with cuts to the ears, and the sheep are sheared twice a year. The shearing is done with knives, and the wool is washed and dried in the sun before being spun into yarn. If the animals are infested with worms, they are bathed with infusions made from the bark of mistol or from poroto del monte. The sheep breed annually, while the goats are expected to breed twice a year. Once they are three or four years old, they are usually slaughtered.

Pigs are managed in the same way as sheep and goats. During the summer months they forage freely close to the house; they return to their pens at night and, if shade and water are available, during the hottest hours in the middle of the day. In winter the forage is sometimes insufficient, and the pigs are fed with maize or sweet potatoes kept over from the harvest. The need for winter feed may account for the limited distribution of pigs among the Nivaclé and Manjuy.

Despite what has been said above, most Indians show an interest in owning livestock, particularly cattle. Many men, particularly in the Lower Chaco, have the skills to manage cattle, but fewer have sufficient land or the capital needed to build fencing, corrals, or drinking ponds. Indeed, the only people who until recently have shown no interest in cattle are the Ayoreo, who traditionally owned no livestock.

Few men ever manage to accumulate sufficient cattle to make herding an alternative to wage labor or hunting. The men who have large herds are often ranch hands or foremen who live and work on the land of their employers. On some ranches the permanently employed hands, especially those in positions of trust, receive sheep or cattle as payment or gifts from the owner, and one or two have managed to build up considerable holdings. Few are wealthy by Paraguayan standards — as table 3 shows, less than 2 percent of households have more than ten head of cattle — but there are men among the Chamococo and the Guaraní who own over a hundred head of cattle.

Although ranch hands make no payment for grazing, the arrangement is not entirely one-sided. Most Indians have no registration marks of their own — and no incentive to brand the ranch owner's calves with their own marks — and are dependent on the owner to the extent of not being able to sell their cattle without his or her signature. The ranch owner has the benefit of an indebted, hopefully trustworthy employee — particularly important if the owner is absent for much of the time — who is less likely to become involved in disputes over payment or rations.

In Pedro P. Peña some of the Guaraní have built up flocks of sheep and goats and herds of cattle through an arrangement known as *partija*. Men with a reputation for hard work and honesty are entrusted with the animals of a neighbor, usually one of the Argentine *criollos*, and the offspring are divided equally with the owner. One of the Guaraní is reputed to own four hundred head of cattle, and another owns three hundred sheep, which he has now begun to entrust to some of his neighbors under the same arrangement. Most of the Indians who have acquired large holdings of livestock are estranged from their communities, however, and this is a theme that I take up in a later chapter. But first I shall discuss the Indians' participation in the market economy.

CHAPTER FOUR

The Market Economy

Economic Activity and Occupations

TABLES 5–7, taken from the 1981 Indian census, provide an overview of the economic activities and occupations of the Indian population. The information is presented in conventional census categories and should not be interpreted as an accurate reflection of the Indians' own perceptions of what constitutes "work."

Table 5 shows the economic activity of the population of twelve years and over, distinguishing the economically active and inactive sectors of the population. In all, 56 percent (9,474 people) were classified as economically active. There was a marked difference between the sexes: 89 percent of men were classified as economically active as against 21 percent of women. This is an ethnocentric definition, since the "domestic duties" carried out by 73 percent of the female population are not classified as economic activities, but it does reflect the limited involvement of women in the market economy. It should be noted that the questions on economic activity refer to the week before the enumeration, which was carried out in June, when there was little agriculture or gathering, and as a result women's participation in agriculture is not reflected in the census.

The economically inactive include people who were studying, performing military service, and a category of "others" that includes the sick, disabled, and aged. Few children were at school after the age of twelve, although this varies slightly between the regions.

In the High Chaco, 8 percent of women and 10 percent of men were in school. The figures for the Central Chaco were 4 percent of women and 7 percent of men; in the Lower Chaco, they were 4 percent of women and 5 percent of men. These figures reflect the differing attitudes to education shown by the missionary organizations that work in the Chaco—particularly the emphasis given to education by the Oblates of Maria,

Table 5: Economic activity of the population age 12 years
and over, by region and sex

| | Active | | Inactive | | | | Total |
	Employed	Unemployed	Studying	Involved in domestic duties	Performing military service	Other*	Total
Lower Chaco							
Men	2,479	407	162	13	15	102	3,178
Women	675	65	116	2,121	—	29	3,006
Central Chaco							
Men	3,194	618	292	19	6	181	4,310
Women	414	225	154	3,121	—	19	3,933
High Chaco							
Men	946	79	121	9	9	57	1,221
Women	350	22	101	820	—	29	1,322
TOTAL	8,058	1,416	946	6,103	30	417	16,970

Source: INDI 1982: Table 19.

* Includes the sick, disabled, others, and the census returns that lack sufficient information to allow classification in any other category.

who work in Mariscal Estigarribia and the missions situated on the Pil-comayo. The figures also reflect the difference between the dispersed and nucleated populations. In the Lower Chaco much of the population is dispersed, and few people have access to schooling, especially after the first and second grades, which most children should have completed by the time they reach twelve. In the High Chaco, on the other hand, much of the population is concentrated on missions and in Indian colonies.

Only thirty men were engaged in military service. According to the law on indigenous peoples (Law 904/81), the Indian population is exempt from compulsory military service, but some young men join up to acquire their *baja,* a discharge book that serves as an identity document and can be useful when seeking employment. In Paraguay compulsory military service is usually carried out at the age of seventeen and lasts for two years, but in the Chaco it lasts for only a year, since the conditions are considered to be more arduous than in the rest of the country. Conscripts receive no payment but are provided with rations and a uniform. The only indigenous people who regularly perform military service are the Guaraní Occidentales, who usually serve with the Third Army Corps in Mariscal Estigarribia or with the police in Pedro P. Peña.

Of the 8 percent of the population (1,416 people) registered as unemployed, most were men. Unemployment was highest in the Central Chaco, where 14 percent of the men and 6 percent of the women had done no work in the week before the census. If one looks at the age groups of these people, however, it appears that many are children or young adults, who remain dependent on their parents up to quite a late age (INDI 1982:table 19). This also accounts for the contrast between the sexes, since girls are engaged in domestic activities from an early age, while boys, if they are not studying, are under no obligation to help their families or engage in any other activities.

In the age groups from thirty to sixty there is a small but consistent percentage of men, and a few women, who were registered as unemployed. Some may have been farmers who were resting during a slack period in the agricultural cycle. Others, however, would have been land-less laborers who depend on wage labor but who had been unable to find any work. Without any possibilities other than the goodwill of kin and neighbors, the situation of these people and their families may well have been desperate.

In table 6 people who were registered as having worked are classified according to occupational category. The table shows that salaried labor (including labor paid in kind) predominates over other modes of employment, with 69 percent (5,559) of the total classified as salaried, 24 percent (1,934) as self-employed, and 6 percent (514) as unpaid family labor.

In every region the majority of men were salaried, although the proportion varies from 83 percent in the Central Chaco to 50 percent in the High Chaco. This is surprising, since one would expect a higher proportion of independent producers in the Central Chaco, where more than half the population has been settled in agricultural colonies and has suitable land for cultivation, as well as technical assistance and other benefits.

The enumeration took place during an inactive period in the agricultural cycle, and this may account for the relatively low proportion of independent producers in the Central Chaco, although it fails to explain why such a high proportion of the population was engaged in wage labor. Had the colonization programs succeeded in providing for subsistence needs and income, the households in the agricultural colonies would have had no need to work outside the colonies. Moreover, if seasonal factors were significant, one would expect the proportion of independent producers to be lower in the other regions. In fact, even in the Lower Chaco, where few communities have land of their own and where conditions are less suitable for agriculture, 28 percent of men were classified as independent producers.

It may be that the demand for labor, rather than land tenure or the existence of colonization programs, determines whether or not men will engage in wage labor. This does not imply that men engage in wage labor whenever the opportunity arises, but it does point to a more complex relationship between the regional economy and the community's dependence on wage labor than is often supposed. It is likely that the figures reflect a certain level of failure in the colonization programs, but they also suggest that households rely on independent means of production only when other alternatives are unavailable. This is, I believe, an important issue if one is to understand the forms that economic integration takes in the Chaco, and I shall return to it in the next chapter.

Table 6: Occupational categories of the economically active population, by region and sex

	Salaried	Self-employed	Unpaid family labor	No infor-mation	Total
Lower Chaco					
Men	1,784	594	94	7	2,479
Women	235	381	57	2	675
Central Chaco					
Men	2,660	379	720	35	3,194
Women	315	54	43	2	414
High Chaco					
Men	474	368	99	5	946
Women	91	158	101	0	350
TOTAL	5,559	1,934	514	51	8,058

Source: INDI 1982.

Some 6 percent of the working population were classified as unpaid family labor. Most would have been adolescents working with their parents, principally in subsistence activities. In the Lower and Central Chaco only 4 percent of men were registered as unpaid family labor, as against 10 percent in the High Chaco. This reflects the greater importance of subsistence activities and the limited opportunities for wage labor in the High Chaco, and may indicate a cultural difference between the Guaraní Occidentales, most of whom live in the High Chaco, and the other Chaco societies. Among the Guaraní, who rely more on agriculture and stock raising, young men, before they marry, often work with their fathers or paternal uncles, and this may even continue after they are married.

In table 7 the working population is classified according to occupation. Overall, ranching was the most important occupation for men. Some 33 percent of working men were employed as ranch hands, a figure almost three times as high as the next most important occupation, logging, in which 11 percent of working men were engaged. Logging is a rather general category that includes contract laborers, employed to cut fence posts or clear the scrub from overgrown pasture, as well as the men employed to cut quebracho for the tannin companies. A further 11 percent of the working male population were employed as agricultural laborers, mainly in the Central Chaco, while 6 percent were employed as construction workers, and 5 percent in manufacturing industries. The main salaried occupations for women were agricultural labor (18 percent), closely followed by domestic service (17 percent).

In the independent sector, 12 percent of the working male population had been hunting or fishing in the week before the census, followed by 8 percent who had worked in agriculture (on their own plots); another 6 percent had worked at handicrafts. This was the most important occupation for women, employing 47 percent of the working female population. In contrast, only 6 percent of the women had been working in their own agricultural plots.

The occupations shown in table 7 reflect the differences between the regional economies. In the Lower Chaco, 47 percent of working men were employed as ranch hands, and 11 percent in logging, both as *contratistas* and as employees of the tannin companies. The main source of salaried employment for women was domestic service, in which 23 percent were engaged. This would have included women who work in nearby Paraguayan towns, as well as the women employed as cooks on the ranches.

In comparison, 13 percent of the working men in the Lower Chaco had been hunting or fishing in the week before the census, 5 percent were engaged in agriculture, and a further 5 percent in the manufacture of handicrafts. This latter figure reflects the importance of handicrafts for one group, the Mak'a, who at the time of the census were living opposite the Botanical Gardens of Asunción and lived by selling their handicrafts to tourists. The manufacture of craft items was also the main occupation for 55 percent of working women in the Lower Chaco.

The more dynamic economy of the Central Chaco offers greater diversity of employment. Ranching was still the main source of employment, with 26 percent of the working male population engaged as ranch hands. A further 17 percent were employed as agricultural laborers — although this underestimates the importance of employment in agriculture because the census was taken at a time of little agricultural activity — and 13 percent were engaged in logging, mainly in clearing forest and cutting firewood. Another 9 percent were employed in manufacturing industries, which include cotton gins and factories producing edible oils, dairy produce, tannin, and essence of palo santo. Finally, 7 percent were employed in the construction industry; these would have included a number of skilled men working as builders and carpenters in Filadelfia, Loma Plata, and Mariscal Estigarribia.

In the Central Chaco 50 percent of working women were employed as agricultural laborers. They were probably contracted to clear weeds or gather grass seed; had the census been taken at the time of the cotton harvest, the number of women employed as agricultural laborers would undoubtedly have been much higher. Few women were employed in other salaried occupations: 9 percent were registered as domestic servants and another 9 percent as workers in manufacturing industries.

The proportion of the population working as independent producers was low considering that over half the population of the Central Chaco is settled in agricultural colonies. Only 7 percent of the men were working in their own agricultural plots, 7 percent were engaged in manufacturing handicrafts, and another 7 percent were either hunting or fishing.

Table 7: Occupations of the working population age 12 years and over, by region and sex

	Total	Hunting, fishing, etc.	Agriculture, self-employed	Handicraft	Ranching	Farm labor	Logging
Lower Chaco							
Men	2,479	320	119	121	1,175	143	282
Women	675	4	37	371	22	40	16
Central Chaco							
Men	3,194	210	239	237	834	529	416
Women	414	2	37	41	30	207	11
High Chaco							
Men	946	233	179	65	180	42	40
Women	350	—	6	258	4	7	—
Total							
Men	6,619	763	537	423	2,189	714	738
Women	1,439	6	80	670	56	254	27

Table 7 – Continued

	Manufacturing	Construction	Domestic service	Other*	No Information
Lower Chaco					
Men	21	157	31	72	38
Women	2	4	155	20	4
Central Chaco					
Men	287	223	34	79	106
Women	35	2	36	8	5
High Chaco					
Men	44	40	22	80	21
Women	—	3	56	16	—
Total					
Men	352	420	87	231	165
Women	37	9	247	44	9

Source: INDI 1982: table 21.

*These include the categories shown in the original table as professional workers (here mostly teachers), administrators, office workers, and store employees.

Of the working female population, only 9 percent were working in agriculture (self-employed), and 10 percent were engaged in manufacturing handicrafts.

There was a greater emphasis on independent production in the High Chaco: 25 percent of the working men had been hunting or fishing, 19 percent had been cultivating their own plots, and 7 percent had been working at handicrafts. This was also the occupation of 74 percent of the women.

There are fewer opportunities for salaried employment in the High Chaco. Ranching was the main source of wage labor for men, and 19 percent of working men were employed as ranch hands. A further 4 percent had been working in the logging industry, mostly as *contratistas* on the ranches. The only other sources of employment were the missions and the military bases, especially the headquarters of the Third Army Corps in Mariscal Estigarribia and the nearby mission of Santa Teresita. Most of the men employed in the construction and manufacturing industries would have worked here, principally in the brick kilns run by the Catholic mission. The only salaried employment for women was domestic service, which occupied 16 percent of the working female population, most of whom would have been employed by missionaries or the families of military officers.

Cash Crops and Independent Producers

The most striking aspect to emerge from the census is the importance of wage labor. This is true not only of the landless populations, found in much of the Lower Chaco, but also of the populations settled in the agricultural colonies of the Central Chaco.

The reasons for the Indians' participation in wage labor are complex. One important factor is their dependence on items that can only be acquired through the market, including basic foodstuffs, yerba maté and tobacco, and manufactured goods. Wage labor can at times seem almost compulsory, particularly where the Indians' right to settle or even to enter land is dependent on the goodwill of the landowner or his representatives.

As table 7 shows, the main alternatives to wage labor are agriculture, hunting, and handicrafts. Agriculture and hunting are largely subsistence activities, however, and are of greatest importance in the High Chaco, where there are few possibilities for wage labor. Cash crops are never grown in this region, since the markets are too distant and the terrain is unsuitable for large-scale cultivation.

Table 8 shows the distribution of cash crops. These are virtually nonexistent outside the Central Chaco. Even in the agricultural colonies of the Central Chaco the scale of production is small, and many households grow no cash crops whatsoever. Indeed, at the time of the Indian census 51 percent of the households in these colonies grew no cash crops, while a further 15 percent grew less than half a hectare.

In the preceding chapter I examined some of the reasons why wage labor is an attractive alternative to agriculture in the Central Chaco, and I emphasized environmental factors and the Indians' perception of agriculture as a marginal enterprise. These factors also limit the production of cash crops, but there are other elements that should be considered: lack of secure land titles, shortage of capital, insufficiency or absence of credit, and the difficulty of gaining direct access to the market.

In the agricultural colonies of the Central Chaco, households occupy plots of around twenty-five hectares, which are held in usufruct. The plots comprise an area of about five hectares of natural grassland, suitable for agriculture, and a further twenty hectares of forest or scrub, which can be cleared for pasture. The small size of these plots is one of the factors limiting the potential of commercial agriculture. Households tend to be large: Hack (1978–80) estimates the average at 6.8 persons. On five hectares, even in a good year, it would be hard to expect the household to cover all its subsistence needs and produce a surplus of cash crops.

The system of land tenure is a further disincentive. The title to the land is vested with ASCIM, the Mennonite agency responsible for Indian colonization programs; and the colony's Indian administrators allocate the individual plots of land in newly established villages — possibly with guidance from their Mennonite advisers. According to Stahl (1974:139), this system was originally adopted because Indians were not regarded as competent under Paraguayan law, since they lacked identity cards, while the cooperatives that administer the colonies lacked the legal personality (*personería jurídica*) required for holding land titles. Stahl adds that

Table 8: Household production of cash crops, by area cultivated and region

Region	Area cultivated					Total no. of households
	0 ha	<0.5 ha	0.5–2.9 ha	3.0–4.9 ha	>5.0 ha	
Lower Chaco	1,535	4	2	1	1	1,543
Central Chaco	1,126	263	404	152	19	1,964
High Chaco	591	0	0	0	0	591
Total no. of households	3,252	267	406	153	20	4,098

Source: INDI 1982: table 30.

the system has the advantage of protecting the inexpert Indian small-holder from unscrupulous traders who would take advantage of times of drought to get the Indian into debt and then take his land.

These arguments may have some validity, but the legal situation is not well understood by the Indian colonists, and this generates a feeling of insecurity. The insecurity also owes something to the rules that are applied in the colonies: alcohol is strictly forbidden, and acceptance of the Mennonite Church is, if not mandatory, undoubtedly perceived as such by most of the colonists. Indeed, the statutes of at least one cooperative, Nich'a Toyish, explicitly state that all members should be "baptized members of the Mennonite Church." Moreover, the administration of each colony imposes certain demands—for example, payments for the schools and hospitals, and the obligation to market through the cooperative—that are not always well understood. Through its control over retail stores, credit, agricultural machinery, and marketing, the administration has the power to sanction any colonists who infringe the rules and, in the case of more serious infractions, can expel individuals from the colony.

Shortage of capital is another factor limiting the expansion of commercial agriculture. When a new colony is established, the Indians receive assistance, in farm implements and provisions, from the Mennonite agencies responsible for the program, but this aid is often insufficient, and many of the colonists fail to establish themselves and fall back on wage labor for at least part of the year.

In the colonies that were founded between 1961 and 1968, each household received a horse and harness, two rolls of barbed wire, and provisions for six months. They were also given a half share in a plow, a quarter share in a cultivator, a fifth share in a cart, and a tenth share in a well (Hack 1978–80). The provisions were intended to support the colonists and their families from the time they moved into the colony until they harvested their first crops, although, as Hack mentions, in some cases the supplies were inadequate and had to be continued for a few more months. The sharing of implements also appears to have been problematic. Plots, in nearly all the villages, were allocated on a first-come first-served basis, with no regard for the family ties or even the origin of the colonists. As a result, implements had to be shared between neighbors who, although they invariably belonged to the same ethnic group, came from different areas and identified with different communities. Sharing neither kinship nor common origin, neighbors often viewed each other with suspicion or mistrust, and at times this led to conflicts over the use of implements, with some households believing themselves to have been cheated by their neighbors or the village authorities.

In subsequent settlement programs, such as Paz del Chaco, the colonists were provided with more supplies and equipment, on the condition that they no longer work outside the colony. In these colonies the Indians managed to establish themselves on a firmer basis, but even here problems have arisen in years of drought. Lacking the Mennonites' capacity for long-term planning and their resources, the Indians have been unable to subsist exclusively from agriculture in years of drought and have found themselves forced back into the cycle of wage labor, inadequate preparation for the following season, poor harvests, and continued wage labor.

Certain lines of credit are available to the established colonists, but these are intended for the purchase of equipment or for the improvement of infrastructure, and tend to favor the colonists who have already achieved a reasonable level of production. Some of the credits are financed directly from the Indians' cooperatives, while others, including a scheme to finance forest clearance and the introduction of pasture, are financed from special funds donated by international development agencies and administered by ASCIM. Each application for credit is vetted by a committee from the applicant's cooperative, and once granted, the loans have to be repaid at interest rates set slightly below commercial interest rates.

There is no specific line of credit for the production of cash crops, and although the cooperatives may provide seed or insecticides on credit, money cannot be borrowed to cover the needs of the household in the period between planting and harvest. This appears to be a deliberate policy, perhaps because the repayment of such loans cannot be ensured in the uncertain conditions of the Central Chaco. In effect this means that the existing credit programs benefit only the producers who are already fairly well established, and do not help the poorer colonists who are still trying to break free of their dependence on wage labor.

The system of marketing has less direct impact on the level of production than prices, but it is sometimes a cause for complaint. All cash crops have to be marketed through the Indians' cooperatives and are sold directly to the Mennonite cooperatives that own the cotton gins and edible oil processing plants in Filadelfia and Loma Plata. Although the prices received by the Indians' cooperatives are the same as those paid to the Mennonite farmers, the Indian producers receive less than the Mennonites because their own cooperatives discount an additional percentage to cover the costs of storage, transport, and administration.

The principal cash crop is cotton. When seed cotton is sold, the Mennonite cooperative withholds part of the payment. At one time this was in the order of 20 to 30 percent and was paid once the cotton had been graded and the prices for each grade finally established. In subsequent years, however, the amount withheld has increased to 40 or even 50 percent and is only paid once all the cotton from the Mennonite Colonies has been sold on the international market. This procedure is a response to fluctuations in the price of cotton and the exchange rates, as well as to a crisis of liquidity in the Mennonites' own cooperatives. However, it has caused problems in the Indians' cooperatives, since some producers are tempted to sell their cotton to itinerant traders who offer prices similar to, or just below, those paid by the Mennonites but who pay directly in goods or in cash. This practice, which in effect cheats the Indians' own cooperatives, is regarded as a serious offense and, if repeated persistently, can lead to expulsion from the colony.

The production of handicrafts can provide another source of income, but its potential is limited by the difficulties of marketing. In some cases the raw materials are also difficult to acquire. In the more densely populated regions of the Chaco, it is hard to find the varieties of caraguatá that are used for the manufacture of hammocks and string bags. And the raw wool used by the Nivaclé and Guaraní for the manufacture of ponchos, blankets, and *fajas*—the wide woolen belts worn for support and protection—has to be purchased from the few families who own sheep. In the Upper Pilcomayo, where handicrafts are one of the few means of acquiring cash, many women find that even the small sums needed to acquire the wool are beyond their means.

At present most of the handicrafts produced in the Chaco are sold to missionary organizations, which export them to Europe and the United States. The Oblates of Maria purchase the handicrafts produced by the Nivaclé and the Guaraní on the Pilcomayo and in Mariscal Estigarribia, and in the Alto Paraguay the Salesians purchase the items produced by the Ayoreo. In the Mennonite Colonies, ASCIM and one or two private buyers acquire most of the handicrafts that are produced, although the New Tribes Mission buys from the Ayoreo of Campo Loro and Montecito.

Throughout the Chaco prices tend to be low. There is some variation in the prices paid by the different institutions, and private buyers are usually willing to pay a little more. The low prices are not simply a result of the virtual monopoly that each organization exercises in its particular area of influence but are also a reflection of the difficulty of balancing supply with demand. Unlike storekeepers or small traders, the missionaries find themselves under a certain moral obligation to purchase all the handicrafts they are offered—provided they are of the required quality—and they are expected to pay immediately, either in cash or in goods. In places such as Bahía Negra and Fuerte Olimpo, where the only buyers are storekeepers or itinerant traders, the prices are often absurdly low, since the women, once they have finished an item, are usually desperate to sell it to get something to eat. Baskets that may take a Chamococo woman several weeks to finish are sold for only a few guaranies, although by the time they reach the souvenir shops of Asunción, their price may have increased tenfold. Because of the low prices—and the difficulty at times of being able to sell any items at all—the Chamococo have found it difficult to develop handicraft production as an alternative to wage labor.

The Colonia Mak'a, just outside Asunción, is the one community where the manufacture and sale of handicrafts has become the main occupation of the population. Here, unlike anywhere else in the Chaco, both men and women produce and sell handicrafts, and they enjoy a level of income that is probably higher than that of many urban Paraguayans. The handicrafts produced by the Mak'a are in no sense traditional and consist of cheap items woven from brightly colored cotton thread, bags made from animal skins or armadillo shells, and toy bows and arrows. The Mak'a also sell items they have acquired from other indigenous groups—caraguatá string bags made by the Nivaclé, and Ayoreo feather work, which is bought from the New Tribes Mission. The Mak'a sell these items to the tourists that visit their colony, and they also sell in the streets of Asunción and at the airport. In recent years some have moved farther afield: a few families have settled in Ciudad del Este, from where they can cross to Foz de Iguaçu in Brazil, and others in Encarnación, from where they visit the Argentine city of Posadas.

The Mak'a are content to live from the sale of handicrafts and from tourism and have shown little or no interest in any of the agricultural programs that have been attempted in their colony. Nowadays the guides in the colony are Mak'a—and present a picture of Indian life different from the lurid one that used to be portrayed by their old Paraguayan *patrón*. The combination of tourism and handicraft production, plus the sale and resale of live rattlesnakes and other unusual items (they are reputed to sell dog meat to the Koreans), have allowed the Mak'a to remain economically independent. This has clearly helped them resist the pressures from missionaries and other outsiders, with the result that in many respects the Mak'a are one of the groups that have retained the greatest pride in their ethnic identity.

In recent years hunting has become less important as a source of income, and today few Paraguayans live from hunting or trapping. For the Indians who live in the most isolated parts of the Chaco, however, hunting still provides one of the very few means of acquiring some cash income.

The decline in commercial hunting is due to legal restrictions, collapsing export markets, and the scarcity of the more valuable commercial species. In the Chaco animal skins are still bought and sold openly—although there is a risk of their being confiscated at military checkpoints—while in Asunción the dealers no longer advertise themselves as openly as before (most advertise as buyers of hair for wigs). Prices have declined dramatically, however: a full-sized jaguar pelt, which at one time could have fetched over US$800, is now only worth US$5, and ocelot pelts have fallen in value from around US$120 to US$2. Other items also fluctuate in price. In October 1982, for example, when the first iguanas of the summer were being taken, a full-size skin was worth up to US$15.

By the beginning of December, when they were at their most abundant and large quantities of skins were being offered for sale, the prices had fallen to around US$1.50. Similar fluctuations affect the prices of other commercially valuable species, including rhea, fox, caiman, and margay.

Commercial hunting is often organized along lines similar to temporary wage labor, and men who devote a lot of time to hunting often work for a patrón, almost invariably the owner of a small store. The patrón provides the hunter with rations and the other items he needs, such as clothing, traps, and munitions, on credit. In some cases the hunter's wife also receives provisions from the store, either a weekly ration or purchases that are registered in a notebook and discounted when the hunter is paid off.

On his return the hunter is under an obligation to sell his skins or rhea feathers to the patrón, at prices determined by the patrón, at least until the hunter has paid off his outstanding debt. Once the debt has been covered, the hunter can in principle sell the remaining skins to whomever he likes, but he must avoid offending the patrón if he intends to work with him or her again.

A hunter is sometimes unlucky and is unable to pay off his debt. Then he has to talk to his patrón and explain his situation—or the patrón will assume he is selling his skins elsewhere—and ask for more credit until his luck changes. In Bahía Negra some Chamococo have run up debts of over US$400 in this way. Eventually, the patrón loses faith in his client, and the hunter has to work for him or take other employment to pay the debt off. Alternatively, the patrón can denounce the hunter to the authorities, in which case the hunter is likely to receive a beating or spend some time in jail. If this happens, though, the debt is never paid off, and the patrón loses his capital.

Wage Labor

We have already considered how the Indians' dependence on wage labor is determined by their need for manufactured goods and other items they have to purchase and by the limited potential of the kinds of independent production described above. There is another element that has to be considered, however, and this is the almost compulsory nature of many types of wage labor. Wages in the Chaco are low—at times so low that the Indians are hardly able to cover even their most basic subsistence needs — and wage levels are held down by a number of mechanisms that tie the Indians into disadvantageous relations with their employers. These include a system of land tenure that gives the landowners control over all the productive land, including the sites where the Indians are settled, and systems of credit or payment in kind that allow employers to control both the means of production and the means of consumption.

By far the largest proportion of the salaried male workforce of the Chaco is employed in occupations directly associated with ranching; indeed, outside the urban areas, the missions, and the Mennonite Colonies, the ranching industry offers virtually the only source of employment.

There are two kinds of labor employed on the ranches. The permanently employed hands include the *estancieros,* who work on horseback, and the *playeros,* who carry out the menial tasks, while the *contratistas* or *changadores* are employed on a temporary, usually piecework basis for tasks such as erecting fencing, clearing overgrown pasture, or planting artificial pastures. So far, these occupations have been integrated on only a few small family ranches that employ a fixed number of ranch hands and occupy them in repairing fences or clearing pastures outside the periods of more intense activity.

The most prestigious occupation is that of the *estanciero.* It requires skill and at times considerable courage. Indeed, it is said that a good *estanciero* never ponders the consequences of his actions — an ethic that is equally respected outside the corral. The Indians of the Lower Chaco have a high regard for those who are skilled at working on horseback and in the corral. This reflects a tradition that perhaps goes back to the colonial period, when the Guaicuruan-speaking, and possibly some of the Lengua-Maskoy-speaking, tribes adopted the horse and took to raiding the Spanish and *criollo* settlements on the fringes of the Chaco.

Much of an *estanciero*'s time is occupied riding around the property of the ranch, checking the boundary fences and making sure that the cattle are safe from thieves or other dangers. At certain times of the year the activity is more intense. The cattle have to be rounded up and vaccinated, calves have to be branded, young bulls castrated, and, particularly on the more remote ranches, cattle driven to the embarkation points on the highway, to be taken to market. At these times, the smaller ranches especially have to take on extra personnel, who are often brought in from the missions or from neighboring ranches. They are paid a daily rate, with the best rates being paid to the men who bring their own horses and saddles.

The *playeros* are usually either older men — *estancieros* who are no longer able to work the long hours on horseback — or young men, frequently the adolescent sons of the *estancieros,* who still lack the necessary strength and skills to work on horseback. The *playeros* are occupied mainly in menial tasks such as cutting firewood, milking cows, and preparing meals, tasks that are beneath the dignity of the *estancieros,* although at times the *playeros* may assist the other ranch hands, especially when there is a lot of work in the corral. On some ranches women are also employed to cook and milk the cows.

The *estancieros* and *playeros* are paid *libre* — that is, they receive a weekly ration or, if they have no family on the ranch, take their meals together with the other unattached ranch hands. On top of this they usually receive a monthly salary, which can vary from Gs 200,000 (US$80) to virtually nothing. The best wages are paid to the more experienced *estancieros,* while the *playeros* generally receive less. Wages vary greatly between different ranches, as does the regularity of the payments. On some ranches the Indian ranch hands are never paid in cash, a practice justified on the grounds that it prevents them from "spending all their money on *caña.*" On other ranches they receive less than the Paraguayan hands employed to do exactly the same tasks. A further injustice, practiced by some of the larger ranching companies, is to discount social security (IPS) payments from the Indians' wages, even though there is obviously no possibility of the Indians ever getting any benefits in return.

The lot of the *contratistas,* who are employed on a temporary basis to cut fence posts, erect fences, or to clear the forest and plant pasture, is generally less favorable than that of the regular ranch hands. There is little prestige attached to these tasks, and payment usually does not include any meals or rations.

The *contratistas* are sometimes employed through subcontractors, who may be Indians, although it is more common for Indian *contratistas* to be employed directly by the ranch owner or foreman. The employer usually provides some rations and even cash advances, but these are discounted from the final reckoning, and the *contratista* is often left with little in the way of net earnings. Indeed, it is not uncommon for a *contratista* to find that he still owes his employer, in which case he has to continue working or run the risk of imprisonment. Many employers simply assume that the *contratistas* will end up with very little in their favor, and may not even keep enough cash available to pay them off.

Typical is the case of a Toba from Cerrito who was hired to put up a fence on a ranch on the Río Negro. He spent his spare time hunting in order to avoid drawing rations on credit, and when he had completed the agreed length of fencing, he demanded the Gs 30,000 owing to him. The ranch owner, a Colorado Party politician from Benjamín Aceval, refused to pay on the grounds that the bill was "exaggerated." The *contratista* made a number of trips to the owner's house in Asunción—from which she was all too frequently "absent"—but in the end gave up, having received only part of his payment.

The difficulty in getting paid is perhaps the most disagreeable part of the contract, worse than the physical hardship of the job. The problem is complicated by the fact that most *contratistas* are illiterate and are unable to understand the accounts that are kept of the work performed and the rations received. Such is the mistrust that even if he is treated honestly, the *contratista* feels cheated, especially since it is all too easy to forget or underestimate the value of provisions taken on credit. At times mistrust gives way to violence—although this is true more of Paraguayan than Indian workers—with either the patrón or the *contratista* ending up dead or seriously wounded. In fact, it is likely that the high rate of homicide and other crimes of violence typical of the ranching areas of the Chaco owes as much to problems over payment as to hard drinking or fights over women.

The ranching establishments of the Chaco vary in their scale and methods of production, as well as in their requirements for labor and conditions of employment. In the eastern half of the Lower Chaco, most of the ranches used to belong to large companies that practiced extensive cattle raising on natural pastures; most have now fallen into decline owing to the collapse of their traditional export markets. Some still own vast holdings: the Casado company may have 500,000 hectares (1,235,000 acres), and Colón until recently had 300,000 hectares (741,000 acres); others, such as the International Products Corporation and Liebigs, have sold off their holdings to more modern, capital intensive enterprises. Up until the 1960s a number of these companies combined ranching with the exploitation of quebracho for the production of tannin, but only Casado continued to produce tannin into the 1990s.

The decline of the traditional ranching and tannin companies has resulted in continual migration to the more dynamic region of the Central Chaco. In addition, wages on the traditional company ranches are lower than in other parts of the Chaco: Casado, for example, pays half wages to the Indians working on the company's ranches, as if they were minors. The company's administrators justify this on the grounds that the Indian employees work only half the day and spend the rest of their time hunting. In fact, Indian ranch hands work the same hours as anyone else, but if they hunt they can survive even though their wages and rations are insufficient to provide for their families' subsistence needs. In fact, it is the ranching companies' control over land, rather than any strictly economic factors, that determines the Indians' wage levels and conditions of employment. At one time the ranching companies encouraged Indians to remain on their properties, since the Indians provided a pool of cheap labor that could be called on when necessary. Today most ranching companies try to evict all but the permanently employed ranch hands and their dependents. Having nowhere else to go, the families that are thrown off the ranches either remain as a nomadic workforce, moving from work camp to work camp in search of temporary employment, or migrate to the worker villages in the Mennonite Colonies.

The expulsion of Indian families is partly motivated by fear of the agrarian reform laws. These include the *prescripción treintenaria,* which provides for the expropriation of land in favor of anyone who has lived on and worked an area of land for thirty years or more, and the more recently passed Indian laws 904/81, 1372/88, and 43/89. These latter laws explicitly state that the land traditionally occupied by Indian communities is of "social interest" and can be expropriated on their behalf. In fact, the only property in the Chaco to have been expropriated is the 30,000 hectares (74,000 acres) of Riacho Mosquito, which belonged to Carlos Casado. The existence of Indian settlements can affect the value of the land, however, and it is usually when a company is intent on selling off blocks of land that evictions take place. This was the case when the Casado company expelled the Guaná from the Estancia Maria Casilda in 1977, and the owners of the Estancia Colón have taken similar action in recent years (Kidd 1992).

On the traditional ranches of the Lower Chaco, large areas of pasture have become overgrown with thorn scrub, and many of the cattle have run wild. Indeed, on the Casado ranches it is estimated that the cattle accounted for in the roundups represent only about a third of the total number that graze on the company's property. On ranches of this type, many of the ranch hands are engaged in the dangerous task of capturing wild cattle, either with lassos or in traps constructed around the water-holes where the cattle come to drink.

There is a limited demand for contract laborers on the traditional ranches. Much of the itinerant workforce of the Lower Chaco is concentrated on more modern ranches, such as San Antonio (Kilometer 160) and Loma Porã, owned by the Fiduciaria Transatlantica Alemana. These ranches employ large numbers of contract laborers to clear the forest, erect fencing, and plant pasture. Once the work is finished, however, the ranches have little need for casual labor, and the Indians have to move on.

The more modern ranching establishments also require a stable, more skilled workforce to manage the herds and the different areas of pasture. Many owners prefer to employ Paraguayans because they are considered more stable and work-oriented; where Indians are employed, they work alongside Paraguayans rather than forming teams on their own as on the traditional ranches. The exceptions here are the smaller, Mennonite-owned ranches, mainly because the Mennonites regard the Indians as more trustworthy and less likely to cause trouble than the Paraguayans.

In the Lower Chaco Indian ranch hands tend to be employed on the smaller, family-owned ranches: ranches of 1,000 to 30,000 hectares (2,500 to 75,000 acres), which are often located in the less accessible areas. The owners of these ranches may have difficulty finding suitable Paraguayan ranch hands and may not be able to pay the best rates.

On these smaller ranches the relations between the owner and his Indian hands often assume a paternalistic form. The owner may provide the Indians with rations, regardless of whether or not they work. He may try to provide an education for the children: it is quite common for owners to take the daughters of their ranch hands to Asunción, where they work as servants in the owner's house, and they may have the opportunity to attend school for a few hours each day. He may even allow the Indians to keep small herds of cattle or flocks of sheep. No charge is made for the right to pasture these animals, but the cattle often bear the ranch owner's mark. These practices create ties of dependence between the Indians and their employers, and although this restricts the mobility and limits the bargaining power of the Indian employees, it does provide them with more security than they would find on other ranches.

Where the Indians lack any rights to land, they are completely dependent on the landowner. The dependence is further intensified through other mechanisms, such as payment in kind or credit, which oblige the Indians to purchase all their necessities from the employer.

I have already described how contract laborers receive provisions on credit and even cash advances, and have shown how this tends to ensnare them in a cycle of debt. This practice appeared in its most extreme form in the camps of the tannin companies. Here, as in the traditional yerba maté and lumber companies of Eastern Paraguay, subcontractors recruited the workforce, offering advances of cash and goods. The workers were not allowed to leave the camps until they had paid off their debts. This was difficult, since they were cheated both by the foremen responsible for estimating the tonnage of quebracho they had cut and peeled, and by the company stores, which provided even the most essential supplies at extortionate prices. In some camps Indians were not paid but simply received a basic ration supplemented by fuel alcohol, which was provided as a cheap substitute for *caña*.

In recent years few Indians have worked cutting quebracho, and by 1994 the only logging camps in operation were those worked by subcontractors of the Casado company in the region of Toro Pampa and San Carlos. In the late 1970s another camp operated in Kilometer 40, Bahía Negra, but the Chamococo who lived in the area, and who at that time depended almost entirely on wage labor, would accept almost any other kind of work rather than seek employment there. In fact, only one Chamococo worked there—running the camp store—and the only other Indians in the camp were a team of Angaité, brought by a subcontractor from Puerto Casado. The other workers were Paraguayans who, from the way they refused to give their names even to the parish priest, appear to have been mostly fugitives from the law.

The Casado company also engaged in another practice: payment by credit note or *vale,* which, although illegal, is quite widespread in the Chaco. In Puerto Casado the Indian employees of the tannin factory received half their weekly wages as a credit slip that could be redeemed only at the company store. Here prices were usually higher than in any other store, and the range of goods more limited. When an employee takes goods worth less than the full value of the credit slip, either they are given another one to cover the amount outstanding, or the storekeeper gives them extra items—whatever happens to be left over—to round the amount off. Surprisingly, payment by credit note enjoyed the support of the Salesian missionaries, who believed that it prevented the Indians from spending their earnings on alcohol. In fact, the supplies issued by the company storekeepers were often rounded off with a bottle or two of fuel alcohol.

In the Mennonite Colonies credit notes have for years been the standard mode of payment in the cotton gins and edible oil and tannin factories of Loma Plata; they were also reintroduced, despite considerable protest, in the cotton gin and the other industries in Filadelfia. The reappearance of credit notes in Filadelfia was apparently due to a liquidity crisis in the Fernheim cooperative. But as the Indians of Filadelfia were quick to realize, it was only the Indian employees of the cooperative who were paid in this way, not the management or the Mennonite staff. The credit notes issued by the Fernheim cooperative were redeemable in a well-stocked cooperative store where the prices compared favorably with those of Asunción. One of the impacts of this method of payment, combined with strict controls on the sale of alcoholic drinks, was the collapse of many of the small cooperative and privately owned stores that were run by the Nivaclé and Guaraní in the Barrio Obrero of Filadelfia.

Outside the industries, economic relations between Mennonites and their Indian employees tend to assume a more paternalistic form. Many Indian laborers in the Mennonite Colonies try to associate themselves with a particular patrón—a Mennonite who can find work for them whenever they need it, and who in turn is assured of their labor whenever he requires it. This arrangement benefits both parties, since it tends to counteract the seasonal fluctuations in the demand for, and supply of, unskilled labor. In the winter, when there is little essential work to be done on the Mennonite farms, the Indians can find some work and are employed clearing pasture or cutting firewood; conversely, in the critical months of the summer, during the cotton and castor bean harvests, the Mennonite patrón can rely on his employees, Indians he considers trustworthy who are familiar with his methods, style of working, and the layout of his farm. Moreover, this kind of relationship tends to limit the competition between Mennonite farmers at harvest time and assures that the piece rates paid to agricultural laborers are kept at reasonably low levels. This is in marked contrast to the smallholder cotton-growing areas of Eastern Paraguay, where, during a good season, the rates paid to agricultural laborers rise until the less productive smallholders find it more profitable to abandon their own cotton and work in their neighbors' fields.

Apart from the harvest and certain tasks, such as cutting firewood, that are paid on a piecework basis, most agricultural work in the Mennonite Colonies is paid on a daily rate, and the Indians receive supplies on credit, the value of which is discounted when they are finally paid. It is also fairly common for the Mennonites to provide their Indian employees with small advances of cash or provisions to cover the needs of their families from the time they start work until they receive their first payment. Unless they live in worker villages or colonies situated close to where they are working, the Indians spend the week living in temporary camps on the farm and return to their homes only on the weekend. Often the Mennonite employer takes his workers back to their village on the Friday night and collects them again early on Monday morning.

The Indians who enjoy permanent relations with their Mennonite employers mainly come from established worker villages such as Sandhorst, Cayin'o Clim, or Colonia 8 of Fernheim. The relations that were established when the Indians were living in the worker villages are often maintained, even after they have been settled in agricultural colonies. Here, the small scale of production and low level of capitalization often make it advantageous for the Indians to work as wage laborers during the slack months of the winter. Unfortunately, the mutual obligations between the Indian and his employer sometimes result in the Indian having to leave his own plot at critical periods in the agricultural cycle, since these are precisely the times when the Mennonite farmer requires the extra labor. Indeed, it is not unknown for Indians to abandon their own cotton harvests to work in the fields of their employers.

Not all day laborers are able to rely on a regular patrón, and particularly in the more marginal worker villages, many people have to take whatever employment they can find. One of the most marginal groups is the Ayoreo—the last group to arrive in the Mennonite Colonies—many of whom live in Montecito, a camp situated on what used to be a garbage dump on the outskirts of Filadelfia. The Ayoreo have a reputation as hard workers; indeed, when they first moved to the Mennonite Colonies, they were so keen to find employment—or so desperate—that they offered to work for lower wages than other laborers. This caused tension with other Indians, particularly the Toba-Maskoy, but endeared the Ayoreo to the Mennonite farmers. Because of their reputation, some privately owned stores in Filadelfia and Loma Plata began to offer credit to the Ayoreo, and this allowed them to stay in the Mennonite Colonies when they were unable to find any work. In time, however, this led them into a cycle of debt, forcing them to remain in the Mennonite Colonies to pay off the money they owed. Even the Ayoreo from the Colonia Maria Auxiliadora, who had traveled to the Mennonite Colonies with the intention of staying only a few weeks, ended up residing almost permanently, living on Mennonite farms or camping on a piece of waste ground next to the airstrip in Loma Plata.

Skilled and semiskilled laborers are able to command better wages, and the highest paid are the Nivaclé and Guaraní of the Barrio Obrero of Filadelfia, many of whom work as bricklayers, carpenters, and even truck drivers. The Indians employed in the building trades generally work for Mennonite contractors and are paid on a piece-rate basis, although there are times when Indian construction workers make their own contracts. In both cases the conditions of employment are similar to those made with other contract laborers in the Chaco and involve advance payments—to cover the cost of materials and provisions for the workers—or the offer of supplies and materials on credit. Such arrangements seem to be indispensable for Indian contract laborers, since even the best paid lack the resources to cover their expenses from the time they start work until they receive payment.

Domestic service is virtually the only sector in which credit relations are absent. This category covers both residential domestic service, where girls or women live with a household and receive a small monthly salary, and temporary employment, such as washing clothes or carrying water, which is paid on a piece-rate basis.

It is usually the younger, unmarried women who work in residential domestic service. In some cases, local ranchers or military officers take the girls to Asunción, and the girls may use the opportunity to further their education. In other cases, the girls go from a desire to provide something for their families, to see the outside world, or simply to be able to eat every day. Conditions of service vary greatly: in some households the girls are well treated, while in others they are used as cheap labor and may be physically or sexually abused by their employers. After a few years in the city, the girls are often unwilling to return to the poverty and monotony of life in the Chaco, and some eventually marry Paraguayans and are assimilated into the urban lower classes.

In towns such as Puerto Casado, Bahía Negra, and Mariscal Estigarribia, many of the women have temporary employment, *changas;* this is particularly important for women whose husbands are absent for long periods working on the ranches or hunting. The women's *changas* are badly paid: for washing clothes they receive around Gs 1,000 (US$0.40) per dozen articles, and they can expect to earn a similar amount for a morning's work carrying water or cleaning floors. They are paid as soon as the task is completed, however, and the payment is generally in cash. The money is insufficient to provide for all the needs of the family, but it helps the women manage while their husbands are away.

The alternative to this kind of work is for women to acquire provisions on credit from local storekeepers. Most small stores in Paraguay operate on credit, both with their customers and with the wholesalers that supply them, and if they were to demand cash from their customers, they would almost certainly go out of business. The relations between storekeepers and their regular clients are of a personal, often paternalistic nature. The storekeeper is often a buyer of animal skins and may employ Indians in other activities; some also own small ranches, while others are cattle buyers or dealers in caranday palms and other forest products. Store-keepers have to be able to judge the capacity and the situation of their clients, and offer them credit according to their ability to pay. Purchases on credit are registered in a notebook that is usually held by the client, and when the client gets paid, the storekeeper tries to persuade him or her to settle part of the account. Part of the debt is left outstanding, however, and this obliges the parties to continue with the arrangement (see Reed 1991).

The Impact of Development Projects

Table 9 offers some insight into the impact of development projects in the Chaco at the time of the 1981 census.

Table 9 should be regarded as a crude indicator for various reasons. First, there is some overlap between the communities classified as "missions" and those classified as "assisted communities." The former category includes the more traditional missions with resident missionaries, some of which, like the Colonia Maria Auxiliadora, were the subject of economic development programs. The category of assisted communities includes all the agricultural colonies of the Central Chaco, as well as colonies such as Pablo Stahl and San José that were supported by the Equipo Nacional de Misiones (ENM). Second, the census was carried out during a slack period in the agricultural cycle, with the result that self-employment in agriculture is almost certainly underreported. Finally, there are a series of intervening factors, other than the presence or absence of economic development projects, that determine whether or not people will work in wage labor or take up self-employment. As I have indicated earlier, perhaps the most important is the existence of opportunities for wage labor. This, I believe, as much as anything else, helps to explain why fewer men are engaged in wage labor on the missions (66 percent) than anywhere else.

In spite of these considerations, it is clear that the positive impact of development projects has been very limited. Indeed, one finds the highest proportions of both men (78 percent) and women (71 percent) working in wage labor in the assisted communities. For men, the figures are

Table 9: Occupational categories by type of settlement and sex

	Wage labor	Self-employed	Family labor	No information	Total
Missions					
Men	1,072	444	95	9	1,620
Women	185	215	113	2	515
Assisted communities					
Men	2,296	452	146	35	2,929
Women	279	74	41	1	395
Dispersed and others					
Men	1,550	445	72	3	2,070
Women	177	304	47	1	529
Total					
Men	4,918	1,341	313	47	6,619
Women	641	593	201	4	1,439
TOTAL	5,559	1,934	514	51	8,058

Source: INDI 1982: table 26.

similar to those for the whole of the economically active male population (74 percent), while the figures for women are considerably higher
than the overall proportion (45 percent). This suggests that most of the
development projects that were carried out in the years before 1981 failed
to offer the Indians an acceptable alternative to the poorly paid sources
of wage labor described above.

There are various reasons for this failure, and some of the social and
cultural issues will be taken up in later chapters. At this point, however, I would like to emphasize that most of the economic development
projects in the Chaco have failed, not because of social or cultural issues,
but simply because the projects were poorly designed and badly imple-
mented. In recent years the tendency has been to blame the Indians for
the failure of these projects. Volker von Bremen's (1987) paper describing
development projects as "modern sources for hunting and gathering" is
often unfairly cited as evidence that the peoples of the Chaco are inherently incapable of planning ahead or organizing any economic activity.

Most of the development projects that had been carried out up to
the mid-1980s were either paternalistic missionary enterprises or poorly
thought-out colonization programs. The first category includes enterprises that would barely merit a mention as "development projects" were
it not for the fact that they were financed by international development
organizations. The paternalistic "projects" included the brick kilns, car-
pentry shops, and ranches found on most of the established missions,
where the missionary was little different from any other patrón. In some
cases the missionaries made their own demands. I can remember the
priest in Maria Auxiliadora refusing to pay the Ayoreo their weekly wage
(of Gs 500, then equivalent to about US$3) unless they attended mass
on Friday evening. I would also include the agricultural development
programs organized by the Mennonites in the category of paternalistic
projects, since the programs showed — and still show — little or no sensi-
tivity to indigenous culture or aspirations and were also linked, perhaps
less blatantly, to religious demands.

The alternative approach was to encourage self-determination, which
in practice often meant simply abandoning a community to its fate. API
was the first institution to experiment with projects of this type, as part
of its *Plan Económico* financed by the Inter-American Foundation be-

tween 1976 and 1978. Later projects taking a similar approach—although without so much public emphasis on the idea of self-determination—included the Ayoreo and Ñandeva Guaraní projects, supported by AIP and the Misión de Amistad, and the latter phases of the Anglicans' La Herencia project. The projects that were directly managed by the Catholic ENM, such as Casanillo and Riacho Mosquito, were probably similar. Virtually all these projects involved the resettlement of Indians who had been living as wage laborers, either on the ranches, or in peri-urban areas such as the worker villages of the Mennonite Colonies. In fact, the only exception to this that I am aware of is API's agricultural credit and handicraft programs, which were initially a success at the village level but were marred by institutional conflicts with ASCIM and by corruption in API's office in Asunción.

In some cases the imperative behind the colonization programs was the need to acquire or regularize title to land that belonged either to the state (*tierras fiscales*) or to absentee owners. In other cases the land was purchased using donations from overseas agencies. In general, the aim of the projects was to defend and extend rights over land rather than to raise income or improve standards of living. In some projects, certainly in the early years of API, there may have been an underlying assumption that indigenous people would be better off if they could recover their access to land and revert to their traditional economic activities. Little attention was given to the fact that even the least acculturated Indian communities were dependent on products and services that included basic items of diet (flour, rice, sugar, noodles), health services, and education. This led to inadequate planning for long-term income generation or the provision of basic services. In the initial stages, supplies were provided to allow the Indians to develop the basic infrastructure for the community, basically housing, fences, and a school or a health post, and to plant gardens. Once this was completed, however, it was expected that the Indians would be able to provide for themselves.

API's projects were characterized by a complete misunderstanding of the agricultural potential of the Chaco. The land that was purchased in Diez Leguas and Buena Vista had no agricultural potential; indeed, Diez Leguas was a useless, low-lying area of palo santo and cactus that was not even suitable for hunting. It soon became, and remains, a worker village, providing temporary agricultural labor for the Mennonites. Buena Vista was better. Once their supplies were exhausted, the Chamococo families who had moved there from Fuerte Olimpo were able to hunt, and for a while they generated enough income to live on from the sale of quebracho fence posts. Later, however, most of the families moved back to Olimpo, and some of the larger Chamococo cattle owners moved in. At present the Chamococo use the colony as a ranch and keep their families in Olimpo or Puerto Esperanza.

Later colonization projects went to more effort to identify areas that would be suitable for subsistence agriculture. The availability of cultivable land determined the areas that were chosen by the Anglicans for La Herencia and by ENM for Casanillo and Riacho Mosquito. None of these projects, however, appears to have seriously considered the need to generate a regular cash income. Once the housing and basic infrastructure were in place, there were no resources left to invest in income-generating activities. The Anglicans left some cattle for the Angaité in La Patria, but most died in an epidemic of bovine rabies because the Indians either could not obtain or could not afford to buy the vaccines. In fact, the only alternative source of income that has emerged in any of these colonies is bee keeping. In general, the projects have slowly ground to a halt as the funding agencies have lost interest in them. The Indians have been forced to look for wage labor on the neighboring ranches, or have abandoned the colonies and returned to the worker villages they originally came from.

The description in this chapter of the external factors that account for the Indians' dependence on wage labor is only partially satisfactory in trying to account for certain features of their economic situation. In particular, it fails to fully explain why people engage in casual wage labor even in communities that are relatively free from outside pressures and that have sufficient land to practice stock raising or cultivation. This is an issue to which I shall return in the next chapter, where I look at the Indians' own system of economic values, and examine how these values inform their perception of the market economy.

Smoking out a bees' nest, Riacho He'e (Toba/Lengua)

Butchering a peccary, Buena Vista (Chamococo)

Net fishing in the Pilcomayo, Mistolar (Nivaclé)

The house of Siriaco Pérez, the administrator in Mistolar (Nivaclé)

An *estanciero* and his wife, Cerrito (Toba)

Branding cattle on the colony's ranch, Cerrito (Toba)

Families of Indian factory workers being paid, Puerto Casado

Nivaclé cooperative store, Barrio Obrero, Filadelfia

Indian children, Salesian mission, Puerto Casado

Cecilio Baez, Chamococo shaman, Puerto Diana

Guaná family in the Salesian mission, Puerto Casado

CHAPTER FIVE

Equality, Natural Resources, and Concepts of Property

I N THE PREVIOUS chapters I have considered the economy of the Chaco societies from what might be labeled an ecological perspective. In describing the Indians' economic activities, I have stressed the importance of ecological factors—related to the natural environment and the regional economy—in determining their choice of activities. I have drawn attention to the importance and variety of activities that provide immediately available returns—particularly hunting and in some communities fishing—and have contrasted this with the rather limited scope of agriculture and stock raising, both of which provide delayed returns. I have argued that this disparity is due to the uncertainty of agriculture and stock raising and to the lack of any perceived need for long-term planning, since the Indians of the Chaco assume that their needs can be met on a day-to-day basis. Similarly, in describing the Indians' participation in the market economy, I have emphasized the factors external to the Indian societies—land tenure, lack of capital, and reliance on credit—that limit the potential of these modes of production and push the Indians into dependence on wage labor.

But a description of the economy of the Chaco societies in terms of purely ecological or external factors is, I believe, in some sense incomplete and may even be misleading, suggesting as it does some kind of ecological determinism. The emphasis on the exploitation of immediately available resources is not something that has been imposed by the natural environment, as is illustrated by the contrasting strategy of the Guaraní. Rather it is an alternative that reflects an underlying system of values, one that is shared by all the truly indigenous societies of the region. In this chapter I shall try to elucidate something of this system of values by looking at the Indians' concepts of equality and personal autonomy, their attitudes toward natural resources, and their notions of property.

Equality and Sharing

One of the features that strikes even the most casual visitor to any of the Indian communities in the Chaco is the remarkable uniformity in the material conditions of life. Between communities, it is true, one does find considerable variation — a variation that reflects the way the community is integrated into the regional economy as much as any other factor — but within each community one finds little if any obvious difference between the constituent households. Moreover, in the few settlements where one can distinguish any real variation in the material circumstances of the population — the most notable examples are the missions of Pedro P. Peña and Santa Teresita — the variation reflects the ethnic composition of the population. In both these settlements, the Guaraní appear materially better off than the other ethnic groups (Nivaclé, Manjuy, and Guaraní Ñandeva).

In general, the houses in any Indian settlement are almost identical. The materials tend to be the same: split palm trunks in the Lower Chaco, and adobe, wattle and daub, or simple poles in the Central and High Chaco. Their size and layout are also similar: the houses are rarely more than a single room intended for storage and for sleeping in times of bad weather. The only exceptions are those houses occupied by some large extended households that may comprise various nuclear families. There is likewise little variation in the possessions to be found in each house. The furniture, if any, is usually limited to one or two beds — cheap wire-sprung *catres,* or beds made from strips of rawhide stretched across a wooden frame — some mattresses, perhaps a wooden chair or two, and in all but the poorest households, the seemingly indispensable mosquito nets. The other possessions are generally limited to clothing and a few personal items. For men, these might include an ax, a machete, and perhaps a rifle or a revolver; for women, their cooking pots and possibly an earthenware water jar. In some households one might also come across a rather battered radio or cassette recorder, or perhaps a bicycle.

This uniformity in material possessions cannot, I believe, be explained simply in terms of poverty. Rather, I would argue that it also responds to a strongly held egalitarian ethic, an ethic that predisposes the Indians of the Chaco to view the accumulation of material possessions — beyond a certain, limited level — as a threat to the social order. The idea of equality is not merely the absence of social stratification but a positively affirmed moral principle, one that is ultimately linked to a vision of the individual as an autonomous being, responsible for all of his or her actions. From this perspective the affirmation of rights over property, whether individual or corporate, is viewed as a restraint on the freedom of the individual, and the accumulation of material goods is seen as potentially coercive. As Woodburn notes in his characterization of egalitarian societies:

> In these societies equalities of power, equalities of wealth and equalities of prestige or rank are not merely sought but are, with certain limited exceptions, genuinely realized. But, the evidence suggests, they are never unchallenged. People are well aware of the possibility that individuals or groups within their own egalitarian societies may try to acquire more wealth, to assert more power or to claim more status than other people, and are vigilant in seeking to prevent or to limit this. The verbal rhetoric of equality may or may not be elaborated but actions speak loudly: equality is repeatedly acted out, publicly demonstrated, in opposition to possible inequality. (1982:432)

Although the Indian societies of the Chaco are in many respects different from the mainly African hunter-gatherer societies that are the focus of Woodburn's concern, they do seem to share some of the same structural preconditions that, Woodburn argues, permit the realization of a high degree of social equality. In fact, these structural features, along with an emphasis on equality and personal autonomy, appear to be widespread in Lowland South America (Rivière 1984:4; Clastres 1972, 1977).

In the first place, as I have described in the previous chapters, production is, within the limits of the sexual division of labor, organized on a largely individual basis. In principle, most subsistence activities can be carried out by a single man or woman, and even where cooperation is necessary, as in the case of net fishing in the Upper Pilcomayo, the groups that work together are formed on an informal, day-to-day basis. Second, there are no enduring social or "corporate" groups that hold any tangible rights to property, to land, or to the labor and reproductive capacity of women. The Ayoreo clans, the *cucharane,* are perhaps an exception here, but as I shall discuss in the next chapter, they have nothing whatsoever to do with productive activities. Finally, the Chaco societies are characterized by considerable freedom of choice in questions of residence and political allegiance. The pattern of residence, as I shall discuss in the following chapters, is the outcome of a series of individual choices that are determined by certain principles but not by any clearly perceived rules. This allows a high level of mobility and effectively prevents anyone from imposing their authority through physical coercion or control over resources.

In the traditional context, there appears to have been little or no possibility of an individual's accumulating property, let alone of using property as means for acquiring prestige or political power. There appear to have been virtually no prestige items and little intercommunity trade, while the resources that the Indians of the Chaco exploited were available to all and were generally unsuitable for storage. Moreover, given the seminomadic pattern of settlement in much of the Chaco, the accumulation of possessions was always limited by the need for mobility, with people not owning, or wanting to own, more than they were able to carry by themselves. In the modern context, however, there are greater opportunities for the emergence of inequality, particularly in the ownership of goods acquired through the market economy. Differences in household composition, in earnings, and in dependence on purchased foodstuffs might all be expected to affect the household's access to industrially manufactured goods, but in practice one finds remarkably little variation in the distribution of property within any given community. This is in marked contrast to even the poorest and most marginal sectors of the Paraguayan population, among which one finds considerable variation in both housing and material possessions.

The Chaco societies' commitment to the idea of equality is manifest in the emphasis they place on sharing and generosity. These concepts are rather more complex than they at first appear, however, since the Indians of the Chaco stress a notion of reciprocity that, although often expressed in an idiom of kinship or affinity, is in fact perceived as existing independently of such ties.

In practice, the distribution of foodstuffs and the lending of personal property tend to follow lines of affinity, especially within the uxorilocally extended household, and kinship, typically outside the household. But the obligation to share is seen, ideally at least, as extending beyond one's own household and kindred to all the members of the community or residential group. This is not merely a question of kinship being manipulated. It is recognized that ties of kinship or affinity can be manipulated to gain advantage, and although people will complain about this, they are unlikely to refuse a request from those who claim to be their distant kin or affines.

The Indians of the Chaco sometimes emphasize the local residential group as the people with whom one should share. This reflects the real networks of redistribution and does not necessarily negate the importance of kinship, since the more clearly bounded residential groups are typically composed of uxorilocally extended households linked together by ties of kinship. In reality, though, the composition of residential groups is usually more complex than this simple model would suggest; moreover, such groups are rather unstable, with households and individuals coming and going all the time. They move in search of wage labor or to hunt, they often abandon a community if a member of the household dies or if there are conflicts with other households, and they may leave simply from a desire for change. Given this situation, the networks of distribution within any community tend to be very flexible. They are capable of incorporating people who may be neither kin nor affines, who may not be identified as members of the same community or residential group, and who may even belong to a distinct ethnic group. Indeed, it might be best to represent the obligation for sharing as one that places the onus not so much on kin or affines but rather on anyone who, at a particular moment, happens to have a surplus available for redistribution.

The distribution of surplus foodstuffs—typically portions of large game or agricultural produce—is on occasion determined by a simple notion of restricted reciprocity. One gives meat to those who have given meat previously, and, perhaps less frequently, one may give to those from whom one expects some kind of a return. This is, however, by no means the principal criterion taken into account when distributing surplus. Indeed, the practice of giving in the expectation of a return is more characteristic of the way the Indians of the Chaco deal with outsiders, such as missionaries or anthropologists, who are never permanently integrated into the networks of exchange, than of the way they operate among themselves. In general, need is perceived as a more important criterion than short-term reciprocity: one gives to those who are in need, and one expects to rely on the goodwill of anyone who has a surplus when in need oneself. This is certainly an explicit ideal. In criticizing the economic individualism of the Mennonites—what he calls "the White Man's religion"—one of the Nivaclé of Pedro P. Peña asks, "How is it that the Mennonite pastors always insist on our saving when the Bible tells us that we should help those in need?"

This is well illustrated by the practice, found in those colonization schemes where the Indians have genuinely had a hand in deciding policy, of distributing rations to every household, regardless of whether the members actually participate in any of the activities of the project. When the colony of Buena Vista was first established, the Chamococo received a monthly supply of provisions from API which were distributed to every family, regardless of the effort they put into the project. The decision was taken against the advice of the Paraguayan agronomist supervising the project, and many of the more influential men in the community were aware that it might be a disincentive to work. The decision was supported by the whole community, however, on the grounds that distributing rations in payment for work was not the Chamococo way of doing things—it was a form of coercion and would discriminate against the widows and elderly. Rather, they felt it was a matter of personal responsibility whether an individual worked or not, and the unity of the group, and the success of the program, were dependent on each individual's comprehending the aims of the project.

In the traditional context, the emphasis on generalized exchange would have helped to balance the fluctuations in individual returns characteristic of a hunting economy. However skilled he is, a hunter will have days when he returns empty-handed, while on other days—if he encounters a herd of peccary or kills a couple of deer—he will have as much, if not more, meat than he can carry. Generalized exchange helps to minimize this element of chance and ensure that everyone in the group has something to eat. The same logic is not lost on those communities that nowadays rely mainly on wage labor. The low levels of employment, the low pay, and the uncertainty of being paid all combine to reinforce the survival value of sharing. A casual wage laborer or ranch hand often has to leave his family for long periods, and although his family may manage for a time with credit from local storekeepers or money received in advance, they eventually have to fall back on their kin and neighbors. Once the wage earner is paid off, though, the family will usually have more than enough for their immediate subsistence needs, and this gives them a chance to support those of their kinsmen and neighbors who in the meantime are unemployed or awaiting the return of their wage earners.

The Indians of the Chaco do not, however, view sharing simply as a strategy for survival. Rather, it is a positively valued ethic in itself. Indeed, one often finds foodstuffs being exchanged between households that have no need to share at all. Among the Nivaclé of the Upper Pilcomayo, for example, households continue to exchange smoked fish and agricultural produce even during the months when these products are in abundance and each household has ample supplies of its own. In the same way, many of the Guaraní in Pedro P. Peña invite their neighbors to harvest from their gardens, even though most have gardens of their own. In these cases sharing is obviously not determined by any sense of economic "rationality" but is a function of social relations and is primarily a means by which the group, usually the residential group, defines itself. This exchange of goods is not determined by kinship but provides the practical basis of kinship, the people with whom one exchanges food becoming as it were one's kin (see also Clastres 1977:95).

Rights and Attitudes to Natural Resources

Natural resources and the land on which they are found are not considered to be the property of individuals or even of any clearly defined corporate groups. In the traditional context, land was never a scarce resource. Certain populations were, and to some extent still are, associated with particular areas — areas that in the absence of any significant natural boundaries, such as major rivers, tend to be rather vaguely defined. But the relationship was not conceived as one of ownership in the sense that the group in question held exclusive rights over the natural resources of the area. Indeed, provided that the territorial groups were on friendly terms, it seems that small bands or hunting parties were free to move into the territory of neighboring groups and to exploit the natural resources as they wished.

In the modern context, most of the Chaco is privately owned, and the Indian population is concentrated in missions or colonies with clearly demarcated boundaries. Unlike the official colonies for Paraguayan farmers, established by the Instituto de Bienestar Rural (IBR), the Indian colonies are not divided into individually titled family plots. There is no legal restriction, other perhaps than the lack of personal documentation, that prevents Indians from holding land in the same way as other Paraguayan citizens. Indeed, many people in government would like to settle the Indian population in neat and manageable family plots of the kind found in the colonies for Paraguayan smallholders. Rather, the system of tenure in the Indian colonies reflects the Indians' resistance to the idea of individual landholding, a resistance that is so strong that the desire to hold individual title is taken as evidence that a person wants to adopt Paraguayan rather than Indian identity.

Until the law on indigenous peoples (Law 904/81) was passed in 1981, there was no legal provision for communal landholding other than by institutions with legal personality (*personería jurídica*) such as formally constituted cooperatives and limited companies. The titles to most Indian colonies were held by private institutions, such as the Asociación Indigenista del Paraguay (AIP), or by the missions. In some cases the missionary orders were the owners of the land and were entitled to use it and even to sell it—the Anglican Mission sold off much of its land in the 1950s—while others held the land in trust for the Indian communities. In the years since Law 904/81 was passed, many of the Indian communities in the Chaco have acquired their legal personality and are now the owners of the land on which they are settled. The process involves the election and registration by INDI of three or more "leaders" who represent the community, followed by a formal request to the Office of the President of the Republic. Despite their initial opposition, some religious missions—but not the Mennonites or the Oblates of Maria—have now transferred the land titles to the Indian communities.

In practice, there are two systems of land use in the Chaco. The first is essentially the same as the traditional system and is found in all the communities situated outside the Mennonite Colonies. Here, rights to house plots and gardens exist only through usufruct, and in principle anyone, even those with only the remotest of links to other members of the community, can exploit the natural resources of the area as they wish. The second system is that found in the agricultural colonies of the Central Chaco, where the Mennonite administration assigns households individual plots of agricultural land.

In areas outside the Central Chaco, the location of house plots and gardens tends to be determined by considerations of kinship and affinity. House plots and gardens are sometimes fenced in, but this is done not so much to demarcate the plot as to deter marauding pigs or goats. The construction of a house or the preparation of a garden does not, however, confer any rights other than those of usufruct, and indeed, given the kin-based nature of most residential groups, it is perhaps a mistake to describe land use in terms of individual rights. In fact, in those rather infrequent cases where conflicts arise, they are perceived not as conflicts over the rights of individual households but as conflicts between larger residential groups or political factions.

In the agricultural colonies of the Central Chaco, the system of land use appears to resemble a system of private landholding. Each household is allocated its own plot of agricultural land and a small area of scrub forest and is also able to use areas of common grazing land that belong to the village or the colony. Like the agricultural economy it is intended to foster, this system of land use has been imposed from outside and is based on the Mennonites' own cooperatives rather than on any indigenous system. The Indians who live in these colonies have generally accepted the religious doctrines of the Mennonite Church, but there is little evidence to suggest they have accepted the Mennonites' economic values. There is not much open criticism of the system of land use as such, but the Indians' resistance seems to be expressed through the rather lackluster economic performance discussed in previous chapters and through continual complaints about the lack of land titles and resources for the colonization programs. In fact, the one group that has opted out of this system, the Nivaclé of Mistolar, most of whom were previously settled in Yalve Sanga, are quite explicit in their rejection of what they see as the creeping individualism characteristic of life in these colonies. The issue is not simply that households are allocated individual plots—even in communities such as Mistolar gardens generally belong to individual households—but rather that the bureaucratic allocation of the plots has tended to break up the residential unity of extended households and kin groups.

The Indians also note that the system is leading to the creation of *mini-fundia* (smallholdings). As the household increases in size and daughters marry, typically bringing their husbands to live with them, the plot becomes insufficient for the needs of the extended family. The young couple may try to acquire a plot of their own, a process that can involve some years of waiting, but the members of the family often prefer to remain together even though the five-hectare plot is insufficient for their needs.

The only situation in which a concept of "ownership" of natural resources appears to have emerged is with the permanently occupied fishing sites on the Upper Pilcomayo, such as Lhvi, Tinayfas, Mistolar, Jo'ot (Lomitas), and Pedro P. Peña. At the height of the fishing season, in May and June, the people of these settlements were joined by other groups of Nivaclé from the interior, who apparently would ask permission to fish there. Permission was always granted, and the same groups would return year after year. There is no evidence of conflict over fishing rights between members of the same ethnic group, and indeed the sharing of fishing sites appears to have been one of the features that defined the political unity of the Nivaclé territorial groups.

Fishing rights were, and still are, however, a potential source of inter-ethnic conflict. Indeed, in the winter of 1983 the Nivaclé of Mistolar were complaining that the Mataco had constructed fishing weirs farther upstream, preventing the fish from passing into the lower reaches of the river. The construction of fishing weirs is mentioned by Nordenskiöld (1912) as one the main causes of conflict. The groups living downstream would try to destroy the dams constructed upriver, and fighting would ensue; people would be killed and captives taken, and this would provide a motive for further raids. Indeed, when Nordenskiöld visited the region, large stretches of the Pilcomayo were deserted because the Nivaclé and Choroti had been driven away by the Toba, who had managed to acquire repeating rifles (Nordenskiöld 1912:chap. 8).

It is apparent from the emphasis on communal landholding that the Indians of the Chaco regard natural resources as being available to anyone who cares to use them and that, even in the contemporary context, they view the natural environment as bountiful and potentially inexhaustible. The Chaco is as it were a vast storehouse, and the Indians show little concern for the conservation even of resources such as timber that are quite clearly nonrenewable. They are, it is true, well aware that overexploitation has resulted in the depletion of certain species, and they sometimes claim that traditionally they would have limited the numbers taken. This is perhaps more of an ideal than a historical fact. I have heard hunters among the Toba comment that in the past young rhea would have been left to maintain the species, although nowadays it is recognized that they are never spared—if they were, it is argued, someone else would come along and kill them. This is not, I believe, merely a response to the present scarcity of game. The Anglican missionary Grubb, writing at the turn of the twentieth century, notes precisely this argument among the Lengua. He recalls coming across a rhea's nest and suggesting to his companions that they leave a few eggs to maintain the stock. At this his companions laughed. "The wolf, if he finds the nest," they replied, "will consume what we leave, and if an Indian comes along he will take them," and they proceeded to sit down and gorge themselves (1911:190).

This same attitude has been noted among other societies in Lowland South America, including some of the relatively sedentary societies of the tropical forest. Paul Henley, for example, writing about the Panare of the Middle Orinoco, remarks on their "prodigal" attitude to the natural environment. He notes that this attitude is perfectly rational in a situation, such as the Panare traditionally enjoyed, where the natural resources that they exploited were to all intents and purposes infinite (1982:52). While this appears to contradict those accounts that have presented the societies of Lowland South America as ecologically balanced or even conservation minded (e.g., Reichel-Dolmatoff 1976), the issue is, I would argue, really one of perspective. The Indians of the Chaco, and in all probability the Indians of the tropical forest, are not, I believe, consciously concerned about the conservation of natural resources in the course of their day-to-day subsistence activities. At a different level, however, these societies have managed to maintain a balance between population and resources, and this has been due, at least in part, to a system of values that explicitly rejects the accumulation of surplus.

Concepts of Property

In order to understand how the egalitarian values of the Chaco societies are manifest in their attitudes to material possessions, it is worth examining their concepts of natural resources and property in more detail. These concepts are very different from the dominant Western notions of resources and property. Indeed, one almost hesitates to use the term *property* to describe the way the Indians of the Chaco view the relations between people and things, and implicitly the relations between people and others. The Western concept is imbued with the idea of property as commodity, whereby property is alienable and exclusive rights are held by individuals, married couples, or corporate groups endowed with some kind of legal personality. The Western concept is familiar to most of the Indians of the Chaco, but it has not been internalized, and I would argue that it is the indigenous categories that still dominate the Indians' ideas about material possessions.

The Chaco societies appear to distinguish three separate categories of "property." They are not referred to by any generic terms, but they seem to be clearly differentiated. First is personal property: a rather limited range of items that are not simply "owned" but are intimately associated with an individual, being largely inalienable and regarded almost as a part of the person. Second, there are what I shall term consumable items: the produce of hunting, fishing, gathering, agriculture, the meat of domestic animals, and purchased foodstuffs and other consumables such as yerba maté, tobacco, and *caña*. Finally, in the modern context, there is money (including cash and credit notes), an anomalous form of property that by its very nature is impersonal but remains outside the sphere of generalized reciprocity.

In most Indian households one does not, as I have already mentioned, find much in the way of durable property, and what there is, is almost always considered to be the property of specific individuals. There is

168

little or no elaboration of the concept of joint ownership, for example, between spouses or perhaps among the members of the extended household. Even houses and furniture are regarded as the personal property of specific individuals rather than as the common property of the household. As a result, one finds a marked sexual division in the ownership of personal property. Seelwische (1974), for instance, notes that among the Nivaclé a married woman's property would typically have included her loom, woolen blankets, caraguatá-string carrying bags, earthenware cooking and water pots, and personal ornaments. The house, which was constructed by the women, was also considered a woman's property; the owner was usually the elder woman in the typical uxorilocally extended household. Since the women were responsible for the flocks of sheep and goats, these too would be considered their property. A man's property would be more limited—the Nivaclé would have had to carry all their property with them when they moved between settlement sites— and would have included his arms, skin carrying bags, and, among the riverine Nivaclé, fishing nets. Both men and women sometimes owned horses, which were also considered their personal property.

Today the category of personal property also appears to include a number of industrially manufactured items. For men, these can include tools (axes, knives, machetes, hoes); firearms; items of clothing, including such things as leather chaps and gun belts; saddles and other riding equipment; and personal ornaments, including items like wristwatches and sunglasses. The purchased items that belong to women are more limited and usually include clothing, aluminum or iron cooking pots, furniture, and a variety of personal ornaments. It should also be mentioned that all personal documents, such as identity cards, Colorado Party affiliation papers, personal recommendations, and vaccination certificates, also fall into this category of personal property.

All these items appear to be viewed as in some sense a part of an individual's persona and are, strictly speaking, inalienable. The relation between an object and its owner is a metonymic one. This is perhaps seen at its clearest in the traditional context, where almost all the artifacts that were produced were destined for the producer's own use, there being no clear distinction between the creator of an object and its "owner." It was the owner who gave the object its particular form, and so the personal nature of such property was especially clear with items such as woolen blankets or caraguatá string bags that bore their maker's own designs. Nowadays, however, the category of personal property appears to have been extended to include all the tools and utensils that a person uses in daily productive activities, as well as those items, such as personal documents, that in a literal sense represent the person (see also Crocker 1985:112; Clastres 1972:212).

Although personal property is inalienable in the sense that it is identified almost as a part of the owner, this does not prevent the Indians from lending or giving away their personal property. In fact, precisely the opposite is the case, since the Chaco societies place a high value on generosity, both in lending and in giving away items of durable property. Tools, firearms, and even clothes are continually lent and borrowed, and most people would find it difficult to refuse a reasonable request for any of their personal possessions. Such requests, it should be noted, are often phrased in terms of the would-be borrower's need and not, directly, in terms of kinship, affinity, or political allegiance; in turn, when a request is refused, the refusal is typically justified in terms of the owner's need for the item in question.

The importance of lending and giving does not necessarily contradict the idea that personal property is inalienable. Seelwische (1974), in discussing the Nivaclé, provides two examples that illustrate this concept. The first is that if a couple separate, they will return any gifts they have given each other. At first sight this appears unremarkable, but in fact it seems to suggest that a gift is never completely divorced from the person who gives it. Once the relation, in this case the marriage, between the person who gave the gift and the person who received it is broken off, the gift should revert to its original owner. The second example is more surprising. Seelwische notes that if a Nivaclé gives away or even sells a goat or sheep, any offspring that the animal has will be considered the property of the original owner and not of the person who bought or received the animal. This latter example should, perhaps, be treated with a certain caution, since it is reminiscent of the practice of *partija*, where animals are lent out, not given away, and their offspring divided between the original owner and the person put in charge of the animals.

The association between an individual and his or her personal property is seen at its most explicit in the way that such property is treated on the death of its owner. Among the Chaco societies virtually all a person's possessions—including any industrially manufactured items and, very specifically, their personal documents—will be destroyed on their death or interred with the corpse. Traditionally, any dogs or horses that belonged to the deceased would also be slaughtered. In fact, as Grubb (1911:125) notes, the death of the owner is the only occasion when the Indians of the Chaco would kill a dog or a horse. The house where the deceased resided will be burned or, more usual nowadays, demolished and later re-erected close by. The name of the deceased will no longer be mentioned—the person is referred to indirectly as "he or she who was"—and the deceased's close relatives will often leave the settlement where the death has occurred, and not return for some months.

The explicit reason given for these practices is that they help the relatives forget the deceased and overcome their sorrow. From this, it is clear that the Indians of the Chaco are intent on effecting a separation between the living and the dead, and that the personal property and the names of the dead are seen as an intrinsic part of their owner's being. Underlying these ideas, perhaps, is a notion that the dead, and by extension those things associated with the dead, represent a danger to the living.

Grubb (1911) and Loewen (1964), writing about the Lengua, refer to the belief that the spirits or souls of the dead, which Grubb calls *aphangak* and Loewen *jangauck,* may try to take the souls of the living (*vanmongcama*), causing them to die. They note that the souls of the dead are believed to haunt the place of death or burial, and may even haunt the objects that the deceased used to own. Loewen cites the example of a Lengua who found an old iron cooking pot lying in a field. He picked it up, intent on taking it, but was immediately confronted by the soul (*jangauck*) of its long dead owner. The man threw himself into the cactus then ran off into the forest. A few minutes later he returned and fainted in front of his companions; they feared his soul had been taken by the *jangauck,* but eventually he came to and explained that he had shaken off the spirit in the forest (Loewen 1964:38). Ideas of this kind seem to be widespread in Lowland South America; for instance, the Aché of Eastern Paraguay believe that the souls of the dead will try to take the souls of their close relatives, causing them to sicken and eventually die (Clastres 1972:180).

The intimate association between a person and his or her personal property does not extend to those consumable items, such as game, fish, honey, or agricultural produce, that are taken or cultivated by an individual, or to purchased foodstuffs, yerba maté, tobacco, *caña*, and so on. Indeed, it would appear that some of the Chaco languages actually lack a direct possessive form for items of this kind. In both Ayoreo and Guaraní, for instance, the possessive prefixes that are applied to parts of the body, relationships, personal property, and positions cannot be used for most consumable items, and the action that relates the individual to the object has to be made specific. An Ayoreo cannot, for example, talk of the peccary he has killed as "my peccary" but has to refer to it as "my killing, the peccary" (*yuje yacore*). Similarly, in the case of cultivated produce an Ayoreo will talk of "my bringing, the squash" (*yui dutue*) rather than employing a direct possessive prefix.

While linguistic evidence of this kind should be treated with caution, it does suggest that consumable items cannot really be regarded as the property of individuals. In practice, these items are usually distributed among all the members of the extended kin or residential group, although the networks of distribution may extend well beyond this level. Moreover, and in marked contrast to the model of bridewealth societies posited by Collier and Rosaldo (1981), the produce acquired by men is almost invariably redistributed by women, either the wife or, in the typical uxorilocally extended household, the mother-in-law. On returning from a hunt or from a fishing expedition, a group of men may, it is true, make an initial and usually equitable division of their game, but once the game has been butchered and cleaned, its redistribution becomes the prerogative of the women of the household. In this way men, who are the providers of most of the household's subsistence needs, are, to use Woodburn's phrase, systematically disengaged from the product of their labors (1982:431).

A similar process is also effected by a number of alimentary prohibitions—varying in their details among ethnic groups—that restrict the kinds of game or the parts of animals that can be consumed by the young or able-bodied, thus favoring the older and less active members of the community. The Chamococo and the Toba claim that the nine-banded armadillo used not to be eaten by the young; this is one of the fattest game animals, and its flesh was believed to make the young less resistant to hardship. Similarly, the Nivaclé believe that the flesh of the three-banded armadillo is unsuitable for young people. Among the Nivaclé, people of reproductive age still do not eat the largest of the ducks, the *pato bragado* (*Dendrocygma viudata*), as it is believed their children would be born with red blotches on their skin, like those found on the duck's head. However, unlike the situation reported for some Lowland South American societies, including the Aché, the Chaco societies do not recognize any explicit prohibition on the hunter consuming the game he has taken (Clastres 1972:210).

Purchased foodstuffs and rations are treated in much the same way as the produce of foraging and agriculture, but money itself is regarded very differently and is generally considered the property of the person who earned it. It does not fall into the category of an individual's personal property. A person's earnings would not, for instance, be destroyed on their death, and no particular concern is attached to money that belonged to the dead, but it is specifically excluded from the networks of sharing that characterize economic relations within the extended household or residential group.

Wage earners have considerable freedom to dispose of their money, and it is often spent in a way that to an outsider appears irrational, the purchases being motivated by simple curiosity or a desire to imitate one's employers. Indeed, the Indians of the Chaco show remarkably little interest in acquiring industrially manufactured items. The possession of such goods, even those that are of obvious use such as firearms or bicycles, does not constitute a source of prestige but instead tends to be problematic, drawing unwanted attention and the continual demands of neighbors. In fact, an Indian wage laborer, once he has covered his immediate subsistence needs, will sometimes spend the earnings that are left over on the most unnecessary items. For example, a Lengua ranch hand, having spent some weeks driving cattle to an embarkation point on the Trans-Chaco Highway, finally took the bus to Asunción, where he was paid off by his employer. On his return, he was approached at the bus station by a street vendor who talked him into spending the whole of his earnings, as well as some of the earnings of a companion, on an elaborate watch that could tell the time in Rio, Johannesburg, and Hong

Kong. The man had no need of a watch and was in fact unable to tell the time. He was satisfied with the purchase—perhaps a little concerned that he had been overcharged—and he remarked that he would give the watch to his children as a plaything, and that when they broke it, it would be no great loss.

Purchases of this kind, not to mention the money that is sometimes spent on drink or gambling, may leave the wage earner's immediate family short of essential foodstuffs and other items. But they tend to be accepted—although not always without comment—as a consequence of the value that the Chaco societies place on personal autonomy. Indeed, it would appear that a wage earner's immediate family members are not necessarily seen as his "dependents," since mutual dependence is a function of the extended household, or even of the community, defined in terms of common political leadership, rather than the nuclear family as such.

This attitude to material possessions is, I believe, implicit in the way the Indians of the Chaco often describe themselves as "poor." This concept is always somewhat ambiguous. On the one hand, it is an expression of the Indians' very real material poverty, and of their aspiration to a better standard of living, one that at least satisfies their subsistence needs. On the other, it is an assertion of their social or cultural identity, associated with an egalitarian system of values, which sets them apart from the rest of the national society. The idea of poverty as a positive ethic, an idea expressed in Guaraní as *mboriahú porte*, "the way the poor behave," is seen at its most explicit when it is used to confer a sense of common identity on people with whom one has no ties of kinship or affinity. One sometimes hears it said of Indians from other ethnic groups, or even on occasion of Paraguayans with whom the Indians are on friendly terms, that "they are poor, just like we are." This is not really an incipient sense of class consciousness, in the sense of perceiving common class interests opposed to those of the landowners or industrialists. Rather, it focuses attention on the idea of a shared system of moral values, which contrasts with the value system of the dominant sectors of Paraguayan society.

The Indians of the Chaco are often at a loss to explain exactly why it is that money is so different from the produce of foraging and agriculture, and even to food that has been purchased from a store. In fact, when questioned directly on this issue, they often laugh, which suggests perhaps that the answer is so obvious as to defy further explanation. The point seems to be that money is inherently unsuitable for sharing. It is strictly quantifiable and is a unit of exchange rather than being of value in itself—one of the principles of any system of reciprocity being that one can never return a gift identical to that which one has received.

Money is also perceived as potentially coercive. In a myth that explains the poverty of the Nivaclé, Fisoc'oyich, the Creator, having offered the First Nivaclé a variety of industrially manufactured goods, finally presents him with a handful of banknotes, saying, "Look my son, this is for you. You can exchange it for anything you like. You can get others to work for you, and they will bring you all the provisions that you and your kinsmen need to live with." The First Nivaclé refuses the offer, laughing, and he goes off to look for honey, while Fisoc'oyich, now angry, goes off and gives all the money to the Europeans and Paraguayans (Chase Sardi 1981:211).

Attitudes toward Wage Labor

Although it may seem paradoxical, it is this perception of money, and indeed of the accumulation of any kind of surplus, that, I would argue, helps to account for the Chaco societies' apparent preference for wage labor. In the modern context, where nearly all the Indian population is in some way integrated into the market economy, it might seem surprising to suggest that the Indians are not interested in the production of surplus. But as I have already noted, the Indians' participation in the market economy has not necessarily resulted in their adopting the values of the market. In the first place, the Indians of the Chaco still view the natural environment as bountiful and see no merit in accumulating resources or, to use Grubb's phrase, in "saving against the day of adversity" (Grubb 1911:189). The accumulation of surplus is, moreover, viewed as a threat to the Indians' egalitarian system of values, since it may favor particular individuals or households and allow them the possibility of coercing others through their control over resources (see also Clastres 1977:165–68).

The initial incentive for participation in the market economy usually seems to have been the desire for industrially manufactured goods; some of the elder Nivaclé remember the first time they saw the cheap cotton cloth brought back by the people who had been working in the cane fields of Argentina. They were astonished by the bright colors and the softness of the cloth — so different from their own garments woven from caraguatá fiber — and were eager to acquire cotton clothing of their own. Once they began working as wage laborers, other needs soon asserted themselves, and they found themselves being increasingly drawn into dependence on the market economy. Even today, though, the Indians' "needs" are by no means infinite and are still essentially defined in subsistence terms. Indeed, as I have already mentioned, an Indian wage laborer, once he has covered his immediate subsistence needs, will be relatively unconcerned about how he spends what remains. In fact, on some of the more isolated ranches where there is little opportunity to spend cash, one sometimes hears it explicitly acknowledged that the purpose of wage labor is to acquire the rations provided by the ranch owner rather than a cash income.

In many respects the opportunities for wage labor are not unlike the opportunities for foraging provided by the natural environment, and indeed decisions about whether an individual works as a wage laborer or, for example, goes hunting tend to balance the relative expectations of each activity. As one of the Manjuy of Pedro P. Peña expresses it:

> If you go to the Mennonite Colonies, and are able to find work, you can eat well every day, and you may even have some money left to buy new clothes and a few other things. Once the work comes to an end, however, there is nothing to do. You have to wait and bear your hunger until another *patrón* comes along.
>
> Here, there are hardly any opportunities to earn money, and no chance of acquiring a new set of clothes for yourself or your family. It is difficult to find even enough money for half a kilo of sugar or yerba. On the other hand, you never have to listen to your children crying of hunger. Even in the hardest months of the winter, when the fish have gone and there is little game in the forest, you can always find some lianas and caraguatá to fill your stomach. (Ruíz Mateo, Loma Alegre)

Wage labor nearly always provides some immediate return in the form of provisions, credit, or advances of cash. Permanently employed ranch hands receive weekly supplies as part of their payment, while temporary laborers—engaged in erecting fencing or clearing pasture—usually expect to receive provisions on credit. The variety of supplies is limited, and the prices are usually much higher than those in a store. But it is the Indians themselves who often demand rations, credit, or advances of cash, a demand justified by the laborer's need to support himself and his family during the period he is working.

The provisions provided by an employer are not only immediately available but also, unlike cash, easily integrated into the system of exchange on which the economy of the Chaco societies is founded. There is always a limited supply. The provisions are never abundant in the way that natural resources sometimes can be, and are probably never distributed as widely as the produce of a successful hunt or fishing expedition. However, they do not provoke any contradictions and can be treated in more or less the same way as the produce of most day-to-day hunting, fishing, or gathering.

Moreover, there is little apparent contradiction between the Chaco societies' emphasis on generosity and the fact that wage labor is carried out for payment. Sharing and generosity are characteristic of relations within the extended kin or residential group—the means, as it were, by which the group defines itself. Outside this group, however, the model no longer applies, and there is no expectation of generosity; rather, the relation between a wage laborer and his or her employer is perceived as one of restricted reciprocity defined in the narrowest of terms. Even where the relation between an Indian and his employer is of a fairly personal nature, as on some of the ranches and at times in the Mennonite Colonies, the Indians expect their employer to be fair rather than generous.

It should be noted, however, that wage labor is almost always performed for outsiders, whose values are perceived as distinct from those of their Indian workers. It would not be acceptable for an Indian to employ anyone from his own community on the same terms as are offered by Paraguayan or Mennonite employers. Indeed, on the rare occasions when Indian subcontractors employ people from their own communities—the subcontractors are usually skilled men who have been contracted at piece rates for a specific task, such as erecting fencing—the terms of employment are more equitable than those offered by outsiders.

Typically, an Indian subcontractor will provide his laborers with supplies, acquired on credit from the ranch owner, and, having deducted his expenses, will make an equitable division of any profits that are left.

As we saw in the previous chapter, independent means of earning money, such as cultivation of cash crops, stock raising, and commerce, are of less importance than wage labor for most Indian communities. These activities, unlike wage labor, do appear to present some contradictions for an economy traditionally based on the exploitation of immediately available resources, where the networks of sharing are determined by coresidence rather than by any specific ties of kinship or affinity. I am not suggesting that these contradictions are the only reasons for the Chaco societies' marked dependence on wage labor, and they have to be understood within the context of the ecological and economic constraints considered in the previous chapters.

The potential of agriculture is limited by environmental factors and by the present system of land tenure. In the Central Chaco, the Mennonites have made an effort to help the Indians develop their agricultural production so as to stabilize the population and reduce the Indians' dependence on direct aid, and they have provided equipment, technical assistance, and small loans to stimulate the production of cash crops. Despite these advantages, a significant proportion of the Indian population do not even practice agriculture at a subsistence level. This suggests that they perceive wage labor as an attractive alternative to agriculture. One of the reasons seems to be that agriculture, unlike wage labor, provides delayed returns on the time and labor invested. Furthermore, the agriculture practiced in the Central Chaco requires a level of accumulation that conflicts with the emphasis on sharing. The consumption of agricultural produce demands careful management, because seed has to be maintained for the next season's planting, and, more important, the household has to have a surplus sufficient to cover everyone's needs from the end of the harvest until the next season's crops are ready. This means that even though they are seen as having a surplus, the members of the household must limit their own consumption and resist pressures from their kin and neighbors who feel they have a claim on the harvest.

Stock raising poses problems similar to those of agriculture, and significantly, the few Indians who have managed to acquire large holdings of livestock are to some extent estranged from their communities of origin. Some are ranch foremen, who have to represent the interests of the ranch owner, which brings them into conflict with the other Indians employed on the ranch or with people who want to hunt on the owner's land. The estrangement is also a direct result of their wealth. The other members of their community try to pressure them, through gossip or direct requests, to slaughter their animals or to provide gifts and money to their neighbors and relatives. If they give in, the pressures continue until they have nothing left, and if they refuse, they will be accused of meanness or of "behaving like Paraguayans." Often they tend to isolate themselves, and they avoid participating in activities that might lead them into conflict with the rest of the community.

Men in this position are often potential leaders. They are capable, hardworking, and well able to deal with Paraguayans, but these qualities are seen to be ambiguous: their wealth is taken as evidence that they work for themselves rather than for the community, and their ability to handle Paraguayans is interpreted as over-friendliness. Any efforts they make to help the community are as likely as not ignored, and this can lead them to adopt the same outlook as the Paraguayans for whom they work. They come to regard their own people as lazy, thriftless, and lacking in initiative. Unfortunately, such men are sometimes pushed into positions of authority by military officers, missionaries, or the staff of development projects, and when this occurs, the tensions in the community can lead to open conflict.

Commerce is an even more contradictory activity than either agriculture or stock raising, since it implies the deliberate negation of generosity, with market relations taking the place of sharing. Commerce is virtually unknown in the Indian communities of the Chaco. This is in striking contrast to Paraguayan settlements, where, even among the poorest sectors of the population, one finds a proliferation of petty commerce: small stores, street vendors, shoeshine boys, and so on. Indeed, on the few occasions when individuals have tried to engage in commerce, they have either lost money or have provoked serious conflicts within their communities. Most small stores have disappeared within a few weeks, since their owners have felt obliged to give credit to their kin and neighbors until the entire stock was used up. In the Mennonite Colo-

nies a few individuals have, rather than sharing, taken to selling game or
the meat of domestic animals they have slaughtered. Some Nivaclé interpret this as evidence that the social order is breaking down, and they
cite this as one of the main reasons why a significant number of households from Yalve Sanga have abandoned the Mennonite Colonies and
returned to their traditional territory along the Upper Pilcomayo.

In this chapter I have argued that in order to understand the economy
of the Chaco societies one must look beyond the external constraints
that determine the Indians' economic situation and consider the system of values that underlies the economy. This system of values, with
its emphasis on equality and personal autonomy, is, I believe, a defining
feature of the Indians' sense of ethnic identity. An understanding of the
Chaco societies' economic values, especially their conceptions of property and their attitudes to natural resources, also helps shed light on
their apparently anomalous preference for wage labor over other forms
of production for the market.

Wage labor is often interpreted as evidence of a distinctly Western
or capitalist mode of production. In the Chaco, however, I would argue that it indicates precisely the opposite, since it offers an alternative
that allows indigenous societies to maintain their own system of values
while providing access to those industrially manufactured goods that
are now regarded as necessities. Unlike other forms of production for
the market, wage labor offers a relatively quick return on the time and
labor invested, and its products — wages or rations — can be integrated
into the networks of exchange through which the Chaco societies define
themselves without seriously challenging their insistence on equality.

This type of situation is probably common among small-scale, rural
societies situated on the periphery of the global economy, societies that
maintain their system of values but at the same time are part of an economic system that extends well beyond regional or national boundaries
(see Taussig 1980:chap. 1). The value systems of these societies may be
challenged and are probably subject to change over time. But the main
cost associated with this meeting of value systems is the poverty into
which the small-scale societies fall, the result of an unequal relationship
not truly based either on reciprocity or on market values. The causes of

this poverty are complex. It is not something that the indigenous societies have brought on themselves. The Indians of the Chaco recognize a link between their poverty and their system of values, but this does not imply that they want to be poor or are satisfied with their poverty. Rather, it is an inability to compete on equal terms with other sectors of the national society. This is not simply a question of economic competition, but of creating social and political space in a difficult environment, where a small and powerful elite has almost complete control over the political and economic processes. These are issues that I shall address later. First, however, I have to provide a more detailed description of the social and political organization of the Chaco societies.

CHAPTER SIX

Household and Kin

THE SOCIAL organization of the Chaco societies is characterized by a high degree of flexibility. The composition of residential groups and individual households can change from day to
day—often for little apparent reason—while the details of biological,
as opposed to social, kinship are often unknown, sometimes ignored,
and may even be deliberately negated. Few people have any depth of
genealogical knowledge, and although this perhaps owes something to
a general unwillingness to evoke memories of the dead, it also indicates
the relative lack of importance given to descent or to any strictly genealogical reckoning of kinship. Above the level of the household there
are no groups that are defined exclusively in terms of kinship, and the
ways in which kinship is used tend to be determined more by pragmatic
considerations than by any abstract set of rules.

Despite this, there are certain principles that underlie the composition
of the household and wider residential groups. I shall begin with a discussion of residence, looking at the household and at the organization of
production, distribution, and consumption. I then examine the development cycle of the household, considering how demographic factors,
marriage strategy, and political considerations affect the composition
of extended kin or residential groups. I shall then look at the kindred,
the ego-focused network of kin, which in the Chaco is by definition an
exogamous group. This concept is, I believe, universal in the Chaco, but
among the Ayoreo and Chamococo it coexists with a system of exogamous patriclans, which I consider briefly in a separate section. Following
this I shall look at the relationship terminologies of the Nivaclé and the
Toba (Qom), using them to outline a general model for the Chaco societies. One of the issues here is the apparent contradiction between the
solidarity of the household and the distinction between kin and affines,
and in the final section I look at how this is resolved through the use of
teknonyms.

Residence: Practice and Principles

It is often difficult to get the Indians of the Chaco to formulate ideas about residence or household composition in abstract terms. The most explicit statement that the Ayoreo of Maria Auxiliadora would give me about postmarital residence, for instance, was that it depended on which of the partners showed the stronger resolve. If the husband were more determined, the wife would reside with his kin, while if the wife were more insistent, the husband would reside with hers. The Ayoreo are able to discuss specific situations; they can usually explain why they or their close kin choose to live where they do, and they appear to use cognitive models that provide a frame of reference by which particular situations can be judged. The models I use to explain residence, which I have elaborated on the basis of what the Indians say and what they do, are not, I would argue, systems of rules. They do not directly determine the choices made by individuals: the Chaco societies lack any institutional means for enforcing rules, and they emphasize the individual's independence. Rather, the models should be envisaged as conceptual systems that offer a framework for understanding the social relations between individuals or between groups of people.

Residence can be considered at three distinct levels. The first is that of the household, defined strictly in terms of coresidence in the same dwelling. The importance of this level should not be overemphasized: in the Chaco housing is simple, and the people who share the same roof are not necessarily the same people who cooperate in domestic or productive activities or who eat together. This latter group may in fact correspond to the extended kin or residential group. In dispersed populations this can be the whole settlement, but in larger communities these groups generally occupy a distinct area within the settlement. The third level is the community or territorial group, a level that nowadays corresponds to the Indian colonies or the larger nucleated settlements.

The household provides a starting point for consideration of residence. Table 10 shows the types of coresident household found in three, fairly representative, nucleated communities: the Colonia Maria Auxiliadora (Ayoreo), Fuerte Olimpo (Chamococo), and Mistolar (Nivaclé).

The households have been grouped into general categories to draw attention to the principles underlying their composition rather than to

184

Table 10: Household composition in three communities

Household composition	Colonia Maria Auxiliadora (Ayoreo), Feb. 1977	Fuerte Olimpo (Chamococo), May 1977	Mistolar (Nivaclé), Nov. 1982
1. Nuclear families	38	14	45
2.1 Uxorilocally extended families including DH	2	1	4
2.2 Uxorilocally extended families including WM or WF	5	4	7
3.1 Virilocally extended families including SW	0	0	3
3.2 Virilocally extended families including HM or HF	2	0	3
4. Others	8	4	1
Total no. Households	55	23	63

demographic variations between them. The nuclear families include childless couples, single parents and their children, and households where some or all of the children are of only one of the spouses (children of previous unions) or have been adopted. Nuclear families, defined strictly in terms of coresidence in the same dwelling, predominate in all three communities (69 percent in Maria Auxiliadora, 61 percent in Fuerte Olimpo, and 71 percent in Mistolar), as they do throughout the Chaco.

The uxorilocally extended families are those in which a couple live with the wife's parents or other close relatives of the wife. They can be divided into two categories, representing different stages in the development cycle of the domestic group. The first category is one in which the household typically includes a mature couple, their married daughter(s), son(s)-in-law, grandchildren, and any unmarried children. This type of household, if it is strictly defined in terms of coresidence in the same dwelling, is not particularly common (4 percent in Maria Auxiliadora and Fuerte Olimpo, 6 percent in Mistolar). The second category, which represents a later stage in the development cycle of the domestic group, is rather more common (9 percent of households in Maria Auxiliadora, 17 percent in Fuerte Olimpo, and 11 percent in Mistolar). Here the daughter and son-in-law are now the dominant couple, and the daughter's parents are elderly and attached to their daughter's household. Most of the households in this category comprise a couple, their children, and the wife's elderly mother or father, but some include other collateral relatives of the wife, such as the wife's mother's sister or the wife's own, often separated or widowed, sisters or even brothers.

Virilocally extended households are those in which a couple live with the husband's parents or other close relatives of the husband. They are less common; in table 10 they have been divided into two categories, again representing different stages in the development cycle of the domestic group. The first would typically consist of a mature couple, their married son(s), daughter(s)-in-law, grandchildren, and any unmarried children. No examples of this type were found in Maria Auxiliadora or Fuerte Olimpo, and they made up only 5 percent of the households in Mistolar. The second category, consisting of a couple, their children, and the parent(s) or collateral relatives of the husband, was again not very common: there were none in Fuerte Olimpo, and they constituted only 4 percent and 5 percent, respectively, of the households in Maria Auxiliadora and Mistolar.

The households classified as "others" varied from community to community. In Maria Auxiliadora they were composed of two or more men belonging to the same exogamic patriclan (*cuchárai*), with their respective wives and children. Some of these men may have been patrilateral parallel cousins (FBS or FFBSS).[1] But I have not classified them as virilocally extended households, since the term used to denote the relationship, *iguios,* refers, as I shall discuss later, to a relationship of categorical similarity rather than to a genealogically defined one.

The four households in Fuerte Olimpo classified as "others" included one that consisted of an elderly couple who lived with their married son and his wife, a married daughter and her husband, their grandchildren, their daughter-in-law's child from a previous union, and an unmarried son. In the second case an elderly single man was living with his sister, now separated from her husband, and her children, one of whom was separated from her husband and had a daughter of her own. In the third case a couple were living with the husband's unmarried brother and with the wife's sister's daughter. In the last case a couple and their son lived with an apparently unrelated couple. In Mistolar there were no complex households of this kind, and the only household classified as "other" consisted of a man with no close kin in the community who lived alone.

It is important to remember that the households in table 10 are nothing more than the people who live in the same dwelling at a particular moment in time. Residence at this level tells us something about a people's conception of social space and social order, but we should be careful not to interpret the information out of context. Housing is fairly simple, and people decide to construct dwellings of their own, or to move from one house to another, for reasons that often appear trivial.

In most communities the Indians' houses are similar to those of the poorer sectors of Paraguayan society or, in the Central Chaco, copy the houses that were constructed by the Mennonites when they first settled in the Chaco. This reflects the more sedentary lifestyle in the present-day communities and suggests a desire to conform, at least superficially, to some of the values of the national society. It does not, however, indicate any real change in social organization at the level of the household.

187

Traditional dwellings were made of easily available materials and could be quickly and easily erected. The Ayoreo built huts (*guiguijnane*) during the wet summer months, when they lived in large semipermanent villages. The huts were circular in plan, having a diameter of around two or three meters (six–ten feet), and were constructed by leaning poles against each other, covering them with branches and earth to form the roof, and leaving the sides open. During the winter months they lived in the open, sometimes sleeping on platforms or beds (*mochapiode*) made of poles, under which they could place hot embers to keep themselves warm at night.

The traditional round huts of the Nivaclé are still found in some of the missions on the Pilcomayo and in some worker villages in the Central Chaco. They are constructed from a circle of large branches that have been stuck in the ground, bent over, and covered with palm leaves or dry maize stalks. In communities such as Misión Esteros, Laguna Escalante, and Pedro P. Peña, they coexist with the houses copied from the Argentine *criollos,* just as described by Metraux (1963:267), who worked in the area over sixty years ago. The dwellings of the Lengua described by Grubb (1911) were even simpler, being little more than windbreaks made of reeds and branches, and are still found in the temporary camps built by Lengua and Toba contract laborers when they are working on the ranches. The shelters provide shade to rest and work in, and storage for household items, but they are used for sleeping only during the winter or in times of bad weather.

Given the limited symbolic importance of housing, it is worth examining the household in more general terms. Here, I shall consider the household, and the extended kin group into which it develops over the generations, in terms of two distinct, and to some extent contradictory, models. The first is that of the uxorilocally extended household, and the second that of the household or extended kin group formed around a group of coresident siblings of both sexes.

The Development Cycle of the Domestic Group

In the communities considered in table 10, there are more uxorilocally extended households than virilocally extended ones; indeed, the latter rarely constitute more than a small proportion of the households in any community. Extended families are more likely to be found in communities where there is a shortage of housing, or where other external factors favor coresidence. Where the members of a community are free to choose, they are more likely to reside as separate nuclear families.

In the larger nucleated villages, houses are often separated into fairly discrete clusters. In some cases two or more houses share a common fence—intended to keep out pigs or goats—and in others the houses are grouped together along a path or track. The smaller clusters of houses tend to be occupied by uxorilocally extended families. Typically, a mature couple live with their unmarried children in one of the houses, and their married daughters, sons-in-law, and grandchildren live in the others. The larger clusters of houses show more variation. They may be occupied by uxorilocally extended families of up to three generations in depth, or they may be composed of extended families formed around a group of siblings of both sexes, some of whom may live with their own married daughters and sons-in-law.

The variations can best be described in terms of the development cycle of the domestic group, although it must be remembered that this is an ideal type and in reality demographic factors and other circumstances, such as political factionalism, can lead to considerable divergence from the model. Here I shall describe four stages in the development cycle of the household. In the first stage, when a couple are newly married, they are likely to reside with, or close to, the parents of the wife. In time, as they have children of their own, they move farther away from the wife's parents. Typically, in the second stage of the development cycle they retain some links with the wife's kin, while in the third stage they may choose to cooperate more closely with the husband's siblings. Eventually, in the fourth stage of the cycle, usually after one of the wife's parents has died, the remaining parent may come back to live in what has now become the daughter's household.

When they first live together, a young husband and wife usually choose to reside with the wife's parents. This is not, I believe, seen as an obligation but is regarded as normal practice—a statistical norm rather than a rule. Indeed, in the traditional context, it was only when the young man took up residence with the wife's family that the union came to be considered a marriage. Today, however, marriages are often legitimized by whichever church happens to be present in the community, and they may be noted in the civil registry (see Alvarsson 1988:100).

At this stage the couple may live in the same house as the wife's parents, although they may equally well live in a separate dwelling situated in the immediate vicinity. Coresidence in the same house is more common on the ranches, where Indians are allowed to settle only if at least one member of the household is working. Similarly, young couples in the agricultural colonies of the Central Chaco often have to live with the wife's parents for some years before they can acquire a plot of land of their own. When they moved to Mistolar, however, many of the young couples from Yalve Sanga, who had been living with the wife's parents, moved out and set up their own houses.

Whatever the dwelling arrangement, the household tends to function as a single unit of production, distribution, and consumption. Even before marriage, the young man is expected to provide something for the family of his future wife. Among the Ayoreo, a young man would traditionally present his future wife's parents with gifts of meat and honey, and today it is not uncommon for the young man to give them cloth or foodstuffs and even occasional gifts of cash. Once the couple have settled with the wife's parents, the young man continues to provide for the whole household, and either gives most of what he produces or earns to his wife's parents or works alongside his father-in-law. The young man will accompany his father-in-law, and perhaps his unmarried brothers-in-law, on the longer hunting, fishing, and honey collecting expeditions, but he may hunt or fish separately if he only goes for a day or two.

The game, fish, or honey that the son-in-law brings back is given to the wife or her family to distribute or consume. The young man may give the larger game or fish to his father-in-law, who will gut, clean, and divide it up, and the mother-in-law will distribute the portions. Smaller game or portions of large animals are often given to the wife, who in turn may give it to her mother to divide and share out. In some societies the relations between the young husband and his mother-in-law are marked by a certain reserve. Among the Ayoreo this is almost a relation of avoidance, and the young man is not supposed to give his mother-in-law anything directly or to address her more than is absolutely necessary.

Young men often work alongside their fathers-in-law. When they work as *contratistas*, they share their provisions; in fact, when wives and families are absent, *contratistas* usually share their provisions and eat together regardless of kinship or affinity. If they work as ranch hands, they share their weekly rations but treat the money they earn as their own. Both the wife's father and the son-in-law, however, are expected to provide for the household as a whole, and the wife's parents may ask their son-in-law, either directly or through their daughter, to give them small sums of money or items such as clothing whenever they need them. Equally though, if the young man is out of work, he can expect to be supported by his wife's father or any other member of the extended household.

In the agricultural colonies of the Central Chaco, some households have adopted a strategy whereby the older members of the household, usually the wife's parents, work in agriculture to provide for the household's subsistence needs while the sons-in-law, and sometimes the unmarried sons, work as wage laborers. Where there is a greater emphasis on the production of cash crops, the wife's father and the son-in-law work together in the same plot, and the income is regarded as the wife's father's, although he usually gives the son-in-law any money he needs. This was not a traditional practice and reflects the particular circumstances of the Central Chaco, where young families often have to wait some years for a plot of their own. In other settlements, where Indians practice subsistence agriculture, the son-in-law is more likely to have a separate plot, which will be harvested by his wife for the whole household, or even given over to the wife's parents to use as they wish.

The relation between the young husband and his father-in-law is generally an easy one, and sharing within the uxorilocally extended family is not marked by the tension that sometimes characterizes sharing between distantly related kin or neighbors. This reflects the way in which the uxorilocally extended family is perceived, at least in this stage of the development cycle, as a single unit of production, distribution, and consumption in which the individual members are dependent on one another. The wife's father has no effective control over his son-in-law or, for that matter, over his own daughter. The daughter's choice of partner is entirely her own, and there is little that her father or mother can do or say, even if they disapprove of her choice. The wife's father can, at best, only drop hints or make suggestions to his son-in-law, and requests, for small sums of money or other items, are invariably phrased with great tact or are made indirectly through the daughter.

Uxorilocal residence and the demands, or rather expectations, of the wife's parents are only rarely a cause of marital problems. Marriages, particularly in the early years, can result in strife, and separation and remarriages are common; infidelity, on the part of the husband and sometimes on the part of the wife, is the one of the main causes of disputes. The opportunities for affairs—or for one of the partners to suspect the other of engaging in an affair—are increased in those communities where men spend much of their time away from home. It is not unusual, though, for the wife's parents to try to bring the couple back together rather than take their daughter's side in the dispute. If there are children, it is in the wife's parents' interest that the marriage be a success, since they, rather than their daughter, will be faced with supporting the children if the couple separate.

Although the wife's father has no explicit authority over his son-in-law, he expects his political support, and the son-in-law may act as his representative. Many of the young men who served on the local and regional councils organized by API represented the factions of their fathers-in-law. Some were effective representatives in their own right and had a better understanding of the outside world—or were better able to express themselves in Guaraní or Spanish—than their fathers-in-law, but they always tried to consult their fathers-in-law before taking any decisions.

The young wife cooperates closely with her mother. This is the continuation of an existing relationship: the young wife, her mother, and the other married and unmarried sisters may work in the gardens, manufacture handicrafts, or collaborate in wage labor. In Mistolar some mothers would prepare caraguatá string or raw wool for their daughters to manufacture bags, blankets, or ponchos. In Fuerte Olimpo the Chamococo women would sit together at the riverside washing clothes for the better-off Paraguayan families, and the money they earned was spent on food for the whole household. The women also collaborate in domestic activities: collecting firewood, carrying water, preparing and cooking food, washing clothes, and looking after small children. Here, the mother is a great help to her married daughter, who, when she first marries, may not be capable of carrying out all the domestic tasks by herself. Girls frequently marry and bear children when they are only sixteen or seventeen, and they lack the strength and experience to manage the arduous daily routine on their own. Moreover, if the husband is absent for long periods, hunting or working on the ranches, the young wife looks to her mother and sisters for company as well as for support with the domestic chores.

It is the importance of the relationship between a mother and her newly married daughter that helps explain the tendency for uxorilocal residence. It is not perceived as an obligation, and most couples consider themselves free to choose where they reside. In the public domain decisions are supposed to be the prerogative of the husband, but in practice the relation between a man and his wife is an egalitarian one, and decisions relating to the domestic sphere, and often to the public sphere as well, are based on mutual consent. In regard to residence, the young wife has practical and emotional reasons for wanting to live with her mother and sisters, while the husband has, at least in this stage of the development cycle, little justification for wanting to live with his parents and siblings.[2]

In the second stage of the development cycle, the extended household may break up. As the young wife gains experience, she relies less on her mother and her sisters, and as they grow older, her own daughters start to help with the domestic tasks. From an early age girls learn to assist their mothers, preparing food, cooking, washing clothes, and helping to care for their younger siblings. Boys, on the other hand, do little or nothing and spend much of the day with their peers. The Ayoreo boys' peer group (*disiode*) includes all the adolescent boys in the settlement, who play and eat together; in other societies, particularly in the heterogeneous communities of the Lower Chaco, the boys' peer groups mirror the factions of adult life and are kin or neighborhood based. The boys provide little or nothing for the household—any fish or game they catch will be consumed among themselves—and they expect the family to feed them and provide anything else they need, an arrangement that often continues into late adolescence or even beyond.

By the time a couple have growing children, they will usually have

moved to a separate dwelling and may live in another part of the community. They share fewer meals with the wife's parents, perhaps on a feast
day or after a successful hunt, and although they exchange food and gifts
and continue to help each other, they no longer perceive themselves as
a single household.

It is in the next stage of the development cycle, when the elder children
have reached adolescence or adulthood, that one finds the greatest variation in residence and cooperation. In some cases the family maintains its
uxorilocal orientation and continues residing close to, and cooperating
with, the wife's parents and her married sisters. In other cases the family
is more closely associated with the husband's siblings, residing in the
same part of a settlement, and the men, the brothers and their brothers-
in-law, hunt, fish, or work together, while the women, the sisters and
sisters-in-law, collaborate in domestic tasks.

In the final stage of the development cycle, the elderly parents, or other
elderly relatives who have no children of their own in the community,
move back with the daughter's family. In some cases the uxorilocally extended household maintains itself through the generations; in others,
the elderly couple, or more frequently the surviving spouse, rejoins the
daughter's family after some years living separately. This may happen
when one of the elderly spouses dies and the surviving partner is no
longer able to live independently, or when the sibling group to which the
couple were attached begins to break up as the elder members die off.

Uxorilocally extended households composed of a mature couple and
the elderly parents or other relatives of the wife often live in the same
dwelling. As table 10 shows, they constituted 9 percent of households in
the Colonia Maria Auxiliadora, 17 percent in Fuerte Olimpo, and 11 percent in Mistolar. The arrangements vary, however, and it is not unusual
for an elderly man to occupy a separate, often rather small house next to
that of his daughter. In some cases the dwelling is attached to the daughter's house, forming as it were a separate room, while in others it is independent. Elderly women are more likely to reside in their daughter's,
or sister's daughter's, house, an arrangement that reflects the contribu-
tion they make to the household. Women, at least until they are very old,
take an active role in domestic activities and are regarded with affection,
especially by the grandchildren they have helped to raise. Elderly men

are less active and devote much of their time to social ends, drinking and telling stories. They may cultivate their own gardens, although they have to be helped with the heavier tasks, or occasionally go hunting or fishing with their sons-in-law, who may sometimes organize expeditions simply to humor them.

The elderly are rarely neglected, even though they can be a burden on the household. Traditionally, however, the Ayoreo are reputed to have asked their children to bury them alive if they were unable to keep up with the group (Bórmida and Califano 1978:128; Bernand 1970).[3] Similarly, Grubb reports that the Lengua would abandon the sick and elderly at some distance from the camp once they were perceived to be dying, for fear that the souls of the dead would threaten the surviving relatives (Grubb 1911:160). There is perhaps a present-day parallel in the way the elderly are sometimes left abandoned in the hospital if they appear to have lost any hope of survival.

Residence Strategies

The dynamics of residence can best be illustrated by looking at some specific examples that show how the choices of individual households are determined. Figure 1 represents a small settlement of Lengua families who live on the Estancia Buen Amigo, a ranch near Kilometer 260 of the Trans-Chaco Highway, which provides an example of a residential group formed on the basis of continued uxorilocal residence. Here, in two houses set next to each other, four married sisters and their families live with their widowed mother and with the married daughter of another sister who has died. In one house the two younger sisters, Margarita and Marita, live with their husbands and children; Margarita's two elder daughters are married and live in the house with their husbands and children, as does Marita's eldest daughter. Marcelina, the married daughter of the deceased sister, also lives here with her husband and daughter and with the old widowed mother, Sara. Marcelina's father has left the group and lives in Sombrero Piri, some fifty kilometers up the road. In the other house China and Lidia, the two elder sisters, live with their husbands and unmarried children.

This group illustrates how continued uxorilocal residence can provide the basis for a sizable residential unit, but it would be a mistake to

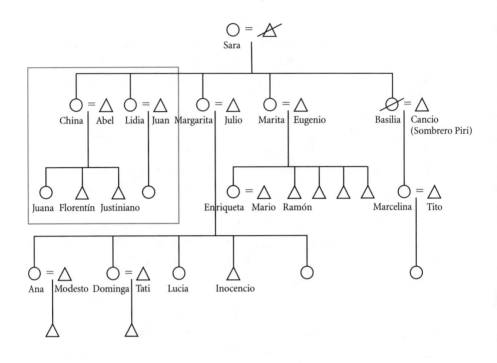

Fig. 1. Estancia Buen Amigo, May 1982

regard it as representing an ideal type. In the first place, it is unusual to find so many nuclear families in the same house: in this case coresidence may be a way of legitimizing the presence of families who might otherwise be expelled from the ranch if they were out of work. In fact, all the married men, with the exception of Tito, were employed as ranch hands at the time the information was recorded (May 1982), as was Ramón, Marita's adolescent son. The demography of the group is also unusual: few women in the Chaco manage to see five of their children reach marriageable age, let alone five daughters. It should also be noted that scattered populations of this type have little involvement in any political activity, and so there is little pressure for men to reside with their adult siblings.

The Manjuy and Nivaclé of Loma Alegre, shown in figure 2, provide another example of a group that has been built up on the basis of uxorilocal residence. Loma Alegre, one of the outlying settlements of Pedro P. Peña, comprises five shelters, constructed of poles, with roofs of earth and branches, situated within a few meters of one another. The first house (no. 1) is occupied by an elderly Manjuy couple, Rubio and Vatay, who live with their daughter Maria, her husband, Martín, a Nivaclé, and their daughter. Opposite them (no. 2) lives another daughter, Mari, her husband, Velasquez, a Manjuy, and their three children; while to one side (no. 3) lives a third daughter, Rosa, her husband, Mateo, of mixed Manjuy and Nivaclé parentage, and their two daughters. Mateo's brother, Lavi, and father, Felipe, also live here, as does Mateo's mother's mother's sister (MMZ), Tomasa, an elderly Nivaclé. In the next house (no. 4) an elderly man, Sargento, lives alone. He is the brother of Felipe and the husband of Vatay's sister's daughter, now deceased. He lives alongside his daughter, Catalina, her husband, Luciano, a Manjuy, and their four children (no. 5).

The members of the group cooperate closely. The women go gathering together and prepare communal meals that are eaten by everyone who happens to be present. The men fish and occasionally hunt together, although more frequently they go off alone and share anything they bring back. Their small gardens are cultivated independently (see chapter 3), but the produce is shared. In some years they travel to the Mennonite Colony of Neuland, where they work as agricultural laborers; the men

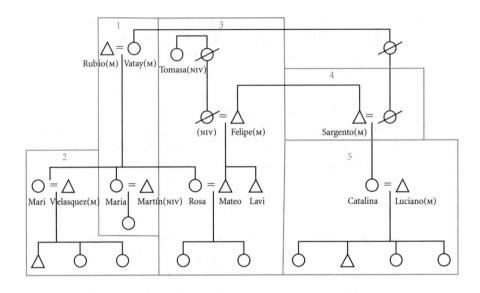

Fig. 2. Loma Alegre (Pedro P. Peña), March 1983

are paid individually and regard their wages as their own, but the provisions they purchase are prepared and consumed by all the group.

The younger married men live uxorilocally, although the situation of Mateo and his father, Felipe, is ambiguous. Mateo shares a house with his father and younger brother, constituting what is effectively a virilocally extended household, while Tomasa, who is Felipe's late wife's mother's sister and a classificatory mother-in-law, also lives with them, giving the household an uxorilocal character. The situation of Felipe's brother, Sargento, is also ambiguous and could be explained by reference to the presence of his brother, his daughter, or his late wife's mother's sister. At the level of the settlement, the residence pattern is clearly uxorilocal, the households being related principally through Vatay, her three daughters, and her sister's daughter's daughter (ZDD).

Despite the multiplicity of ties that bind this group together, it was not particularly stable as a residential unit. Some days after the information was recorded in March 1983, the group split up. The sisters from Pedro P. Peña convinced Luciano and Velasquez to enroll their children in the mission school, and they moved with their wives to Campamento, a Nivaclé settlement situated only a couple of kilometers from the mission, where they were later joined by Mateo. Here they took up residence with Mejias, a Manjuy who was a brother of Luciano's late father and a distant kinsman of Velasquez, and they cooperated with his household, and with that of Mejias's brother Castro, much as they had done in Loma Alegre. The women worked together and prepared meals in common, while the men hunted alone or worked for a local storekeeper but shared everything they brought back. The rest of the group remained in Loma Alegre to take advantage of the gardens, which were still productive, and on weekends the families from Campamento would walk back to harvest what remained.

The Nivaclé households that occupied one side of a "street" in Mistolar in November 1982—shown in figure 3 and map 4—provide a more complex example of residential choices. These households do not form a clearly bounded group or faction, and they can trace links of kinship to households that live in other parts of the community; they also have kin in the Mennonite Colonies, in Sandhorst, Cayin'o Clim, and Yalve Sanga. By and large, the individual households function as inde-

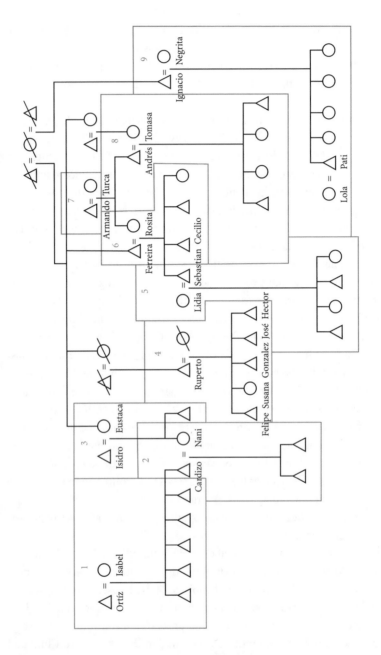

Fig. 3. Mistolar, November 1982

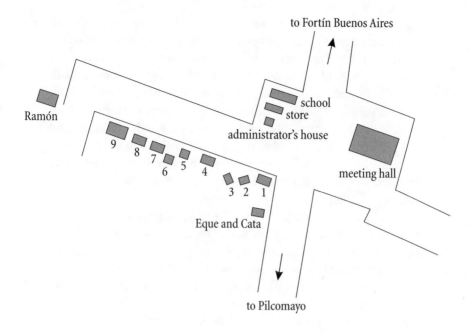

to Fortín Buenos Aires

Ramón

school
store
administrator's house

9
8
7
6
5
4
3 2 1

Eque and Cata

meeting hall

to Pilcomayo

Map 4. Mistolar, November 1982

pendent units of production, distribution, and consumption, although the young married couples cooperate closely with the parents of one of the spouses. Cardizo, Nani, and her parents constitute what is virtually a single household, as do Lola, Pati, and his parents. The men of this group fish together, often with men from other parts of the community, but they hunt alone or with one or two partners and cultivate their gardens independently. The produce from these activities is shared but is distributed, either cooked or raw, to individual families—usually the nearest neighbors—and is consumed within the individual households. The women also cooperate with their neighbors, but they never work together as a single group.

The households are linked around a group of siblings and their immediate descendants. The three surviving siblings—Eustaca, Ferreira, and their half brother, Ignacio—originally came from Catsajshi, a settlement in the interior that was abandoned in the 1940s, as did the father of Lidia, the wife of Sebastian, Ferreira's son. The Nivaclé of Catsajshi numbered some ten households and regarded themselves as belonging to Mistolar, which they visited in the fishing and algarrobo seasons. The second generation—Ruperto, Tomasa, and the elder children of the three surviving siblings—were brought up in Mistolar, although they eventually moved to the Mennonite Colonies with the rest of the community and lived in the worker village of Sandhorst before settling in Yalve Sanga. The families of Isidro and Ruperto were the last to leave Mistolar and remained there until 1972. They, and all the other families in the group, returned to Mistolar in 1980.

The arrangement of the houses reflects the relations between the individual households. In the house on the corner (no. 1) live Ortíz and his wife, Isabel, with their five unmarried children. Ortíz and his wife have no close kin in the community, although his wife regards Cata, an old woman who lives with her husband in the next house on the adjacent street, as a distant relative. Ortíz also considers Siriaco, the administrator of the community, who lives opposite, one of his distant relatives. The position of Ortíz's house, on the corner, is not fortuitous. He is one of the more important figures in Mistolar and is a "leader of work," responsible for overseeing the communal gardens, construction of the church, and clearance of the airstrip. His house, like that of the administrator, is situated in the center of the community, near the church and school.

Next to Ortíz live his son Cardizo (no. 2) and Cardizo's wife's parents, Isidro and Eustaca (no. 3). Despite the proximity of Cardizo's parents, the arrangement is typical of the first stage of the development cycle. Cardizo's family and his wife's parents live in separate houses, situated alongside each other and surrounded by a common fence, but it is difficult to tell which house belongs to which family. At any time of day members of both families will be sitting together; they take their meals together and in good weather sleep outside.

In the next house (no. 4) live Ruperto, a widower, and his five unmarried children. It is unusual for young men or women of this age to remain unmarried—the eldest children are over thirty—and the only comment anyone could offer was that this was a very traditional family in which the sons and daughters waited until they were fully adult before they married. In fact, although late marriage may have been an ideal, the accounts of the older inhabitants of Mistolar provide little evidence to suggest that late marriage was ever a common practice. Ruperto's sons and daughters cooperate closely with their father, and the sons appear rather less independent than most young men of their age. At one time the family owned a number of sheep and horses; indeed, this was the main reason for Ruperto's remaining in Mistolar until 1972. Later, when they lived in the Mennonite Colonies, Ruperto worked with his sons growing cash crops.

The next cluster of houses contains a close-knit group in which the conflicting claims of kin and affines have been resolved through the repetition of marriages between two groups of kin. Ferreira (no. 6) and his sister's daughter, Tomasa (no. 8), have married Rosita and Andrés, who are siblings, allowing the men to live uxorilocally and at the same time to reside close to their own siblings. Although Ferreira and Tomasa belong to different generations, the marriages can be regarded as a variation of sister exchange. This type of marriage, which, along with the repetition of marriage between groups of same sex siblings (BWZ marriage from the male viewpoint), is a fairly common strategy in the Chaco, since it allows both groups of siblings to stay together. But marriage is not permitted with anyone defined as kin, and the strategy cannot be repeated in the following generation. Thus, the systematic use of alliance as an organizing principle—characteristic of much of Lowland South America, where alliance is institutionalized in the two-line terminology—never develops to its full potential.

Armando and Turca (no. 7), the parents of Andrés and Rosita, are elderly, probably in their seventies. They are not entirely dependent on their married children: they are both active, and their situation, as co-residents in the group of their children's affines, may be partly because they have no other close collateral kin living in the community. Armando is one of the few survivors of a group that once inhabited Lhvi, a site on the Pilcomayo some forty kilometers (twenty-five miles) downriver from Mistolar that was decimated by epidemics in the period immediately after the Chaco War. Armando's only brother was taken away by Paraguayans when he was a young boy, and he was never heard of again. Turca, whose mother was also from Lhvi, has two sisters living in Asunción and a brother in Yalve Sanga. From their accounts it seems they were associated with Isidro and Eustaca even before they migrated to the Mennonite Colonies.

Sebastian and Lidia, whose house (no. 5) is situated between Ruperto and Sebastian's parents, live virilocally. This is unusual, since both spouses have strong kin groups in the community. Lidia's parents are an important link in another residential group at the far end of the street that includes her father's brother, her mother's siblings, and various married daughters and sons-in-law. Lidia is the eldest child in her family, and it is possible that her decision to live with her husband's kin was influenced by the fact that she has a younger married sister who, with her husband and children, continues to reside with her parents.

The situation of the two families that live at the end of the street (no. 9) is more straightforward. The elder couple, Ignacio and Negrita, live with Ignacio's half siblings because Negrita has no close kin in the community; their son, Pati, continues to stay with them because his wife, Lola, is an orphan. Lola is from Pedro P. Peña, and the only person with whom she can trace any kinship is Ramón, a Nivaclé from the same community who, with his son-in-law and another distant relative, lives just around the corner.

This residential group in Mistolar is more complex than those considered previously and is founded on the ties between a group of siblings and their affines. However, the Nivaclé describe it with the same term that they use for groups like that of the Manjuy and Nivaclé of Loma Alegre, *velha tolh'e,* which is translated as "a clan of families." The term emphasizes coresidence rather than any specific set of genealogical or affinal ties and is perhaps synonymous with what I have called the extended kin group or residential nucleus; it appears to be very similar to the Mataco bands, *wikyi',* described by Alvarsson (1988:63).

The Kindred

The importance of coresidence is apparent in the way the Indians of the Chaco conceive of the kindred, which among the Nivaclé is referred to as *lhavelh.* The concept is, I believe, universal among the Chaco societies and refers to a group that is bilaterally reckoned—that is, kinship is traced through both males and females—and, theoretically at least, includes all of one's cognatic kin. The kindred is not a corporate unit, even in the sense of being a bounded group with a distinct identity, since it is ego-focused, and the only people who can in principle share the same kindred are full siblings. The kindred, however, is not always defined in strictly genealogical terms, and links with kin are sometimes recognized on the basis of unspecified links that existed in a previous generation. A Nivaclé might, for instance, consider a person to be *lhavelh* because his or her mother or father called one of that person's parents *lhavelh.* There is also a tendency to associate the kindred with particular bands or residential groups. Some Nivaclé will claim that all the people of a particular group or band, such as Utsiyishi or Catsajshi, are their kin, even though they are unable to trace the lines of common descent.

The kindred is, by definition, exogamic, that is to say, marriage is not allowed with anyone classified as kin. Since the kindred is theoretically unbounded, it would seem that individuals, even in the larger communities, might have difficulty finding non-kin of marriageable age, effectively making the community an exogamic group. In fact, this is rarely the case, and a fairly high proportion of marriages take place within the larger communities. Genealogical knowledge is relatively shallow, and an individual's kindred is rarely traced beyond two degrees of collaterality; that is, an individual will usually recognize the descendants of his grandparents' siblings as kin but not the people descended from his great-grandparents' siblings. This is reflected in marriages. Marriages between first cousins are unknown, while marriages between second cousins, although they occasionally occur, are rare and are difficult to detect because the links between the partners are either forgotten or deliberately ignored. Beyond this limit marriages between distant kin are probably quite common, and by redefining the terminology and using affinal terms for the spouse's close kin, the Chaco Indians redefine the kindred itself.

Two other factors limit the boundaries of the kindred. One is the relative instability of marriages. In theory this could widen the group classed as kin, since links can be traced through the half siblings of the parents and grandparents, but in practice it tends to accelerate the loss of genealogical memory. Relations with the children of one's parent's half siblings are not usually as close as those with other first cousins, particularly since the age difference may be greater, and in the next generation the links with their children may well be forgotten. The second factor is the tendency for uxorilocal residence: if the father comes from a different community or territorial group, his children may lose contact with his kin; equally, if the mother's brothers marry out of the community, they and their descendants tend to lose contact with the original group. In some situations this may result in an individual's kindred appearing to have a matrilineal emphasis.

Ayoreo Clanship

The bilateral reckoning of kinship and the lack of any strictly genealogical criteria in the ordering of residential groups are, I believe, general features of Chaco social organization. This is clear among the Nivaclé and the societies of the Lower Chaco, but doubts are raised by the Zamuco-speaking societies—the Ayoreo and Chamococo—who divide their societies into named exogamous patriclans. These are groups within which one is not allowed to marry, and in which membership is inherited in the male line. Among the Chamococo the system of patriclans appears to have fallen into disuse, and only the eldest people can remember their clan affiliation, but among the Ayoreo the system has remained more or less intact (Susnik 1973; Fischermann 1976:91–96; Bórmida and Califano 1978).

Ayoreo society is divided into seven named exogamous groups, the *cucharane*—a term that, in accordance with the literature, I have translated as "clans." The same seven clans—the Chiqueno, Picanera, Posoraja, Cutamoraja, Dosape, Etacore, and Jnumione—are found in every Ayoreo community, and the system crosscuts the political and territorial divisions of Ayoreo society. Clan membership is transmitted in the male line, and both men and women belong to the clan of their biological father. It is biological rather than social paternity that is stressed here, and half brothers of the same mother, who for other purposes would act as full brothers, are distinguished if their respective fathers belonged to different clans. The Ayoreo, however, show little interest in descent as such. Some Ayoreo have difficulty remembering the name of their paternal grandfather, and fellow clan members who stand in a relationship more distant than first, or perhaps second, cousins are often unable to trace their relationship through a common ancestor.

Marriage is prohibited between members of the same clan, and infraction of this rule—the prohibition is quite clearly perceived as a rule—is extremely rare. The Ayoreo, like the other Chaco societies, are also forbidden from marrying anyone classified as kin, kin being traced bilaterally within the limits of genealogical memory. This suggests that any fellow clan member, referred to as *iguios,* is assimilated into the category of kin, and indeed the Ayoreo who speak Spanish often translate the term as *pariente,* "kin." In addition, an Ayoreo should avoid marrying anyone from his or her mother's clan. The close members of the mother's clan, such as the mother's brother's children, are included in the general prohibition on marriage with kin, and such marriages are virtually unknown. But the prohibition is extended, at least ideally, to the members of the mother's clan with whom one is unable to trace any ties of kinship. In fact, such marriages occur, although they tend to meet with disapproval.

Fellow clan members, regardless of which community or territorial group they belong to, are expected to act as kin and assist one another, exchanging food and other items. In reality, this kind of relationship is never extended to all clan members, even within the same territorial group. However, men, particularly when they lack the support of a strong group of siblings, often maintain close relations with one or two of their fellow clan members, and even apparently unrelated fellow clan members may share the same dwelling (see table 10). The concept of clan solidarity is also extended to interterritorial relations. If an Ayoreo is visiting a community where he has no close kin, he can expect to receive hospitality and protection from one of his *iguios;* protection does not extend to enemy groups, however, and apparently there is no prohibition on killing an enemy who belongs to the same clan.

The Ayoreo clans are not divided into moieties. This contrasts with the Chamococo, whose seven clans, in other respects almost identical to those of the Ayoreo, were classed as "warriors" or "thinkers." The Chamococo moieties were ceremonial, although there was a notion that it was preferable to marry into the opposing moiety (Susnik 1969). Ayoreo clans are, however, divided into a series of pairs, between which the men refer to each other as "my wife" (*yacote*). The men of the Dosape and Etacore will call each other "my wife," as will men of the Picanera and Cutamoraja; because there are seven clans, the Posoraja are paired with both the Chiqueno and the Jnumione. The pairing is not related to ceremonial practice or mythology and is something of a joking term. It emphasizes equivalence rather than complementarity and is used reciprocally in the public sphere between men, in contrast to the domestic sphere, where the term is part of a complementary set *yacote/yabai* ("my wife"/"my husband") and is used by men to address women.

The idea of equivalence is also apparent in the relationship between the clans and their "possessions" (*edopasade*), which include a diverse range of animal and plant species, everyday objects, mythical ancestors, clan marks, and so on. They are not characterized by binary oppositions of the eagle hawk / crow type, as described by Lévi-Strauss in his study of totemism (1964) but in theory divide up the world, each clan being distinguished from the rest but not paired with any other. A large corpus of myth explains how the world was originally inhabited by the *Jnani Bajade,* beings who were both Ayoreo and animal or plant species and who came to be divided among the *edopasade* of the seven clans, the species becoming the animals and plants they are today. The members of a clan show no particular respect for their clan "possessions": they are not responsible for the fertility of the animal or plant species, nor are the *edopasade* associated with naming or food taboos. Even the clan marks can be used by anyone for the purpose of design; indeed, the clan mark of the Cutamoraja, a series of parallel lines called *pedopicaidie,* is one of the commonest designs that women use when making string bags.

Although the Ayoreo clans are elaborated on the mythological plane, they do not provide much of a basis for practical social organization. A few households, it is true, are formed around apparently unrelated fellow clan members who are also close friends, but at the higher levels of social organization, the ties of clanship tend to crosscut political and territorial allegiances. At one level, clanship is regarded as an extension of kinship and implies both exogamy and mutual cooperation. But whereas kinship is defined bilaterally and is limited by genealogical knowledge, clanship, which in essence is a relationship of categorical similarity, is defined in strictly patrilateral terms and is not limited by the need to trace common ancestry. As such, it provides a network of ties that extend well beyond the limits of kin and territorial groups and, at least at the ideological level, offer a means of integrating and defining Ayoreo society as a whole. Indeed, it may be no coincidence that the Ayoreo, unlike virtually all the other Chaco societies, are a remarkably homogeneous society with few regional differences and an almost complete absence of interethnic marriages.

Chaco Kinship Terminologies

The kinship categories of the Chaco societies provide a useful insight into the way kinship is perceived. Here, I shall briefly examine the terminologies used by the Nivaclé and the Toba (Qom), which, I believe, illustrate the main features of Chaco kinship categories.

The simplified Nivaclé terminology, shown in appendix 2, is used for reference and address.[4] Other forms of reference and address are also used, including names, nicknames, teknonyms, and generic kinship terms. Names include traditional names, used by older people; Spanish and occasionally German names, taken from the Mennonites or the German priests of the Oblates of Maria; and nicknames. Spanish surnames do not follow the conventions used by the Paraguayan population, where the father's surname is followed by the mother's surname. Children usually take only the father's name, and in some cases the surnames are changed in each generation. Nicknames are usually animal names and reflect some physical characteristic or trait of the individual referred to. Teknonyms are also used, as I shall discuss below, while the members of one's kindred can be addressed by a generic term for cognatic kin, *yi'lhavelh*—"my kinsman" or "my kinswoman."

The form of address is chosen according to context: nicknames are a demonstration of familiarity, while teknonyms are used only within the household. Kinship terms are mostly used among fairly close cognatic kin, especially when the speaker wants to emphasize the relationship with the person he is addressing. With more distant cognatic kin, where there may be doubt about the precise nature of the relationship or a lack of conformity between age and generation, it is more usual for the speaker to use the generic term for kin.

The main features of Nivaclé kinship terminology are as follows. First, all cognatic kin (*lhavelh*) are distinguished from affines, a residual category that includes real affines, potential affines, the affines of one's consanguineal kin, and anyone else with whom one is unable to trace ties of kinship. The Nivaclé have no generic term for affines, and the category is simply referred to as *ni lhavelh'a*, "non-kin." This distinction is in accord with the marriage rules, found throughout the Chaco, which prohibit marriage with anyone classified as kin.

A second feature of the terminology is its bilateral emphasis. In the first ascending and first descending generations, lineal kin are distinguished from collateral kin, but all collateral kin are grouped together and are classified only according to their sex. Thus, the father is referred to by a different term, *tata*, from that used for the father's or mother's brother, *yit'jo'ok*, which is also used for more distant collateral relatives of the parents' generation (FFBS, FFZS, MFBS, MFZS). The mother, *mimi*, is distinguished from the father's and mother's sister, *yit'oj*, who are grouped with more distant female collateral relatives of the parents' generation. Similarly, one's own sons and daughters, *yaos* and *yiase*, respectively, are distinguished from the children of one's brothers and sisters, both real and classificatory, who are referred to as *yitfakl'a* or *yifakche'* according to whether they are male or female.

The same bilateral emphasis is apparent in the affinal terminology, where the wife's kin of her own generation—her brothers and sisters, both real and classificatory—are distinguished only according to their sex: *yika'atjok* for the men, *yikaut'oj* for the women. The wife, *yich'akfa*, however, is distinguished from her real and classificatory sisters. In the first descending generation, the children of the wife's real and classificatory brothers and sisters are again distinguished on the basis of their sex: *yazanach* for males, and *yazanche* for females.

A third feature of Nivaclé terminology is the fairly rigid division of the generations. Great-grandparents are referred to by the same term as grandparents—*yikt'e'ech* for men, and *yikt'e* for women—and these categories include more distant collateral relatives of the second and third ascending generations (FFB, MMB, FFZ, MMZ). Similarly, great-grandchildren are grouped with grandchildren, and with the grandchildren of one's real and classificatory siblings: *yitaukshich'a,* for males, and *yitauklishe'e* for females. All other cognatic kin are distinguished according to their generation.

A final feature of the consanguineal terminology is the division of ego's generation according to relative age. Siblings are grouped with more distant collateral relatives, including all first and second cousins, but they are all distinguished according to whether they are older or younger than ego, as well as by their sex. Thus the older brother, *chikla,* is distinguished from the younger brother, *onaj,* as are all collateral kin of the same generation (FBS, FZS, MBS, MZS), who are distinguished according to their age relative to ego and not according to the age of the linking relative. The father's elder brother's son, for instance, will be referred to as *onaj* if he is younger than ego, while the father's younger brother's son will be referred to as *chikla* if he is older. The same distinction is made with sisters and more distant female collateral relatives of the same generation: if older than ego, they are referred to as *chita'a,* and if younger as *sunja.* The distinction is not carried over into the affinal terminology. The wife's brothers, real and classificatory, are all classed as *yika'atjok* and the wife's sisters as *yikaut'oj* regardless of their age, as are the husbands of ego's sisters, *yifakl'u,* and the wives of ego's brothers, *yifaklis'a.*

The affinal terminology of the Nivaclé can be divided into two distinct subsets: the spouse's kin, and the spouses of ego's kin. In the first ascending generation the wife's father, *yikakt'ech,* is distinguished from the parents' sisters' husbands, *yinjayas'a,* since the children of the latter are classed as siblings and are prohibited as marriage partners. In the same way, the wife's mother, *yikakt'e,* is distinguished from parents' brother's wives, *yinjaozo'a,* since the children of the latter are classificatory siblings. The distinction also applies in the first descending generation, with the wife's siblings' sons, and one's own stepsons, *yazanach,* being distinguished from the daughter's husband, *yitaumit'a,* since the daughter would classify the former as brothers. Equally, the son's wife, *yitaumite'e,* is distinguished from the wife's siblings' daughters, and one's own stepdaughters, *yazanche,* since the son would classify the latter as sisters.

This logic does not apply in ego's own generation. The wife's sister, *yikaut'oj,* is distinguished from the brother's wife, *yifaklis'a,* but there is no prohibition on marriage with the brother's wife's sister. Indeed, such marriages are quite common because they offer the possibility of maintaining the unity of both groups of siblings. The wife's brother, *yika'atjok,* is also distinguished from the sister's husband, *yifakl'u,* but there is no prohibition on sister exchange, which again is quite common.

This is not the only contradiction posed by the affinal terminology. The affinal terminology is applied to anyone not classed as kin and implies a certain social distance. Any male stranger who is older than ego will, for instance, be referred to as *yinjayas'a,* the same term that is applied to the husbands of the father's and mother's sisters as well as to one's own stepfather. When ego is a young man, it is perhaps reasonable for him to refer to his stepfather with a term that implies a certain social distance, but when ego is a child when his mother remarries, it would be inappropriate. In this case the stepfather would be referred to as *tata,* a term usually reserved for the father. The same question arises with the spouses of the parents' siblings. In an uxorilocally extended household or residential group, the relation with the mother's sister's husband will be close, and rather than being addressed as *yinjayas'a,* a term that is used for strangers, he is likely to be called *yit'jo'ok,* "uncle," and assimilated into the category of kin. He in turn will call his wife's sister's son *yitfakl'a* or "nephew" rather than *yazanach,* which strictly speaking is the correct affinal term.

Within the uxorilocally extended household, affinity cannot be blurred so easily. As we shall see in the next section, the use of teknonyms provides one means of overcoming the contradiction between the egalitarian nature of social relations within the residential group and the terminological distinction between kin and affines. With more dis-

212

tant coresident affines, terms of address are sometimes more creative. In one of the households in Mistolar, for instance, an elderly widower who lived with his sister's daughter addressed her husband as *onaj*, literally "younger brother," and the husband reciprocated, calling the old man *chikla*, "elder brother."

The kinship terminology of the Toba (Qom), also shown in appendix 2, is similar to that of the Nivaclé. It is characterized by a bilateral emphasis: in the first ascending and first descending generations, lineal kin are distinguished from collateral kin, but all collateral relatives are classed together and are differentiated only on the basis of their sex and generation. In ego's generation, siblings are grouped with cousins, traced through either parent, and are distinguished according to their sex and relative age. The second and third ascending generations are grouped together, as are the second and third descending generations, and all grandchildren and great-grandchildren are referred to with a single term, *laual*.

The affinal terminology is somewhat different in structure. The first terms shown in appendix 2, part 4, are used only for immediate affines and refer to specific individuals rather than general categories. The terms *lacho'* and *lachodo'* are used for the wife's parents but not for their siblings, potential affines, or strangers. These terms can be used for address, but immediate affines may also use teknonyms.

Unlike the Nivaclé, the Toba refer to some more distant affines with the same terms that are used for kin. The wife's grandparents, for instance, are referred to in the same way as one's own grandparents (both real and classificatory), although they in turn refer to the spouses of their childrens' children with specifically affinal terms. Similarly, distant affines in the first descending generation, including the spouses of one's siblings' children and the children of the wife's siblings, are referred to as *iasoshic* and *iasoshi*, terms that are also used for one's nephews and nieces. This may reflect the tendency—also found among the Nivaclé— for coresident affines to refer to each other with consanguineal terms rather than with the terms used for strangers.

There is some merging of the generations in the affinal terminology, and two terms, *ledaua* and *lauete*, are used for all distant affines in the first ascending and in ego's own generation. The term *ledaua*, used for men, includes the husbands of ego's female kin (FZH, MZH, ZH, FBDH, and MBDH), as well as the male kin of ego's spouse (WB, WFB, and WFBS). The term *lauete* is used for women and includes the wives of ego's male kin and the female kin of ego's spouse. Although the terminological association of the wife's brother and the sister's husband suggests a logic of sister exchange, it would be a mistake to assume that this is a prescriptive or preferential strategy. As I have mentioned, such marriages do occur, but this is because they offer an opportunity for the husband and wife to maintain the unity of their respective sibling groups. In fact, it might be more appropriate to regard *ledaua* and *lauete* as generic terms that can be applied to all distant affines as well as to all those people with whom one is unable to trace any link of cognatic kinship.

The structure of Nivaclé and Toba relationship terminologies is similar to that of the Mataco, described by Alvarsson (1988:81). Two features of the terminologies are, I believe, characteristic of the Chaco societies and help to define the cultural unity of the region. The first is their bilateral emphasis. Siblings are grouped with cousins and are not distinguished according to the sex of the linking relative, while in the first ascending, and usually in the first descending, generation lineal kin are distinguished from collateral kin, the latter being classified only on the basis of their sex. This appears to be a consistent feature of Chaco relationship terminologies, despite the tendency for uxorilocal residence, which can give residential groups a matrilineal appearance, and despite the existence of exogamic patriclans among the Ayoreo and Chamococo. The bilateral emphasis of the terminologies is consistent with the flexibility of practical social organization in the Chaco and permits the formation and maintenance of extensive ego-focused networks of kinship that allow individuals the widest possible choice for residence and mutual cooperation.

The open-ended nature of Chaco social organization is also apparent in the distinction between kin and affines. This reflects the general prohibition on marriage with anyone defined as kin, a rule that is probably universal in the Chaco. This prevents the formation of closed and enduring endogamic groups—that is to say, communities where marriages take place within the residential group—which are seen as an ideal by many societies in the tropical forest regions of Lowland South America

(Rivière 1984). The rigid distinction between kin and affines does result in certain contradictions, however. Affines are by definition non-kin and are assimilated into the same category as strangers, even though residential units are based on ties of affinity. Social relations within the household are egalitarian, and the household or residential group is never conceived of in terms of wife-givers and wife-takers, a perception that would be consistent with a more authoritarian system. To some extent the problem is resolved by redefining close affines as kin. The spouses of collateral kin are sometimes referred to with the same terms that are used for collateral relatives, but with the closest affines—the spouse's parents and the children's spouses—such a redefinition is impossible, and here the use of teknonyms appears to offer a solution.

Teknonyms

The Nivaclé teknonyms, shown in figure 4, are only used between members of the same household or people who reside in close proximity and cooperate on a day-to-day basis. Unlike those reported for some other societies in Lowland South America (Overing Kaplan 1975:169), they take the name of a child as their point of reference. The terms are added as suffixes and are the kinship terms the child would use with the individual being referred to, in the third person possessive. For instance, if the child whose name is used is Maria, her father will be called *Maria lhtata,* "Maria's father," and her mother *Maria lhamimi,* "Maria's mother." The child whose name is used can be male or female and is not necessarily the firstborn; indeed, over time the names of different children may be used.

   Some elderly Nivaclé affirm that teknonyms were once more widely used, and the terms of address may have been modified when the Nivaclé adopted Spanish names. Nowadays teknonyms are used within the household between affines: spouses refer to each other as "mother of . . ." or "father of . . ." a particular child, and in an uxorilocally extended household, the wife's parents address and refer to their son-in-law with a teknonym. When talking to people from outside the household, however, they are more likely to refer to him with the affinal term *yitaumit'a* (DH). The son-in-law will in turn use the teknonyms "grandfather or grandmother of . . ." when he addresses or refers to his wife's parents

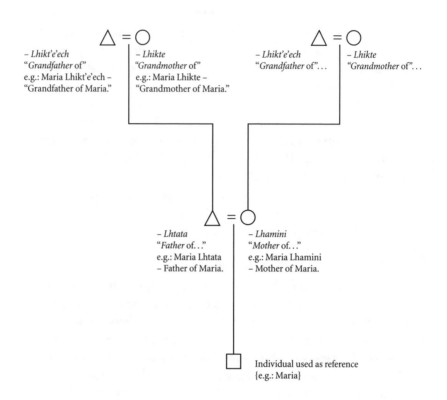

Fig. 4. Nivaclé teknonyms

within the household, but outside he will refer to them as *yikakt'ech* (wf) or *yikakt'e* (wm). In a virilocally extended household, the husband's parents will address their son's wife with a teknonym, and she will reciprocate; outside the household the son's wife and the husband's parents refer to each other with affinal terms. Other affines may also use teknonyms, although they will not be used reciprocally. The wife's brother, particularly if he is coresident, may address his sister's husband with a teknonym, although the sister's husband will address him by name, since teknonyms are never extended beyond the terms given in figure 4. One would, for instance, never hear a person addressed as *Maria lhit'jo'ok,* "Maria's uncle."

In some cases the Nivaclé use teknonymy between affines who are not strictly related to the child in the way implied by the teknonym; the teknonym is consistent, however, with the way the affinal terminology is used. In Mistolar, for example, there was a young couple living next to the wife's adoptive parents; the adoptive father was her real mother's father's brother. Here, the young husband addressed his wife's adoptive father as *Jorgelina lhikt'e'ech,* "Jorgelina's grandfather" (Jorgelina being the name of the couple's only daughter), a usage entirely consistent with the way he referred to his wife's adoptive father as *yikakt'ech* (wf) when speaking to people from outside the household.

The Nivaclé do not use teknonyms between kin. In an uxorilocally extended household, the wife's parents will address her by name and will refer to her as *yiase* ("daughter"); similarly, in a virilocally extended household, the husband's parents will address him by name and will refer to him as *yaos* ("son") when speaking with outsiders. This suggests that the teknonyms are explicitly intended to transform close affines into kin by adopting the perspective of their children, for whom the kin and affines of the previous generation are all kin. Through this transformation the teknonyms overcome, or at least mask, the contradiction implied by the grouping of close, even coresident, affines in the same category as strangers. This allows the household or residential group to conform to a model of kindred-based social solidarity and cooperation (see Overing Kaplan 1975; Rivière 1984:67–71).

The Ayoreo teknonyms, shown in figure 5, appear almost identical to those of the Nivaclé. They are formed in the same way, by adding suf-

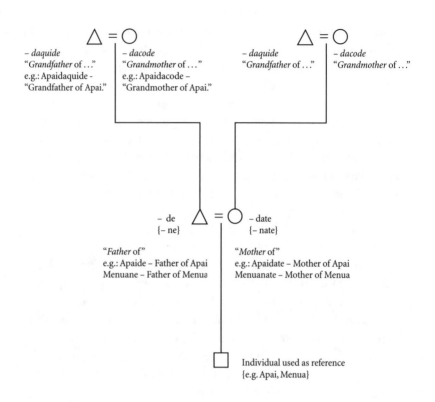

Fig. 5. Ayoreo teknonyms

fixes to the name of a child of the person referred to. For example, if the child is named Apai, his father will be called *Apaide,* "Apai's father," and his mother *Apaidate,* "Apai's mother." If the child's name ends in a nasal consonant, the *d* changes to *n:* thus, "Menua's father" is *Menuane* and her mother, *Menuanate.* The child whose name is used can be either male or female and is frequently, but not always, the firstborn. Nowadays the child's name is often Spanish rather than Ayoreo.

The main difference between the Ayoreo teknonyms and those of the Nivaclé is in the way they are applied. The Ayoreo teknonyms are similar to personal names and are used by kin, affines, and even strangers. They do not entirely replace personal names but are regarded as a mark of respect and are often the most common way of addressing or referring to an individual. The parental teknonyms are the most widely used. In the Colonia Maria Auxiliadora about 10 percent of adults were referred to by their parental teknonyms rather than their personal names. The grandparental teknonyms are used less often and only rarely appear to be substituted for personal names.

It would be reasonable to assume that the teknonyms are intended to transform the relation between affines into one of kinship. But in the Ayoreo case the emphasis seems to be on presenting the community, rather than the household, as a clearly bounded network of kin. Among the Ayoreo, intercommunity relations were often hostile, and in theory, though not always in practice, the Ayoreo viewed community or territorial endogamy as an ideal. Against this background, the generalized use of teknonyms emphasizes the unity of the group by relating people through their children, and stresses common kinship rather than the opposition between affines. As the children are undisputed members of the community in which they are born and brought up, the use of teknonyms may also provide a way of helping to integrate people of different origin into the community or territorial group.

Teknonymy is also a means of indicating full adult status. There are no institutionalized age grades among the Ayoreo, and no initiation ceremonies for either men or women, but traditional games, such as *chacheriñane* and nowadays soccer, are based on a division into age sets, which are distinguished with specific terms and associated with particular kinds of behavior. The *jnacariode*—adolescent and young men—are not considered fully responsible or productive, and it is only when they have established a stable relationship with a particular girl and have at least one child that they achieve full adult status as one of the *jnanione*. In the same way, it is only when a woman has at least one child that she can be considered *cheque,* an adult woman, rather than *gapu,* an adolescent. Here, the use of teknonyms provides a clear and public way of demonstrating that an individual has become fully adult.

In this discussion of the Chaco societies' perception of household and extended kin groups, I have tried to elucidate the models on which the system of kinship and coresidence is based, and have tried to show how they provide a means of ordering a system of social relations that is explicitly based on freedom of choice.

One of the characteristic features of this level of social organization is the absence of any clearly defined "corporate groups." Indeed, the residential units I have described not only lack any definition in terms of rights to land or other productive property (Fortes 1969) but also appear to lack any clearly undifferentiated or unitary identity that is maintained over time (Overing Kaplan 1975:82). In fact, the most clearly defined social groups in the Chaco are the communities or territorial groups that respond to a particular political leadership, and it is to this level of organization that I now turn.

CHAPTER SEVEN

The Community and Political Leadership

I N   T H E   P R E V I O U S   chapter I discussed how extended kin and residential groups provide the basis for social and economic organization in the Chaco. Here, I shall move beyond this level to consider
how these groups are integrated into communities or territorial groups,
above all through their acceptance of common leadership.

At first sight it is perhaps surprising to find that the egalitarian societies of the Chaco can give rise to charismatic leaders who exercise very
real authority. The existence of powerful leaders, of a kind not unknown
in other parts of Lowland South America, is, however, less paradoxical than it appears. I would argue that it is the unstructured, egalitarian
nature of Chaco social organization that gives rise to these leaders, with
the absence of mechanisms for integrating the extended kin and residential groups being counterbalanced by the unifying power of common
political leadership. Political leadership of this kind is, moreover, consistent with the Indians' conception of personal autonomy; it is not based
on coercion but embodies the values and aspirations of the community.

I shall begin by discussing the relation between settlement patterns
and leadership and considering the nature of politics in the Chaco. Underlying the apparent diversity of political organization—some communities respond to a single leader, others are riven by factionalism, and
yet others appear to lack any kind of leadership—is a common conception of legitimate authority. I shall look at leadership in the light of the
Indians' notions of consensus and coercion; I then examine the nature
and qualities of leadership and consider how a leader's following is built
up through kinship, affinity, and coresidence. Having discussed leadership in these rather abstract terms, I then look at two specific cases. The
first is Mistolar, where the leadership has undergone a transformation

221

from warrior chief to *capitán* to the present-day administrator. Then, by way of contrast, I shall look at Puerto Diana, a heterogeneous community where rival factions find themselves representing the interests of different sectors of the national society.

The Community and Territorial Group

At present, most of the Indians of the Chaco live in nucleated settlements, with 85 percent living in localities of more than ten households (INDI 1982:table 4). The tendency for nucleation reflects the pressures on contemporary communities, many of which have been pushed off their ancestral lands and have been resettled in missions, in Indian colonies, or on the outskirts of urban areas. The traditional patterns of settlement were more flexible and ranged from semipermanent villages with populations of up to a thousand, to dispersed bands of twenty or thirty people who had only sporadic contact with other groups.

Nordenskiöld (1912) describes a Nivaclé village near Estero Patiño that had a population of about a thousand people. Similarly, the Ayoreo claim to have lived in large, fairly permanent villages of about the same size; indeed, one of the largest groups was called the Guidaigosode, "people of the village," a reference to size of their population. A state of endemic warfare may have favored settlement in large villages, but populations of this size would have had difficulty finding sufficient resources to support themselves throughout the year, particularly if they lived away from the major rivers. This is a problem in all the larger present-day communities. In fact, it is likely that the more typical settlement pattern was one in which the members of a particular territorial group spent part of the year living in small bands and came together only at certain seasons (Grubb 1911; Metraux 1963; Bórmida and Califano 1978; Alvarsson 1988). Such groups are still in evidence today, although the dispersion and concentration of the population respond more to the opportunities for wage labor than to the availability of natural resources. The Ayoreo of Campo Loro, for example, spend much of their time living as small bands with their Mennonite employers, but they consider themselves a single group and from time to time congregate in the mission, usually for religious meetings. Similarly, family groups of Toba from Cerrito and Río Verde spend months hunting or working on the ranches along the Trans-Chaco

Highway but return to the colony for the cane harvest, which lasts from May to November.

The existence of small autonomous bands is more problematic. The Manjuy of Loma Alegre claim that when they lived in Cañada Milico, their band, comprising some twenty people in all, had no more than sporadic contact with other groups of Manjuy. The Ayoreo of Kilometer 70, Bahía Negra, who numbered only nineteen people, lived in isolation from their original group for over fifteen years and were easily able to provide for their subsistence needs. The seven Totobiegosode who were contacted in 1998 also appear to have lived alone for a number of years. Bands of this kind would, however, have been unable to reproduce themselves, for demographic reasons and because of the prohibition on marriage with kin, and would also have been vulnerable to raiding and epidemics. Indeed, these were the reasons why the Manjuy abandoned Cañada Milico and settled among the Nivaclé of Pedro P. Peña. In the traditional context, most bands may have retained a certain level of autonomy as the allies of larger and more powerful groups—as in the case of a few Manjuy families that settled in Mistolar. It is likely that over time any independent bands would have been integrated into the larger groups through intermarriage.

The Indians of the Chaco conceive of their social and political organization in terms of common residence or association with a particular territory. This is true both at the level of the larger residential or territorial groups and at the level of the smaller residential nuclei, but the larger groups achieve a sense of unity only when they are also defined in terms of common leadership. Traditional territorial groups were often named after some physical feature of the area the group inhabited. Among the Ayoreo, the Garaigosode were "the people of the grasslands," the Tiegosode "the people of the river Timanes," and the Iyapepaigosode "the people of the closed scrub forest," but these areas were only vaguely delimited. Contemporary groups also identify themselves on the basis of locality; the Faromorogosode, for instance, are the group that used to live in the New Tribes mission station of Faro Moro. These groups do not enjoy much permanence over time and exist in a continual state of flux. A close examination of the history and composition of these groups will usually show how the opposing tendencies for fission and fusion be-lie the appearance of stability suggested by the groups' association with particular localities. The smaller groups merge or are absorbed by the larger ones, while the larger ones are split, and eventually divide, as a result of factional conflicts.

The flexibility of this level of social organization is also due to the fact that membership in a particular community or territorial group is determined simply by continued coresidence and not by descent or any other predetermined criterion. As the Ayoreo explain it, one can belong to the group (*-gosode*) of one's father, one's mother, or to a different group if one happens to live there. In practice, the criteria that determine membership are similar to, and in some contexts associated with, those that determine ethnic identity: the individual identifies with the territorial group in which he or she was brought up, regardless of his or her parents' origin. Moreover, individuals can be identified with more than one group if they move to a different community. An Ayoreo brought up among the Garaigosode but who marries into and lives among the Guidaigosode, for example, would be considered a Garaigos by the members of the latter group but would be a Guidaigos to outsiders.

The situation is further confused by the heterogeneity of many of the larger present-day settlements. Some communities, such as the Barrio Obrero of Filadelfia and Santa Teresita, are divided along ethnic lines, while others, like Cerrito, are divided according to where the different subgroups originally came from. In settlements of this latter kind, however, one should be careful not to interpret factionalism in strictly historical terms, since the differences of origin are as much a comment on the ongoing political relations within the community as they are a faithful representation of historical fact.

Political Leadership

Social organization at the level of the community or territorial group has to be considered in terms of political leadership as well as coresidence. The two aspects are interrelated, because the choice of residence is a political act, and politics in the Chaco is based on a notion of consensus that receives its most explicit expression through coresidence.

In practice, the Indian societies of the Chaco present a range of political organization, and the Indians' attitudes to leadership reflect the pattern of settlement. At one extreme are the small autonomous bands that appear to lack any kind of leadership. This is the situation among the small groups that are scattered throughout the area of Pedro P. Peña: the Manjuy of Loma Alegre, for example, express distaste for the idea that an individual should set himself up as leader. This kind of atomism is also apparent in heterogeneous communities like Puerto Diana and Santo Domingo, although it tends to be expressed through rejection of the individuals who aspire to leadership, rather than through rejection of the idea of leadership as such.

A few communities—perhaps not many—come closer to the stated ideal of social solidarity. Here, the various kin groups and potential factions are integrated into a wider community through what is essentially the persuasive power of a single, dominant leader. The interests of particular kin groups are relegated to those of the community as a whole, but everyone is perceived as benefiting from the increased sense of security. It may be that communities of this kind were more common in the traditional context. The state of endemic warfare that existed in much of the Chaco would have been more conducive to strong leadership and social solidarity than the present-day complex and often divisive threats posed by competing sectors of the national society.

Despite the diversity of political integration that one finds in the Chaco societies, there is, I believe, an underlying unity in the Indians' conception of political authority. Two aspects are particularly important. The first is the emphasis on personal autonomy and consensus. The second, in some ways related, is the way in which a leader's authority is divorced from all forms of coercion, whether direct, through physical force, or indirect, through control over productive resources or sources of mystical power.

This is not merely an ideal notion of political authority. Indeed, I would argue that if it is leadership that gives a community its sense of coherence and unity, it is the flexibility of social organization that helps determine and delimit the nature of political leadership. Membership in a community is determined simply by continual residence—there are no a priori kinship qualifications, and individuals or households are free to come and go as they wish. The relation between a leader and the faction or community that accepts him as such cannot in these circumstances be adequately described in terms of rights and duties toward some pre-determined group of people. Rather, leadership should be interpreted as the ability to bring a sense of unity to a group that may be composed of diverse factions, kin groups, and extended households—a potential that is realized in some cases but not in others. This is certainly the explicit concern of most Indian leaders, and aspiring leaders, who try to achieve this sense of unity through a leadership that gives expression to the ideals and aspirations of the whole community.

The Indian societies of the Chaco are not what would normally be understood as democratic societies. In the first place, the convention of the majority vote—the idea that a majority can somehow impose their will on all the members of a community—is alien to them and comes into direct conflict with their fundamental conceptions of personal autonomy. Every decision that affects the community has to be accepted unanimously and has to reflect the will of everyone involved. Even when a public consensus is achieved, the individuals concerned feel themselves under no binding obligation, and anyone who has a change of heart feels free to act as he or she pleases.

This has been apparent on every occasion that outside agencies have tried to introduce democratic models of organization into indigenous communities. The most explicit examples were the local councils (*consejos locales*) promoted by API, but similar models have been adopted by most development agencies. Typically, when such councils are set up, they either reach unanimous decisions or, if this proves impossible, remain deadlocked, and the decision of the majority is never regarded as binding. This has led to frustration on the part of the outsiders involved in these programs. They have tended to see the issue either as one of the Indians' inability to understand the organizational structures they have promoted or as one of personal failings, the Indians being seen as indecisive, untrustworthy, and so on. The issue is not, however, that the Indians fail to intellectually understand these modes of organization, but rather that they refuse, on moral grounds, to accept a system that ultimately restricts the autonomy of the individual.

It is the emphasis on personal autonomy that more than anything else defines the scope of political leadership in the Chaco. A political leader is not simply a man of vision, able to give expression to the values and aspirations of the community. He also has to be capable of making the members of the community understand why, for moral and practical reasons, a particular course of action is desirable. This applies not only to decisions that clearly belong to the political arena and that affect the community as a whole—whether to solicit a title to land or prepare a communal garden—but equally to the judicial arena. A political leader has no power to sanction antisocial behavior and is not a judge or an arbiter of disputes: disputes, should they be serious, are usually resolved by one of the parties leaving the community. He does, however, try to make antisocial individuals see the error of their ways and make them recognize their failure to live up to the values of indigenous society.

In the end, though, it is personal autonomy that prevails. If a leader is unable to convince his followers, he has no means of coercing them—other perhaps than the threat of renouncing his leadership—and he has to abide by their wishes, however foolish they may be. The Chamococo have a tale about their legendary chief Basebuk, who fought the Caduveo for control of the western bank of the Paraguay River. Basebuk always rode on horseback to watch for the Caduveo while the other warriors accompanied him on foot. One day he ran down a deer and killed it with his lance. "Come and skin this animal," he called to his companions. His companions refused. "Who will be watching for the Caduveo if I get down from my horse," asked Basebuk. "If you want the deer skinned do it yourself," his companions replied. Basebuk dismounted, and while he was skinning the deer the Caduveo fell on the party, taking them by surprise. They tried to run, but the Caduveo, who were on horseback, ran them down and slaughtered everyone except Basebuk, who escaped into a swamp and hid among the reeds.[1]

It is surprising, given that even such legendary leaders as Basebuk were unable to enforce their wishes, that a successful leader is sometimes talked of as a "dictator." This is an expression that the Nivaclé sometimes use to describe not only their traditional warrior chiefs but also some of the more respected contemporary leaders. The imagery is taken from Paraguayan society—or perhaps from the German priests who used to celebrate Hitler's birthday—but it reflects another aspect of the Indians' conception of leadership, that a leader should not sit and debate every day-to-day issue but should take decisions for the community, bringing issues up for discussion only when they are of importance or there is likely to be disagreement. This is still leadership by consensus. The members of the community are free to disagree with or to ignore the requests of the leader, but it seems to suggest that by accepting an individual as their leader, the members of the community abdicate what would otherwise be a series of personal or family decisions. These include decisions that at first sight appear to lie outside the political sphere. A leader is, for instance, often expected to provide for the subsistence of his followers, either through his own productive efforts or, in recent years, by acquiring rations from outside agencies. In times of shortage leaders can also call on the members of the community to slaughter their livestock and prepare a feast.

This is, I believe, the essence of what Metraux (1963:303) describes as the leader's obligation to share. Generosity is an ideal that touches on everyone. There is an expectation that everyone should be willing to share regardless of ties of kinship or affinity, but sharing is above all the obligation of a political leader, since generosity is one of the principal features that define the relation between a leader and his followers. This lays a heavy burden on the leader, since the community is dependent on him, and he is ultimately responsible for the subsistence of all the households in the community.

Although the relation between the community and its leader is one of dependence, a leader is not able to coerce his followers. The obligation to share prevents him from establishing control over productive resources or accumulating goods. The values of self-control and non-aggression also limit the possibility of physical coercion. There are no institutional means for sanctioning individuals. Indeed, antisocial behavior such as violence or theft is seen as a personal failing—an indication that there is something wrong with an individual—that can only be put right through the individual's coming to understand his failing, and not through punishment. This is tied to a system of values that views all aggression, particularly within the community, as undesirable and unnatural.

The idea of aggression or anger, referred to in Guaraní as *pochy*, provides, through its negative example, what might almost be considered a model for proper behavior. In writing about the Chiripa-Guaraní of

228

Eastern Paraguay, Norman Anderson (1984) notes that "the idea that Guaraní aren't *pochy* is about the only form of self- definition that these Indians employ." This is, I believe, equally familiar in the Chaco, where the notion of *pochy* is intimately associated with the stereotypes that the Indians hold of the national society.

Aggressive behavior is deplored, even in those contexts where the tensions of the community come to the surface in fights and quarrels, such as dances, drinking parties, and soccer games. In fact, a typical comment on a successful fiesta is "iporã la farra, ndaipori pochy," "it was a good party, no one got angry." If anyone loses control—invariably they will be wildly drunk—they are treated with the utmost tact. Their companions sit with them, talking and trying to calm them down, and physical restraint is resorted to only in the last instance. If a man is armed, with a revolver, a machete, or a razor-sharp knife, his companions try to persuade him to hand it over rather than attempt to remove it by force. The requests usually succeed, and the drunk passes out, watched over by his friends or family. On occasions, however, fights lead to serious injuries and even homicide, and the offender, once he comes to, invariably leaves the community for months or even years. This is not just because he is anxious to avoid punishment at the hands of the authorities—if he is caught by the police or military, he can expect a good beating—but above all because he wants to avoid the shame that his violent actions have incurred.

The term *pochy* is also used to describe the kind of anger, or lack of self-control, that is not necessarily directed toward others but expresses impatience or a lack of endurance. A lack of self-control is not reprehensible in the way that violent behavior is, but it is considered infantile. Impatient and irritable behavior is seen as a characteristic of foreigners and can be a source of amusement, an idea nicely illustrated by the following anecdote of Barbrooke Grubb's: "One day, when travelling with a party of Indians, we camped during the mid-day heat near a forest. The mosquitoes and sand flies were unbearable, and I could not control my irritation. This greatly amused the Indians, and they asked me why I was angry. I told them that the reason was very obvious. On this they asked me if I knew the language of the mosquito. 'Because if you do', they said, 'it would be wise to speak hard words to them'" (1911:200).

Specialist Roles

A political leader's control is limited by the tendency for specialization: the leadership of some activities is left to a "guide" or "organizer" who is chosen for his skill or expert knowledge. When the Mak'a or the Toba hunt as a group, they sometimes elect a skilled hunter or someone with an expert knowledge of the area to act as guide. This man is responsible for daily decisions—where to set up camp, which animals and in which places to hunt—and he may decide to split the group up to cover different areas. He is accorded no special privileges, and once the party returns, his leadership is no longer recognized. Similarly, among the Nivaclé a few individuals are renowned as "organizers of fishing." These are experienced men who study the level, color, and turbulence of the river and can determine when and where the fishing is most likely to be successful. When the conditions are right, the "organizer" visits the houses in the settlement, telling everyone the time and place the fishermen should meet.

Another specialist found in some groups, such as the Nivaclé of Pedro P. Peña, is the "organizer of wage labor." He will be skilled with an ax, or nowadays with a chain saw, and will understand the tools and techniques used for erecting fencing and so on. He may speak some Spanish or Guaraní and will be able to deal with Paraguayans or Mennonites—both to find employment and to understand the inevitably problematic balance between the money owed by the employer and the expenses incurred for provisions, tools, and other advances. The organizer of wage labor is not simply an intermediary between his companions and the employer but may organize the work on a day-to-day basis, allocating tasks and even starting the day with a harangue, urging his companions to work hard and avoid running up excessive debts.

The decentralization of authority is found at its most explicit among the Mak'a, who are reputed to have different chiefs for almost every collective activity, including a "chief of hunting," a "chief of fishing," and a "chief of drinking parties." The same system also functions in communities that at first sight appear to have adopted outside organizational structures. In Cerrito, the colony's ranch is the responsibility of a foreman (*capataz*) who acts independently of the political leaders. Similarly, in Mistolar, the communal tasks—the communal gardens, construction of the church, repairs to the school, clearing the airstrip, and so on — are the responsibility of a "leader of work" who organizes the activities on a daily basis.

The political leaders of the Chaco societies, unlike the leaders of the Guaraní of Eastern Paraguay, are not religious leaders. Traditionally, the only religious specialists were shamans, who were distinguished for their ability and knowledge (when speaking Guaraní, the Indians of the Lower Chaco refer to the shaman as *hi-arandu-ha,* "a person of knowledge"). The shaman does not occupy a specific role within the community, and in the few communities where shamanism is openly practiced, a large number of men, and some women, are regarded as shamans. Only a few, however, are believed to have much power.

Powerful shamans are rarely political leaders: the only leader of recent years who had a reputation as a powerful shaman was Uejai, leader of the Guidaigosode, the Ayoreo who were settled by the New Tribes Mission in Faro Moro. Shamans are regarded ambivalently, and may be outsiders or fairly marginal members of the community. In Pedro P. Peña, of the three men who are regarded as shamans, one is a Choroti and the other two are Nivaclé who have no close kinship with the rest of the community. Similarly, one of the most renowned shamans in the Lower Chaco was a Lengua who lived with the Mak'a in the colony opposite the Botanical Gardens. Powerful shamans are respected, but they are also feared and are often blamed for deaths or misfortune.

Shamans are sometimes believed to be selfish; they may demand whatever takes their fancy and ask for payment for curing or finding lost objects. At times they are suspected of deliberately bringing harm — like the shaman who sends a rattlesnake to bite someone and then offers to cure him for a fee. Moreover, the shaman's auxiliary spirits are believed to impose their own will on the shaman. As a Chamococo shaman explains it, his most powerful auxiliary can appear in a dream and order him to call up a flood or a plague of fleas. He is obliged to obey and has to sing, if necessary the whole night and all the next day, for fear that his auxiliary will abandon him and leave him to die.

Some shamans are believed to control natural resources and are regarded as the "owners" of particular species, like the brocket deer or the rhea. Before setting off, a hunter can ask the shaman for permission to take some of his animals, and the shaman may indicate where the hunter is likely to find them, or may set a limit on the number of animals that the hunter can take. There are also shamans who are "masters" of particular environments, or who enjoy special relationships with the spirit "owners" of particular sites or areas.

In many communities one finds pastors or lay preachers. Where a religious sect operates independently of a missionary organization, a situation typified by the Toba Pentecostalists, the pastor is often reminiscent of the shaman. He may claim supernatural powers, and his preaching will focus on explaining the visions he has acquired in dreams or in a trance. He may cure illness—explained as possession by Satan or other malignant spirits—through the power of the Holy Spirit, a power not unlike that of a shaman's auxiliaries. Some pastors have built up large followings, but such followings tend to be unstable and are typically millenarian-type movements that focus on the imminent destruction of the temporal order and the reassertion of traditional values (Miller 1967).

In the Mennonite Colonies and, until recently, on the Anglican and New Tribes mission stations, the missionary organizations have exercised more control over the Indian pastors. In these communities the pastor is typically an intermediary between the missionaries and the community. The pastor preaches and is usually responsible for the day-to-day running of the Indian church. His situation as an intermediary does not in itself disqualify him from leadership—indeed, the missionaries often try to promote the pastors as political leaders—but it places the pastor in a position that is often irreconcilable with legitimate leadership. The other members of the community see him as representing the interests of the missionaries, while the personal privileges he enjoys—access to the missionaries, and to the goods and opportunities they have to offer—may provoke accusations of meanness and abuse of authority.

The Leader and His Following

The personal qualities associated with leadership are largely implicit in what has already been said. A successful leader has to reason with the members of his community and achieve consensus among divergent groups of interest. He must also have courage and, certainly in the modern context, be able to deal with outsiders, particularly members of the national society, on equal terms. This is perhaps a rather unusual quality; the Indians of the Chaco tend to be reserved in their behavior, especially when dealing with outsiders, and they often appear ill at ease when confronted by the forceful, if not aggressive, behavior of most Paraguayans. A leader, however, must be able to handle even the ugliest situations with calm, and should he shy away from a confrontation—even with an armed and violent drunk or a threatening military officer—he would automatically lose the trust and respect of his followers.

A further quality that should be mentioned is oratory. Since he lacks any other means of persuasion, a leader depends on the power of his words. Some traditional leaders used to address their followers with a formal speech every morning and evening, but nowadays speeches are more often directed to weekly meetings attended by all the men and often most of the women of the community. The speeches are different from the rather quiet and reserved tones of everyday conversation, and it is the more forceful orators who are most admired (Clastres 1977).

Indian leaders also tend to be distinguished by their size, strength, and physical skills. They are not necessarily the strongest men in the community, the best hunters, or the best horsemen; the Indians of the Chaco are not competitive, and they avoid comparing individual abilities in these terms. But usually they are physically strong and excel at the activities that are most valued in their communities. Political leadership is often distinguished from the leadership of hunting expeditions or work parties. Unlike the leaders or "organizers" of these activities—who act with certain bravado and who are clearly in the forefront—the political leader may have only a marginal participation in collective activities, or may even be absent. A leader is, however, expected to take control of the situation should a crisis arise, and it is in moments of crisis, rather than in routine affairs, that his skills and strengths are exercised to the full.

This can be illustrated by an incident that took place in December 1981, when I was traveling with a party of Toba to the newly established colony at San José. We were carrying provisions for the colony in two oxcarts, and since there had been heavy rain during the previous weeks, conditions were difficult and the oxen could only make very slow progress. For the first part of the journey, the *cacique* of the new colony rode on ahead with his young son. His wife's brother—a skilled horseman who had previously been the ranch foreman in Cerrito—was in charge of the oxcarts, the provisions, and the other members of the party. On the afternoon of the second day, we reached a mile-long stretch of track that had been completely flooded. The horses managed to get across, slipping and sliding in the mud, but the oxen, after only a couple of hundred yards, refused to go any farther, and the wheels of the carts sank into the mud. The drivers cursed, and the rest of the party pushed, pulled, and tried to lever up the wheels with pieces of wood, but to no avail. It was only when everyone was exhausted and completely demoralized that the *cacique* intervened. He left his son sitting in the shade and returned to help his brother-in-law unhitch the oxen—a dangerous task, since by now they were frightened and exhausted and were liable to turn and slash with their horns—and he led them out of the water to rest. He then took the lead unloading the provisions and, with the help of the other members of the party, carried them sack by sack to dry land. Once the carts were empty, it was decided to free them one at a time. Three pairs of oxen were hitched to the first cart, which was driven by the *cacique* with the rest of the party pushing. After nearly an hour, with much heaving and cursing, the first cart finally reached the far side. The oxen were then driven back and hitched to the second cart, and after another hour or so of hard labor, the party finally reached dry land. Once the carts were reloaded and everyone had rested, the *cacique* carried on as before, riding ahead and leaving his brother-in-law in charge of the party.

A leader's legitimacy is based not only on his personal qualities but also on the ties that link him to the rest of the community and above all to his group of immediate supporters. A leader's immediate followers may be his kinsmen—his siblings, their descendants, and more distant members of his kindred—or his affines, more often the wife's siblings and their descendants than his children's spouses. In practice, most leaders draw their following from kin and affines, and it is by maximizing the potential of kinship and affinity—by maintaining and strengthening ties with more distant kin and affines—that leaders build up their support. Residence is important, and a leader may consolidate his position by keeping his own or his wife's sibling group together: the in-marrying men living uxorilocally, and the in-marrying women living virilocally.

The flexibility of Chaco social organization offers a leader considerable freedom to build up a following, but there are situations where the demographic weakness or dispersion of an individual's kindred, and of his wife's kindred, prevents him from establishing a group of his own. This was the case with Aníbal, a Mataco man of considerable ability who tried to establish his leadership, first among the Manjuy and Nivaclé of the worker village of Sandhorst, and later among the Nivaclé of Pedro P. Peña. He was never accepted as a legitimate leader, not so much because of his ethnic identity, but rather because he lacked the support of a group of close kinsmen or affines and was regarded as unnaturally assertive when he tried to act on behalf of the group. In the end, the Nivaclé of Pedro P. Peña threatened him, and he was forced to leave the settlement.

Leadership in the more warlike of the Chaco societies was tradition-ally associated with an individual's status as a warrior. Indeed, some of the traditional terms used to describe leadership refer not to the leader's role, even as the organizer or leader of raiding parties, but directly to his prowess as a killer. The Nivaclé term *lhcaanvacle,* which is not used to de-scribe contemporary leaders, refers explicitly to an individual's owner-ship of scalps. Similarly, the Ayoreo term *asuté,* usually translated as "chief," was applicable to those who had killed either a jaguar or a human enemy (Bórmida and Califano 1978:105).

The quality associated with the act of killing, although sometimes de-scribed as "courage," differs from our own conception of physical cour-age. The Ayoreo gave little importance to the physical danger involved in a raid. Ideally a raid would take the enemy by complete surprise, and the Ayoreo would kill men, women, and even children, without assign-ing any particular merit to the killing of an enemy warrior. Cases are described where an older warrior, who had already killed a number of people, held a captive and allowed a younger companion to do the kill-ing (Bórmida and Califano 1978:112). The danger was seen to reside in the act of killing itself, the killer being polluted by the blood of his victim or threatened by the victim's soul. Once he had killed, a warrior had to undergo a series of rites and prohibitions that were intended to cleanse him and give him control of the victim's soul. In the case of the Nivaclé, it seems that mystical power was acquired from the victims' scalps. A warrior would converse with the souls of his victims—an idea reminis-cent of the relation between a shaman and his spirit auxiliaries—and the souls were believed to warn their owner of the approach of enemies and other dangers. The souls were also believed to give songs and the power of oratory to their owners (Chase Sardi 1970:202).

The Nivaclé of the Upper Pilcomayo were organized under the leadership of warrior chiefs until the Chaco War (1932–35), when most groups crossed into Argentina or sought refuge in the missions that had been established by the Oblates of Maria. Some warrior chiefs, such as Caunis, leader of the group that inhabited Pedro P. Peña, and his younger brother Tofai, leader of the group inhabiting Fischat, the present-day Laguna Escalante, initially resisted the Bolivian advance. But the Bolivians bought their good will with presents of cloth and provisions.

Even before the Chaco War, a new type of leadership was emerging in some of the Nivaclé communities. The new leaders, who styled themselves *capitanes,* took their authority from their position as intermediaries between the Nivaclé and the administrations of the sugarcane plantations in northern Argentina. The Nivaclé began working in the cane plantations around the turn of the twentieth century. Nordenskiöld (1912) remarks on the presence of small groups of Nivaclé at La Esperanza, which he visited in 1908, but it was probably not until some years later that large numbers of Nivaclé began to make regular seasonal migrations from the Pilcomayo to the valleys of Salta and Jujuy.

In the sugarcane plantations, each capitán was responsible for a group of workers and took his orders from the company administration. Each group was assigned a particular area, and the capitán would take charge of the work, sometimes with the help of an assistant or *lenguaraz,* an interpreter, who was often the leader of a smaller, allied group of Nivaclé. The capitán did not take part in the work himself and was apparently paid more than the other workers. The Nivaclé do not remember this as causing any jealousy, and they remark that the capitán was treated with more respect than is usual nowadays.

The leaders were not appointed by the administration of the sugar refineries but were chosen by their own communities. In fact, on the one occasion when the administration of the Ingenio San Martín tried to appoint a capitán—following the death of Sixto Quintana, leader of the Nivaclé of Pedro P. Peña—the candidate refused, arguing that he lacked the approval of his group. In the event, his maternal uncle was eventually chosen as capitán, and the decision was accepted by the administration without further question. Unlike the present-day "organizers of wage labor," leaders like Mayor Diaz and Sixto Quintana were recognized outside the cane fields, and they enjoyed considerable prestige and drew their followings from a wide area.

Mayor Diaz, capitán of Mistolar, was recognized as a leader before the Chaco War. He was the first of the new-style leaders, the group having previously been led by a warrior chief. His influence extended beyond Mistolar and was recognized by various villages scattered throughout the interior of the Chaco which came together during the fishing and algarrobo seasons. The largest, Utsiyishi and Catsajshi, included some ten to twenty households, but most were smaller, typically comprising four or five households. They were scattered over a wide area and the most distant, Vashaclay and Atjuyechat, were situated 150 kilometers (over 90 miles), a two-week journey, from Mistolar. There was also a separate but closely allied group led by Capitán Alejandro, who is described as an "assistant" to Mayor Diaz. This group included the villages of Yitauyis, Votsopú, Toyshivoyish, and Tinayfas, the latter a site on the Pilcomayo where the group lived during the dry season. They traveled to the sugar plantations with the people from Mistolar and formed a single encampment where they worked and feasted together.

By the time Mayor Diaz died in 1956, the Nivaclé had begun to migrate to the Mennonite Colonies rather than to Argentina. At first these were seasonal migrations, but over the years more and more Nivaclé stayed in the Mennonite Colonies rather than face the lengthy and arduous journey back to the Pilcomayo. The Nivaclé also began to come under the influence of evangelist preachers. Choroti preachers from the Anglican mission of La Paz in Argentina and Nivaclé preachers from the area of the Mennonite Colonies warned of an imminent catastrophe that could only be averted if they settled with the Mennonites and accepted the Christian faith. At the same time, *criollo* ranchers were beginning to settle in the area along the Pilcomayo. By 1972 only five families were left in Mistolar, and eventually they too moved to the Mennonite Colonies.

When Mayor Diaz died, leadership of the Mistolar Nivaclé passed to his nephew Manuelito, who adopted the title *mayor* (major) for himself.

Even though most of the group had settled in Filadelfia, and his position as intermediary was no longer tenable—the Mennonites preferred to hire individuals or families rather than large groups of workers—Manuelito continued to exercise considerable authority, as was clearly demonstrated in the so-called revolution of 1962.

Until the 1960s the Nivaclé workers in the Mennonite Colonies lived in encampments similar to those on the Argentine sugar plantations. One of the largest was located in Filadelfia, in what is now the Barrio Obrero. The older Nivaclé remember this as a rather exciting place where they could mix with Nivaclé from different areas, take part in feasting, and listen to the evangelist preachers. The excitement, however, soon gave way to hunger, and the Nivaclé became dissatisfied as it became more difficult to find work. The situation was exacerbated by the Mennonites' refusal to allow the Indians to bring their flocks of sheep and goats to the colonies, in order to prevent them damaging the Mennonites' plantations.

The immediate cause of the disturbances was the Mennonites' heavy-handed treatment of a shaman known as Cepillo, who was arrested and accused of counterfeiting banknotes—an extraordinary charge that he may have brought on himself by claiming to be able to manufacture money. As leader of the group, Manuelito Diaz intervened personally, just as he would have done in Argentina, but the administrator of the Mennonite Colonies took no notice. This angered the Nivaclé, and when Manuelito gave the word, the entire Nivaclé population of Filadelfia abandoned their work and marched down the main street to the administrator's office, carrying firearms, machetes, and sticks. These tactics, which the Nivaclé had learned from Peronist Party activists in the Argentine sugar mills, were more successful, and Cepillo was immediately released.

The appearance of soldiers from the Sixth Division of Infantry restored calm to the Mennonite Colonies, but the Mennonites were shaken by the experience, and from 1962 onward, they pushed forward a program to settle the Indians in agricultural colonies. In the following years Manuelito and his group were settled in Yalve Sanga, and some families settled on their own initiative in Campo Nuevo, which became part of Yalve Sanga. The inhabitants of Campo Nuevo—one of the few homo-

geneous settlements in the agricultural colonies—later became disillu-
sioned. They never received definitive titles to their plots, despite making
annual payments; they felt the colony's Indian administrators were dis-
criminating against them in the allocation of tractors and other equipment; and they thought they were paying excessive contributions for
the colony's roads, schools, and stores. The conflict came to a head in
1977 when the people of Campo Nuevo, against the advice of their Mennonite advisers, took out a loan from API to finance their cotton crop.
In fact, the loan was one of the few that API ever managed to recover.
But it created a division in Yalve Sanga that was only resolved in 1980,
when the people of Campo Nuevo, along with other families from the
same group, abandoned the Mennonite Colonies and returned to their
traditional site at Mistolar.

At the time of my fieldwork, in 1982–83, the political leader of Mistolar was Siriaco Pérez. Siriaco, who had been one of the key people responsible for the community's move back to the Pilcomayo, was formally elected administrator—a title adopted from the Mennonites—a
few weeks after the Nivaclé returned to Mistolar. All the members of the
community were present at the meeting, and the decision to elect Siriaco
was virtually unanimous. The two people who were in disagreement with
the decision abandoned the colony a few days later and returned to Yalve
Sanga.

Despite the formality of the title, the role of administrator was not
a bureaucratic one. Siriaco was a leader of ideas who gave voice to the
values and aspirations of the community. This could be seen at its clearest in the community meetings held on Sundays after the church service.
Here he would make a lengthy speech in which he commented on a range
of day-to-day issues, as well as some more general moral ones.

A typical speech might begin with Siriaco reminding the community
that they chose him as administrator. If they dislike what he has to say,
they are at liberty to choose someone else. He believes it is his responsibility to call attention to the faults he sees in the community; perhaps,
he remarks, he is mistaken, and if they think his job is simply to ask fa-
vors from the authorities in Asunción, then he will keep quiet. Having
established his right to speak, he moves to concrete issues. He comments

favorably on the communal work carried out during the week. He was pleased to see that construction of the church has progressed, and that the airstrip has been cleared of weeds. Any visitors will now be able to fly in safely, and should anyone have an accident or fall dangerously ill, a plane would be able to land and take them out. He mentions the tasks that have to be carried out: the roof of the school is in need of repair; classes have to stop when it rains, and if nothing is done the roof could collapse on the children.

He then turns to more general issues. He is glad the people of Mistolar continue to share fish, game, and the produce of their gardens and have not been corrupted by the individualism of the Mennonites. Some of the Nivaclé in Yalve Sanga, he notes, have taken to selling the pigeons they have shot for ten guaranies apiece, an observation that provokes amusement from the audience. Finally, Siriaco mentions issues that involve him as intermediary between the community and the outside world. He reads the results of the tuberculosis tests and remarks that those people who have had a positive reaction should continue their treatment and shouldn't share *tereré* with others because they might pass the illness on. He also talks about the importance of maintaining the quality and traditional designs of the Nivaclé handicrafts, showing his audience a blanket that because of its unusual design—a rather lifelike head of a woman—has been impossible to sell. He then asks if there are any questions. One or two men stand up. What were the results of his last trip to Asunción? Has there been any progress in the negotiations for the land title? In general, though, there is little sign of discussion or disagreement.

Siriaco did not take charge of the communal gardens or the repair and construction of the school and church; these were the responsibility of the "leader of work." This may in part have been because Siriaco was often absent, negotiating the community's land title or purchasing supplies, but it also reflected the distinction between political leadership and the management of day-to-day activities, discussed above. There was a similar division of labor in the community store, where two young people managed the daily routine, while Siriaco handled bulk purchases and the purchase and sale of handicrafts and animal skins.

In Mistolar political leadership was distinguished from church leadership. All the members of the community, with the exception of Siriaco, professed to be Mormons—although he would confide that most had joined the sect in the hope of receiving material benefits. From time to time, Mormon missionaries from the United States would stay in the community, but since they were unable to communicate in Spanish, let alone in Nivaclé, their role was limited, and they offered little more than a bizarre spectacle when they went jogging around the village. The leaders of the church were the president of the Church Council, a position occupied by one of the many preachers, and the leader of the choir, a position that, rather surprisingly, seemed to be the cause of more jealousy than any other in the community.

Siriaco was well qualified in terms of his background and experience. He had been a key figure in Yalve Sanga, where he was a teacher, a pastor in the Mennonite church, and one of the authorities responsible for the distribution of agricultural plots. He had been one of the most active representatives in API, and in the two years before he moved to Mistolar, he had worked for the Equipo Nacional de Misiones in the Nivaclé colony of Yishinachat. He spoke fluent Spanish and had a good understanding of the ways of Paraguayan society. He was descended from influential Nivaclé leaders: his father had been one of the first Nivaclé pastors to preach in the Mennonite Colonies—his preaching had apparently attracted people by the hundreds—and he was the nephew of Manuelito Diaz, himself the nephew of Mayor Diaz. When he was young, Siriaco had studied with the Mennonites. But his background also included what he described as an education in Nivaclé culture, given by his grandparents—especially his maternal grandmother—and he was regarded as one of the most knowledgeable people of his generation as far as the more esoteric aspects of Nivaclé culture were concerned.

Siriaco was recognized as a kinsman or affine by most of the households in Mistolar, and his family occupied a key position, linking the various residential groups that were still to some extent identified with the traditional settlement sites. The location of his house in the center of the community, where the two main streets crossed, was far from accidental and provided a spatial representation of the household's genealogical position (see map 4, in chapter 6). On one side of the crossroads, situated along the street that ran parallel to the Pilcomayo, was the group from Catsajshi who were cousins of his mother. On the other side were the families that originally came from Votsopú, some of whom were kinsmen of his father and others kinsmen of his wife. Along the adjacent street, going down to the river, were the families who originally came from Ujaustiyajavat and Mistolar, including his MMB and descendants. Finally, along the same street, going inland, one found the families of Siriaco's co-affines (WZH and classificatory WZ's husbands) and their descendants.

These extensive networks of kinship were not fortuitous. They indicate that although the members of the community shared a historic identity with the site of Mistolar, the community had to some extent coalesced around Siriaco. He was able to maintain and strengthen his ties with his more distant kin and affines; many of the families in Mistolar have at some time lived with his household or with his father's household, in Filadelfia and later in Yalve Sanga. There were no distant kinsmen living in his house at the time, but the one man who had no close kin in the community had located his house next to Siriaco's and considered him a kinsman—possibly his MMZDDS. The ties with kin and affines were strengthened through the exchange of purchased foodstuffs, which Siriaco usually had in stock, for agricultural produce, fish, or game. These exchanges were not viewed as a strategy to acquire support and loyalty—the Nivaclé were well aware that an aspiring leader might try to buy their support—but were interpreted as a mark of exemplary generosity, a virtue clearly associated with legitimate leadership.

A final aspect that deserves mention is Siriaco's role as an intermediary between the community and outsiders. He had to resolve disputes with other Indians, particularly the Mataco from across the river—who from time to time had been found taking timber from Mistolar—and with the neighboring landowners and Argentine *criollos* who lived in the area. A typical dispute involved some *criollo* cattle that had strayed into a Nivaclé's garden and trampled the crops. Infuriated, the Nivaclé took his ax and split open the head of one of the cattle; the owner then appeared with a revolver in his hand and threatened to kill the Nivaclé. Siriaco was called and eventually managed to calm the Argentine down and convince him to leave the carcass as compensation for the damage to the garden. This was a vindication of Siriaco's policy of maintaining cordial relations with the *criollo* neighbors, allowing them to use the community store and letting their children attend the school in Mistolar.

The situation of Mistolar, as it was in 1982, is an example of a community that had been brought together by effective leadership. In contrast, the Chamococo settlement of Puerto Diana, as it was in the late 1970s, was characterized by the absence of any legitimate leadership, and the kin-based political factions were to some extent associated with particular sectors of the national society.

At the time of my fieldwork, the Chamococo of Puerto Diana regarded themselves as a heterogeneous group. This was as much a reflection of the ongoing political relations within the community as it was an expression of any clear historical fact. Traditionally, the Chamococo who lived on the Paraguay River were divided into two separate groups, the Horio and Ebidoso, while a third group, the Tomaraha, lived in the interior and until the 1980s had no contact with the other communities.

In the late 1970s the distinction between the Horio and Ebidoso was of little real importance, and the younger generation was generally unaware that the separate groups had ever existed, although there may have been some continuity between them and the factions that at the time divided the community. Until the 1950s the Chamococo had lived at two main sites, Puerto Leda and Puerto Esperanza, where they combined hunting, fishing, and gathering with work on the ranches and casual wage labor. Relations with the ranch owners were paternalistic: the Chamococo were given provisions and a weekly ration of beef, and some men were allowed to pasture their cattle on the ranch, although they had to use the rancher's own brand. In return, they worked for little or no payment whenever the owner needed extra hands. At least one of the ranchers also took an interest in the Chamococo girls, and many of his descendants are now living in Puerto Diana and Fuerte Olimpo.

This dependence on the ranch owners was hardly conducive to the emergence of leadership among the Chamococo. Capitán Pintura, a veteran of the Chaco War, enjoyed considerable authority among the Chamococo of Puerto Esperanza, but this may have been partly due to the relations he maintained with the naval base of Bahía Negra. In many respects it was the ranchers who exercised the most effective leadership.

In the 1950s the ranches of Esperanza and Leda were sold, and the new owners evicted most of the Chamococo. In 1955 evangelist missionaries began working in Bahía Negra, and in 1958 they had Puerto Diana reserved as a colony for the Chamococo from Esperanza. The group from Puerto Leda moved to Fuerte Olimpo and Puerto Guaraní, and in 1970 settled in the Salesian mission on the outskirts of Fuerte Olimpo.

The Chamococo of Puerto Diana expressed a desire for unity — some would have liked to see the Chamococo united in a single community where, they said, not a single Paraguayan would be allowed to enter — but in fact they were divided into various competing factions. The factions were composed of kin groups that competed for the colony's resources, for representation of the community, and for the aid provided by outside agencies. They were associated with outside interests, and the conflict between them reflected some of the tensions that existed in the national society, giving the impression that in some respects Puerto Diana was a microcosm of Paraguayan society.

It is said that power in Paraguay rests with the armed forces, the church, and the Asociación Rural — the cattlemen's association. Each of these interests was, with some minor variations, represented in Puerto Diana during the late 1970s. One of the main factions was associated with a Chamococo petty officer (*sub-oficial*), whose authority derived from the nearby naval base in Bahía Negra. The navy dominates Bahía Negra. Navy patrols police the town. The only medical treatment available is that provided by navy doctors, and the navy, through the Bahía Negra Development Commission (CODEBANE), is the major employer of casual labor in the area.

The petty officer, who was sometimes referred to by outsiders as the *cacique,* received all visitors to the community and was responsible for maintaining law and order within Puerto Diana. If necessary he could call on a patrol of armed conscripts from the naval base; at night the patrol would visit the colony on its rounds of Bahía Negra, and any drunks or other offenders would be arrested and held for a few days at the naval base. The petty officer was a veteran of the Chaco War — some Chamococo served as scouts during the war — and he received a small pension from the navy as well as a weekly supply of rations. He was also authorized to impose a fine of fifty guaranies on anyone leaving Puerto

Diana and, as far as I could ascertain, appeared to keep the money for his own use. At one time he may have enjoyed a certain legitimacy, and from time to time he would make requests to the commander of the naval base on behalf of the community. His leadership was no longer recognized outside his own extended family, however, and he was considered to be compromised by his pension and rations, while the fines and the presence of armed conscripts were regarded as an abuse of authority.

A second and rather more complex faction was associated with the evangelist missionaries. Puerto Diana, unlike some other large settlements, was not divided on religious grounds, and apart from one or two elderly practicing shamans, the members of the community were nominally evangelists. A few people, however, were more closely tied to the missionaries. The New Tribes Mission had no permanent presence in Puerto Diana, and the missionaries, two elderly ladies from the United States, spent only short periods in the community. The missionaries did not directly employ any of the Chamococo, but three men had previously been employed by the New Tribes Mission in Faro Moro and had later worked with another evangelist missionary in Eastern Paraguay. One of the men owned a small store that he had set up with funds provided by the missionaries.

None of these men, apart from the storekeeper, were economically dependent on the mission, but they relied on the missionaries for support, especially in disputes with Paraguayans. On one occasion some of the leading men in the community were arrested by the naval police and beaten, allegedly for assaulting a group of conscripts who had come into Puerto Diana at night with some Chamococo prostitutes from a neighboring bar. The Colorado Party politicians in Bahía Negra, who were always in conflict with the navy, registered a complaint, but it was the missionaries who interceded most effectively. They raised the matter with the minister of defense, and all the men were quickly released. Not long after, the commander was transferred from Bahía Negra to a minor post with the customs in Concepción. On other occasions the missionaries would intervene with employers who failed to pay their workers, and they also pressed the Ministry of Education to pay the teachers and provide books for the small school in Puerto Diana.

A third faction responded to the leadership of a retired ranch foreman who had settled in Puerto Diana. He had about eighty head of cattle, which grazed on the small area of pasture within the colony. He was no longer as dependent on his patrón as when he lived on the ranch, but he still maintained friendly relations with him; gossip had it that his daughter was the rancher's mistress. He was a capable man, familiar with the ways of the national society, and could deal with Paraguayans on equal terms. These qualities, however, were regarded rather ambivalently. He tended to adopt the same attitudes as his employers and would complain that the Chamococo were lazy and were always asking him to slaughter his cattle to provide meat for the community. The members of the other factions argued that he was self-interested and would comment that when he was a ranch foreman he never allowed them to hunt on his patrón's property. They also said that he had monopolized the pasture in the colony, and they suggested that his concern with fencing the area was motivated more by worries about his own cattle than by any desire to benefit the rest of the community.

In order to avoid antagonizing the other factions, he refrained from taking a direct interest in the day-to-day affairs of the community and allowed other members of his family to take a more active role. His son-in-law was one of the most effective representatives of Puerto Diana at API meetings, and later his son, a bright and articulate young man, represented the community at meetings in Asunción.

A final faction, less clearly tied to specific outside interests, was formed around Ramón, a leader who had come from Fuerte Olimpo in the 1970s with his extended family; he was an opportunist who tried to build up a following every time a new institution appeared in Puerto Diana. When API began working in the community, he was elected as one of the community's representatives. Ramón went to Asunción, where he was given provisions for the community, which he brought back and divided among his own close kin. Later, during the floods of 1981, he traveled to Asunción and talked the staff of INDI into providing him with emergency provisions, clothing, and a rowboat, which again he kept for his own family.

At first sight, the situations of Mistolar and Puerto Diana appear to be quite different. In Mistolar there was a tradition of strong leadership, founded on consensus and largely divorced from any outside interests. In Puerto Diana, on the other hand, there was no overall leader, and the community was divided into factions that were supported by groups from outside the community. There was, however, a unity in the system of values underlying these differences. These values, which include an emphasis on personal autonomy and a refusal to accept any form of coercion as legitimate, are perhaps seen at their most explicit in the case of Mistolar, but they were just as important in Puerto Diana.

In Puerto Diana consensus may not have been achieved, but consensus and the desire for unity were still recognized as ideals and were a fundamental element in the discourse of factionalism. In part, the lack of unity reflected the heterogeneous origins of the community, but it also responded to each faction's, and each aspiring leader's, dependence on outside interests. The desire for unity foundered on the Indians' refusal to be coerced; this could be seen at its crudest with the faction supported by the navy, but it was equally apparent with the other factions, which not only sought legitimacy from outside but also wielded some economic power. This suggests that the Chamococo were unwilling to accept any form of physical or economic coercion as legitimate, and this refusal was perhaps one of the main features that distinguished them from the rest of the regional society.

Indigenous Organizations and Economic Development

The last twenty-five years have seen an unprecedented growth of indigenous organizations in the Paraguayan Chaco. Until the early 1970s there was only limited contact between different communities and ethnic groups. The migrations to the cane fields of northern Argentina, and later to the Mennonite Colonies, brought some groups into contact. Indigenous leaders also met at the Department of Indian Affairs—INDI's predecessor—at missionary conferences, on hunting trips, or working on the ranches. Although they undoubtedly shared a sense of common identity as "Indians," there was little or no concern to establish formal relations or alliances between the different communities or territorial groups. Indeed, as I have explained above, the highest level of political organization was the community or territorial group, a fragile, transient level of organization defined principally in terms of common residence.

The first national-level indigenous organization, the Consejo Indígena del Paraguay (Indian Council of Paraguay) was set up under the auspices of the Marandú Project. In 1973 Miguel Chase Sardi had organized the Parlamento Indio del Cono Sur, a forum of Paraguayan Indians and Indian leaders from other countries in South America, including Argentina, Bolivia, and Venezuela. The forum provided an opportunity to discuss the situation of the Indian peoples of Paraguay and set out the basic position that was later taken by the Marandú Project — that is, that indigenous people should be allowed to determine their own destiny, in accordance with their own culture, values, and aspirations (Proyecto Marandú 1975). The first meetings of the Consejo Indígena were held during 1974 and 1975. The meetings were suspended for much of 1976, when Chase Sardi and his colleagues were in jail. But by the end of 1976 the council was able to acquire legal personality (*personería jurídica*), although on the condition that it adopt the title the Asociación de Parcialidades Indígenas (API).[2]

From the start, the Consejo Indígena was intended to represent all the Indians of Paraguay. Meetings were publicized in the national press; and at different times key people, including the minister of defense, representatives of various international funding agencies, and even a US undersecretary of state, were invited to address the council. The discussions varied. Initially the council provided a forum to denounce injustices and arbitrary mistreatment: murders, beatings, theft, occupation of Indian lands, nonpayment of workers, missionary prohibitions of cultural expression, and so on. The Marandú Project took up some of these causes, but perhaps more important, the meetings generated a sense that these problems were common to all the Indian communities of Paraguay and had to be addressed through concerted action. Much of the rhetoric emphasized the need for unity and in retrospect can be understood as an attempt to create a coherent vision of Indian self-identity and aspirations. The meetings also reinforced the Marandú courses and provided continuity, following up the issues and ideas that had been raised in the communities. In 1975 the Consejo Indígena became the official board of the Marandú Project, and once the statutes of API were approved, a *junta directiva* was established with a salaried president, vice president, treasurer, and secretary.

Although the Consejo Indígena was supposed to represent the Indian communities of Paraguay, the legitimacy of many of the representatives was open to question, and to this day the issue of legitimate representation remains a difficult one. Chase Sardi always acknowledged than some of the "leaders" were selected by the missionaries or simply attended on their own initiative. However, he used to argue that in the political context of the 1970s it was necessary to develop the organization from the top down, starting with a national-level organization that could create a political opening, and later developing greater organizational capacity at the community level. In the Chaco, it would certainly have been very difficult to build up the community organizations to a level where they could enjoy legitimate representation at a national level. A significant part of the population is dispersed, and the larger communities are more heterogeneous and subject to pressures from a diverse range of outside interests. Moreover, as I have already explained, the Indians of the Chaco do not accept the principles of parliamentary democracy and take all their common decisions on the basis of unanimous consent.

In 1978 I worked on an evaluation of API's *Plan Económico,* an ambitious economic development program started in 1976 that had been funded by the Inter-American Foundation. I analyzed the participation in the council meetings and found little continuity, and no clear relation, between the distribution of the representatives and the distribution of the population. There was a small core of Indian leaders who attended fairly regularly, but otherwise the representation of communities and ethnic groups often changed from one meeting to another. Some of the more accessible communities were represented by a large number of people, while many of the major populations were ignored or underrepresented.

There was, for instance, virtually no participation of the Lengua from the area of the Anglican mission. This was partly due to the missionaries' suspicion of API (the Anglican bishop of Paraguay was concerned that Chase Sardi was a communist), combined with Marandú's and API's failure to make any systematic attempt to establish a presence in the region. Moreover, much of the population was dispersed and at that period lived in fear of the ranch owners, most of whom would have been unwilling

249

to allow Indians from their ranches to attend meetings organized by API in Asunción.

There were more representatives from the area of the Mennonite Colonies, although the Nivaclé from Filadelfia and Yalve Sanga usually outnumbered the representatives from other colonies. This was largely due to the impact of the Marandú courses that had been held in Filadelfia and Yalve Sanga, and to Chase Sardi's friendship with a number of Nivaclé leaders who had worked as informants for his anthropological studies. In 1977 API tried to negotiate an arrangement with ASCIM that would allow the indigenous representatives from ASCIM's board to represent the Mennonite Colonies in API. However, the Mennonites were unwilling to accept this idea, since it would have been tantamount to accepting the legitimacy of API as the representative organization of the indigenous people of Paraguay. In fact, some of the board members regularly attended API meetings, but they came in the name of their colonies or villages rather than as representatives of ASCIM. There were also a large number of representatives from the communities where Marandú had been most active. Cerrito, situated only fifty kilometers (thirty miles) from Asunción, was always represented by the founder members from each of the three groups, the Rosarinos, Cerriteños, and Río Verde, often with others who attended out of interest or perhaps the aspiration to lead groups of their own.

The situation of the Chamococo was more complex. Over a period of two years there was very little continuity among the leaders that represented Puerto Diana, Fuerte Olimpo, and latterly Buena Vista. This was not really the fault of API's technical staff or a failure to understand how a representative institution should work. Rather, the issue was one of factionalism in communities that were, and probably still are, unwilling to accept the leadership of any single individual. The existence of API, as an institution that claimed to represent the indigenous peoples of Paraguay, accentuated divisions that already existed in communities like Puerto Diana. Aspiring leaders argued over the representation of their communities and saw participation in API as a way of legitimating their claims to leadership. Initially, one solution—which API's technical team accepted, despite the high costs involved—was to accept more than one representative from each community. This also resolved the problem of how to deal with leaders whose legitimacy was determined by outside agencies.

Initially, Puerto Diana sent two representatives: the *sub-oficial* recognized by the naval base in Bahía Negra and Ramón, who at this time was a focus of opposition to the navy and the New Tribes Mission. At the meeting to nominate the representatives of the community, it was agreed that it would be necessary to send two representatives to make sure that neither of them would "lie about the meeting." In fact, Ramón was taken ill in Asunción and stayed on for some weeks, and when he returned there was a dispute about what had actually been said in the meeting, and two other representatives were nominated to attend the next meeting. In Fuerte Olimpo, the bishop and Sister Angela organized a meeting to elect the representative who would attend the meeting, and when their preferred candidate was defeated in a secret ballot, they persuaded the Chamococo from the mission to send both the elected representative and their own candidate.

A factor that complicated the issue of representation, and that continues to hamper attempts to consolidate any regional or national indigenous organization, is the unrealistic nature of the expectations that are created. To some extent, I believe Marandú and API are to blame here, for failing to distinguish clearly between promoting the development of a truly indigenous organization, the aims of which are social, cultural, and political, from promoting economic development. However, in the late 1970s, when API was trying to establish itself as the national organization of indigenous people, there was little or no political freedom in Paraguay, and indigenous organizations were tolerated only to the extent that they refrained from challenging the established social and political order. In these circumstances, the only politically acceptable discourse was that of economic development, and after the release of Chase Sardi and his colleagues in 1976, Marandú and then API began to focus much more strongly on issues of economic development.

The antagonism between API and the various interest groups that were working with indigenous people—missionaries, Mennonites, government agencies, and even to some extent the ranchers and the military—was often expressed though promises of economic aid. There was an expectation that the aspiring indigenous leaders who attended the meetings of API would bring economic aid back to their communities. At the same time, the Mennonites and various missionary organizations also promised aid, with varying degrees of subtlety, at times combining a mixture of threats and promises. The bishop of the Alto Paraguay, for instance, offered milk cows to all the families that opted to stay in the Salesian mission in Fuerte Olimpo rather than move to API's colony in Buena Vista. Similarly, the Mennonites promoted a cattle-raising project in their colonies and also threatened to expel anyone who accepted loans from API.

This leads to a situation where economic aid is seen as a reward for political loyalty, and where a leader who fails to deliver "aid" (*ayuda*) is seen as a failure, or worse still as corrupt or compromised. This is one of the reasons for the rapid turnover of representatives. Even the most capable Indian leaders find themselves unable to satisfy the demands of their communities, and many are eventually forced to resign in disgust.

Personally, I am not inclined to believe that the insatiable demand for "aid" is an intrinsic cultural characteristic derived from a hunter-gatherer lifestyle (cf. Von Bremen 1987). Rather, I believe it has more to do with a culture of dependency, where the discourse of reciprocity is used to impose and maintain relations of inequality (see Perafán 1999). Charity becomes the counterpart of exploitation. The patrón or mission-ary provides the Indians on his ranch or mission with provisions and expects their loyalty as well as their labor. There is no question of fair wages, market forces, or employees' rights. I believe both sides usually understand this arrangement. I was initially surprised, for instance, to find that the Nivaclé of Mistolar had adopted the Mormon faith without really showing very much understanding of, or even interest in, the Mor-mons' most basic beliefs. Instead, they explained in a matter-of-fact way that the Mormons were the only group that had consistently provided their community with provisions and other support, and as a result they had all joined the Mormon Church. The issue was one of loyalty. The question of belief or faith was never raised and seems to have been of little or no importance.

From 1976 to 1978 API received over a million dollars from the Inter-American Foundation for the *Plan Económico*, and in many cases com-munities did receive significant amounts of aid, often in the form of foodstuffs, intended to develop productive projects or community infra-structure. As often happens with economic development projects, once the funds have been committed, there is pressure to develop projects and to spend the money as soon as possible. In this particular case, the time frame was completely unrealistic: two years in which to promote local-level organizations and to identify and implement productive projects that would finance the running costs of the organization. Seven agrono-mists were hired to promote productive projects, five of them in the Chaco. Some of the projects involved relocation of communities and the development of subsistence agriculture (Buena Vista, Diez Leguas, and Pedro P. Peña); others involved the development of simple productive infrastructure, such as fencing and drinking ponds; and a few, mainly in the Central Chaco, involved agricultural credit.

None of these can be said to have succeeded as economic develop-ment projects. The Nivaclé of Yalve Sanga repaid with interest the loans they had taken out for agricultural production, but the money was lost or stolen in API's office in Asunción and never became the rotating credit fund that was originally intended. The same happened with the funds for handicraft production. Even the projects for subsistence agriculture were a failure. In fact, some of these projects were completely unsuited to the conditions of the Chaco. In Buena Vista and Diez Leguas the areas that were planted had low-lying heavy clay soils that flooded when it rained and became as hard as brick when they dried out. Not only were most of these projects technically ill conceived, but few, if any, even began to address the more complex issues of how to manage collective activities. There was little attempt to develop systematic procedures to administer the funds or the provisions provided by API, or to determine how the benefits of the project should eventually be distributed.

The failure of the projects led to disputes and recrimination. Initially, many of the communities blamed the Paraguayan agronomists who had been hired by API, and eventually the systematic failure of nearly all the development projects led to a rift between the indigenous leadership of API and the technical (nonindigenous) leadership. Once the project funding ran out, most of the nonindigenous technical staff abandoned API. Some of the agronomists and other staff were sufficiently committed to stay on for a few more months, but financial circumstances eventually forced them to leave also, although one or two eventually found work in INDI.

The problems of community organization and political legitimacy have been accentuated with the passing of Law 904, the Statute of Indigenous Communities (*Estatuto de las Comunidades Indígenas*) in 1981. This law allows indigenous communities to acquire communal rights to their land, offering them the possibility of acquiring legal personality (*personería jurídica*) by registering the community's leaders in the National Register of Indigenous Communities held in INDI. Registration usually involves a visit from one of INDI's staff, who collects basic information about the community (location, population, and so on) and then holds a meeting to approve the nomination of the leaders. There is no limit on the number of leaders that can be nominated, and most communities are represented by at least three or four leaders. Once they have been included on the register, these people become the legal representatives of the community (Law 904/81, chapter I, article 12). The community can then solicit legal personality from the Office of the President of the Republic, a process that may take a year or more; once this has been completed, the title can be transferred to the community. The land titled under Law 904/81 is inalienable and cannot be used as collateral for loans.

Until 1985 the potential of this law remained unexplored, but during the late 1980s some of the Paraguayan NGOs that work with indigenous peoples, particularly Servicios Profesionales Socio-Antropológicos y Jurídicos (SPSAJ), helped various communities in Eastern Paraguay obtain legal personality and titles to their land. During the 1990s INDI began to get more directly involved. Initially, the Register of Indigenous Communities was nothing more than an exercise book kept by the personal assistant to the president of INDI, and even today there is no comprehensive database on the indigenous communities of Paraguay. However, virtually all the major indigenous communities of the Chaco have now been registered by INDI, and many have also acquired legal personality and land titles. In the Central Chaco the titles to the agricultural colonies are still held by ASCIM, and the Mennonites appear unwilling to transfer the land titles, probably because this would allow communities to break away from Mennonite control if they wanted to.

The legitimacy of the registered leaders is often open to question. This is not simply an issue of whether the officials from INDI have held meetings with all the members of the community to approve the nominations — some officials are conscientious and understand the dynamics of indigenous communities, others less so. Rather, the issue is whether any individual or group of individuals is able to represent the interests of all the sectors or factions within a particular community. The Register of Indigenous Communities legitimizes leadership in way that was previously unknown, and this can generate tension, particularly if factionalism already exists. It is true that different groups within the national society have often relied on people exercising the roles of *cacique,* capitán, or *sub-oficial* to help them manage their relations with the indigenous communities. Nowadays, however, the representatives of the community have the legal power to act on behalf of the community. They can, for instance, empower a lawyer or an NGO to represent them, and this often effectively excludes other NGOs from working with the community.

Law 904/81 is flexible enough to allow a number of leaders the chance of representing the community. Where a community is composed of a number of discrete settlements or extended families, each one can be represented. In practice, however, joint leadership rarely functions in unison, and any leader who has been registered by INDI can represent the community without necessarily receiving support from the other leaders or the rest of the community. This leads to one representative working with one NGO or missionary organization, another working with a different one, and so on. This kind of factionalism often makes it difficult for communities to organize themselves to achieve social or economic aims, and reinforces existing relations of dependency, sometimes substituting dependence on a local elite with dependence on a national-level NGO or missionary organization.

Throughout Latin America indigenous people have traditionally been excluded from the political process, and this has limited their ability to lobby for resources or political support. They have been doubly disadvantaged, as both an isolated rural population and a distinct ethnic group, with their interests often represented by NGOs or missionary organizations. In the Chaco, indigenous leaders had little or no involvement in Paraguayan politics during the thirty-four years that General Alfredo Stroessner was in power. One or two leaders achieved minor positions in local-level Colorado Party politics, including one who became the vice president of the *seccional colorado* in Mariscal Estigarribia, but this was because Mariscal is a military base with hardly any permanent "Paraguayan" population. In a few other cases indigenous people voted in local Colorado Party elections, usually in exchange for cash or goods, or to show their loyalty to a particular employer or party boss. This kind of politics had little or no relevance to them, and at best offered an opportunity to vote against local landowners who had failed to pay their workers or who denied hunters access to their ranches. Local political issues focused on personalities, not on questions of land rights or economic development, and any attempt to confront the local power structure was usually interpreted as subversion and was quickly, and sometimes brutally, repressed.

Since Stroessner was ousted 1989, the Paraguayan political system has undergone a considerable transformation. This has not always been a one-way process. There have been moments of crisis, threats, political violence, and systematic corruption, but there have also been important changes that are beginning to allow indigenous people to have some impact on the political decisions that affect them. Indigenous leaders participated in the 1992 Constitutional Assembly and helped draw up Chapter V of the Constitution, which deals with Paraguay's indigenous peoples. Chapter V recognizes that the country's indigenous peoples existed as a group with a distinct identity prior to the establishment of the Paraguayan state, and it guarantees their right to preserve and develop their culture and their habitat. It ensures their right to hold communal property; to participate in the economic, social, political, and cultural life of the country; and to have a system of education that respects their cultures (Cristaldo Montaner 1992).

As voting rolls have improved, indigenous people have become increasingly important in those areas of the country where they represent a significant proportion of the voting population. There are now three elected departmental governments (*gobernaciones*) in the Chaco, all of which to some extent depend on the indigenous vote. Many indigenous leaders, however, face a difficult choice in knowing how far they should engage in partisan political activity that is often of little relevance to their own priorities.

The increasing importance of the indigenous vote has led to the emergence of "political operators," leaders or aspiring leaders who work for local politicians, campaigning for them and making the arrangements to transport their followers to the polls. Some of the operators simply take advantage of the candidates, helping them spend their campaign funds and probably bringing little in the way of votes. Others have helped focus candidates' attention on issues that affect the indigenous population. The most positive developments seem to have taken place in the department of Boquerón (Central Chaco), which has a secretary for indigenous affairs in the departmental government. Funds from central government have been channeled through the *gobernación* into service and housing projects, and although the official discourse of the departmental government is focused on development, it has provided something of a counterweight to the Mennonite-dominated ASCIM. The departmental governments of Presidente Hayes and the Alto Paraguay also have secretaries for indigenous affairs, but so far their achievements have been limited. Indeed, both of those departmental governments have been accused of misusing the funds provided by central government, and the government of the Alto Paraguay has been suspended.

Indigenous leaders are also learning to put pressure on central government. In recent years they have organized strikes and protests outside INDI to press demands for land as well as for changes in INDI's management. At the same time, the attitudes of the national society have changed, and there is greater public support for indigenous peoples, certainly among the more educated population of Asunción and other cities. However, while the situation has improved at the national level, there is little evidence of improvement in the Indians' situation at the community level. If anything, poverty has increased, owing to inflation and the decline of the rural economy, and the political gains have not been mirrored in economic development.

This is perhaps partly due to the lack of a coherent vision of indigenous development. The present political process is one that stresses demands for aid rather than the need to develop the capacity that would allow the people of the Chaco to operate in the market economy in accor-

257

dance with their own system of moral values. Here I believe local institutional capacity is critical to achieving any sustainable social or economic development. Indeed, capacity building—rather than income or service provision—is perhaps the essence of "grassroots" development, because it moves indigenous people in the direction of being able to deal with other sectors of society on equal terms. It helps them establish direct access to resources and to use those resources in a sustainable manner. Essentially this should be a process that moves from an analysis of the community's aspirations and priorities to the proposal and finally to the implementation of solutions.

Ideally this should be the responsibility of a new generation of indigenous NGOs. Rather than claiming to represent the wishes of this or that region or ethnic group, and being dominated by indigenous political operators, these would be organizations of indigenous professionals that would offer their services to indigenous communities and their local leaders, helping them develop their skills and capacity. They would have the advantage of understanding the culture and aspirations of the indigenous communities, but they would remain independent from the local political process and would help the community achieve economic development without creating further ties of dependency.

Conclusion

IN THIS BOOK I have discussed the contemporary economy of the Chaco societies, and have argued that the principles of equality and personal autonomy provide a basis for the ethnic identity of the Indians of the Chaco and help determine how they are integrated into the regional economy. The success or failure of this enterprise is ultimately for the reader to judge, above all in terms of its analytic usefulness—that is, whether it offers a deeper insight into the nature of contemporary Chaco societies than, for example, an account phrased in terms of the "ethnographic present" or one that focuses exclusively on the external factors that determine their social and economic situation.

This approach, which highlights systems of interrelated values rather than social structure or symbolic meanings, and which as a result tends to emphasize continuity rather than change, could, I believe, be usefully applied to other areas in Lowland South America. Space does not permit an extended discussion, but some brief comments should be offered on the similarities and contrasts between the Chaco societies and other indigenous societies in Lowland South America.

The ecology of the Chaco presents similarities with other areas of the Lowlands. Land, certainly in the traditional context, was never a scarce resource, and the environment is perceived as potentially bountiful, offering a multiplicity of opportunities for subsistence. This is typical of the Lowlands, but the Chaco societies represent a rather more extreme example of dependence on immediately available resources. Hunting, fishing, honey collecting, and gathering were traditionally the mainstays of subsistence and continue to be important; nowadays they are combined with wage labor, which, I have argued, is viewed almost as another immediately available resource. Agriculture, on the other hand, is of less importance in the Chaco than in the tropical forest areas of the Lowlands and is a seasonal activity, characterized by only a limited range of crops and techniques.

Conclusion

The emphasis that the Chaco societies place on the exploitation of immediately available resources is consistent with certain features of their social organization. The pattern of settlement is more fluid than in most of the tropical societies, including the Guaraní of Eastern Paraguay (Reed 1987), the societies of the Guianas (Rivière 1984), and the Northwest Amazon (Jackson 1983). Traditionally, most communities or territorial groups would have dispersed or congregated in response to the availability of particular natural resources, and this pattern is still apparent, although the movement of population responds more to the opportunities for wage labor than to the availability of natural resources. The community or territorial group, while often associated with a particular area, is never very clearly defined or bounded. Membership in the group is simply determined by continued residence—there are no other a priori criteria for group membership—and the unity of the group is determined by political leadership as much as any other factor.

At the level of the band or residential group, one again finds considerable fluidity. In the Chaco, residential groups cannot, I believe, be characterized as corporate units that enjoy permanence over time (Overing Kaplan 1975), and their composition varies as the constituent households come and go: to exploit particular natural resources, to avoid the site where a death has occurred, or simply to move to a new spot. Despite the freedom of choice in questions of residence, a freedom consistent with the emphasis the Chaco societies give to personal autonomy, there are certain principles that underlie the composition of residential groups. Two principles, both of which are common to many areas of Lowland South America (Overing Kaplan 1975; Rivière 1984), are important here. The first is the tendency for uxorilocal residence, and the second the desire to maintain the unity of the sibling group. These tendencies can be resolved through the repetition of marriages between two or more sets of siblings, but in contrast to much of Lowland South America, the arrangement cannot be continued over the generations owing to the prohibition, apparently universal in the Chaco, on marriage between anyone defined as kin.

The absence of any kind of marriage prescription, whether moiety based or institutionalized through the use of a "two-line" terminology, is a feature that distinguishes the Chaco societies from those of the tropical forest. Instead of the stable and relatively bounded communities of the tropical forest, in which endogamy is at the very least seen as an ideal, the Chaco societies emphasize exogamy and the development of networks of bilateral kinship and affinity extending well beyond the community or territorial group. This, I believe, helps account for both the peculiarly "open" nature of the Chaco societies and for the cultural unity of the region. There are a high proportion of interethnic marriages—a feature found in many areas of the Lowlands (see Jackson 1983 on the Northwest Amazon)—and there is an ease of communication between groups that may be separated by considerable distance, by ethnic boundaries, and by major linguistic differences.

Another theme that has been stressed throughout this book is the emphasis that the Indians of the Chaco give to the interrelated conceptions of equality and personal autonomy. These ideas are widespread in Lowland South America (Rivière 1984; Clastres 1977) and are, I have argued, of critical importance for understanding the Chaco societies' political and economic organization, including their lack of concern with surplus production and their seeming predilection for wage labor. This is something that I would expect to be widespread in other areas of the Lowlands, and is an aspect that I believe has to be taken into account whenever attempts are made to formulate economic or development programs on behalf of the Indian population.

Finally, when thinking about development, it is important to appreciate that Chaco social organization is kinship based and informal and has not developed in response to the demands of the market economy. Moreover, most people are still disadvantaged in their relations with the rest of the national society by their lack of formal education. As a result, they are often excluded from development because they lack effective institutions with legal personality, or the capacity to administer funds and operate in the market economy. The indigenous organizations that have been established in the last twenty years have been supported by advocacy NGOs, and have developed from the top down, starting at a regional level and only later establishing a presence at the local level. Thus they have typically had more success in achieving political goals than in achieving social or economic development at the community level. If the indigenous communities of the Chaco are to achieve sustainable social or economic development, they need to develop the institutional capacity to manage their own programs. Indeed, sensitively managed capacity building—rather than income or service provision—is perhaps the most critical element in development. It has the potential to transform the ties of dependency and, if adequate resources are available, could eventually allow the Indians of the Chaco the possibility of being able to deal with the rest of the national society on equal terms.

Flora and Fauna

The flora are given with Spanish or Guaraní names, since the same term is likely to be used in either language. The fauna are given with English, Spanish, and Guaraní names; where only a Spanish or Guaraní name is given, it can be assumed that the same name will be used when speaking either Spanish or Jopará Guaraní.

Flora

SPANISH OR GUARANÍ NAME	SCIENTIFIC NAME
Algarrobo blanco	*Prosopis alba*
Algarrobo negro	*Prosopis nigra*
Aromita	*Acacia sp.*
Buffel (grass)	*Pennisetum ciliare*
Caña de castilla	*Arundo donax*
Caraguatá	*Bromelia sp.*
Caranday	*Copernicia alba*
Carandilla	*Trithninax bizlabellata*
Chañar	*Geoffroea decorticans*
Chuza	*Bromelia sp.* (broad-leaved species)
Coronillo	*Schinopsis quebracho-colorado*
Espartilla (grass)	*Elyonurus adustus*
Guaimí piré	*Rupretchia triflora*
Guayacán	*Caesalpina paraquariensis*
Lapacho	*Tabebuia impetiginosa*
Mbocayá (coco)	*Acrocomia totai*
Mistol	*Zizyphus mistol*
Palo blanco	*Calycophyllum multiflorum*
Palo bobo	Unidentified
Palo santo	*Bulnesia sarmientoi*
Para todo	*Tabebuia caraiba*
Payagua naranja (bola verde)	*Capparis speciosa*
Pindó	*Syagrus romanzoffiana*
Poroto del monte	*Capparis retusa*
Quebracho blanco	*Aspidosperma quebracho-blanco*
Quebracho colorado	*Schinopsis balansae*

Sachasandia	*Capparis salicifolia*
Samuhú	*Chorisia insignis*
Sipoi (Yvy'á)	*Jacaratia hassleriana*
Trébol	*Amburana cearensis*
Tuna	*Harrisia sp.*
Viñal	*Prosopis ruscifolia*

Fauna

ENGLISH	SPANISH	GUARANÍ	SCIENTIFIC NAME
Armadillo (nine-banded)		Tatu hũ	*Dasypus novemcinctus*
Armadillo (seven-banded)		Tatu poyjú	*Euphractus sexcinctus*
Armadillo (three-banded)		Tatu bolito	*Tolypeutes matacus*
Bees:			
	La Reina		*Apis mellifica*
	Rubito	Jate'i	Unidentified
		Tapesu'a	*Trigona bipunctata*
Caiman	Cocodrilo	Jacaré	*Caiman sp.*
Capybara	Carpincho		*Hydrochaeris hydrochaeris*
Charata	Charata		*Ortalis canicollis, O. pantanalensis*
Coati		Coati	*Nasua nasua*
Coypu		Kyja	*Myocastor coypus*
Deer, brocket	Venado	Guazú virá	*Mazama gouazoubira*
Deer, marsh	Ciervo		*Blastocerus dichotomus*
Deer, red brocket		Guazú pytã	*Mazama americana*
Fish, armored:			
	Armado (Vieja)		*Dores armatus, D. weddellii, D. maculatus*
	Boga		Unidentified
Catfish	Monjolo	Mandi'í	*Pimelodus charias, P. albicans, P. ornatus*
Catfish	Pastel		Unidentified
Catfish	Surubí	Surubí	*Pimelodus tigrinus*
		Dorado	*Salminus maxillosus*
		Mbusú	*Symbrachus marmoratus*
Lungfish		Mbusú capitán	*Lepidosiren paradoxa*
Pacú		Pacú	*Colossoma sp.*

264

		Pirá-mbocayá	*Hoplosternum littorale*
Piranha	Piraña	Pirãi	*Serrasalmo sp.*
	Sávalo	Carimbatá	*Prochilodus sp.*
		Tare'ỹi	*Hoplias malabaricus*
Fox	Zorro	Aguara-í	*Dusicyon sp.*
Giant anteater	Oso hormiguero	Jurumí	*Myrmecophaga tridactyla*
Iguana	Iguana	Tejú	*Teuis teyou*
Jaguar	Tigre	Jaguareté	*Panthera onca*
Margay	Tirica	Jaguareté-í	*Felis wiedi, F. tigrina*
Ocelot	Gato onza		*Felis pardalis*
Parakeet	Lorito	Ñandai	*Nandayus nenday*
Peccary, collared		Kure-í	*Tayassu tajacu*
Peccary, taguá		Taguá	*Catagonus wagneri*
Peccary, white-lipped		Tañykatí	*Tayassu pecari*
Pig	Chancho	Kuré	*Sus scrofa*
Pigeon	Palomas	Pycasú	*Columba picazuro*
		Jerutí	*Leptotila sp.*
Puma	León		*Puma concolor*
Rattlesnake	Cascabel	Mboí-chiní	*Crotalus sp.*
Rhea	Avestruz	Ñandú	*Rhea americana*
Tapir	Tapir	Mboreví	*Tapirus terrestris*
Tortoise	Tortuga	Karumbé	*Testudo denticulata*
Viscacha	Viscacha		*Lagostomus maximus*

Chaco Relationship Terminologies

1. Simplified Nivaclé Consanguineal Terminology
2. Simplified Nivaclé Affinal Terminology
3. Simplified Toba (Qom) Consanguineal Terminology
4. Simplified Toba (Qom) Affinal Terminology

1. Simplified Nivaclé Consanguineal Terminology
(First person singular possessive, male speaking)

G+2 (AND ABOVE)

Male: *Yikt'e'ech* (FF, FFB, FFF, MF, MFB, MFF etc.)

Female: *Yikt'e* (FM, FMZ, FMM, MM, MMZ, MMM etc.)

G+1
Lineal

Male: *Tata* (Father)

Female: *Mimi* (Mother)

Collateral

Male: *Yit'jo'ok* (FB, FFBS, FFZS, MB, MFBS, MFZD, etc.)

Female: *Yit'oj* (FZ, FFBD, FFZD, MZ, MFBD, MFZD, etc.)

EGO'S GENERATION
Older

Male: *Chikla* (e/B, e/FBS, e/FFBSS, e/FZS, e/MBS, e/MZS, etc.)

Female: *Chita'a* (e/Z, e/FBD, e/FFBSD, e/FZD, e/MBD, e/MZD, etc.)

Younger

Male: *Onaj* (y/B, y/FBS, y/FFBSS, y/FZS, y/MBS, y/MZS, etc.)

Female: *Sunja* (y/Z, y/FBD, y/FFBSD, y/FZD, y/MBD, y/MZD, etc.)

G-1
Lineal

Male: *Yaos* (Son)

Female: *Yiase* (Daughter)

Collateral

Male: *Yitfakl'a* (BS, FBSS, FZDS, ZS, MBSS, MZDS, etc.)

Female: *Yifakche'* (BD, FBSD, FZDD, ZD, MBSD, MZDD, etc.)

G-2 (AND BELOW)

Male: *Yitaukshich'a* (SS, SSS, BSS, ZSS, ZDS, DS, etc.)

Female: *Yitauklishe'e* (SD, SSD, BSD, ZSD, ZDD, DD, etc.)

Note: Consanguineal terminology based on Wicke and Chase Sardi 1969.

2. Simplified Nivaclé Affinal Terminology

(First person singular possessive, male speaking)

1. Wife's Kin

G+1

Male: *Yikakt'ech* (WF)

Female: *Yikakt'e* (WM)

EGO'S GENERATION

Female: *Yich'akfa* (Wife)

Male: *Yika'atjok* (WB, WFBS, etc.)

Female: *Yikaut'oj* (WZ, WFBD, etc.)

G-1

Male: *Yazanach* (Stepson, WZS, WBS, etc.)

Female: *Yazanche* (Stepdaughter, WZD, WBD, etc.)

2. Spouses of Ego's Kin

G+1

Male: *Yinjayas'a* (Stepfather, FZH, MZH, etc.)

Female: *Yinjaozo'a* (Stepmother, FBW, MBW, etc.)

EGO'S GENERATION

Male: *Yifakl'u* (ZH, FBDH, MZDH, etc.)

Female: *Yifaklis'a* (BW, FBSW, MZSW, etc.)

G-1

Male: *Yitaumit'a* (DH)

Female: *Yitaumite'e* (SW)

3. Simplified Toba (Qom) Consanguineal Terminology

G+2 (AND ABOVE)

Male: *Iapi* (FF, FFB, FFF, MF, MFB, MFF, etc.)

Female: *Come'* (FM, FMZ, FMM, MM, MMZ, MMM, etc.)

G+1
Lineal

Male:	*Tade'* (Father)
Female:	*Cheda'* (Mother)
	Iate' ("Mamá")

Collateral

Male:	*Tesqo'lec* (FB, FFBS, FFZS, MB, MFBS, MFZS, etc.)
Female:	*Sodo'le'* (FZ, FFBD, FFZD, MZ, MFBD, MFZD, etc.)

EGO'S GENERATION
Older

Male:	*Pichaqo'olec* (e/B, e/FBS, e/FFBSS, e/FZS, e/MBS, etc.)
Female:	*Pilo'ole* (e/Z, e/FBD, e/FFBDD, e/FZD, e/MBD, etc.)

Younger

Male:	*Noqolec* (y/B, y/FBS, y/FFBSS, y/FZS, y/MBS)
Female:	*No'ole* (y/Z, y/FBZ, y/FFBSD, y/FZD, y/MBD)

G-1
Lineal

Male:	*Ialec* (Son)
Female:	*Iale* (Daughter)

Collateral

Male:	*Iasoshic* (BS, FBSS, FZDS, ZS, MBSS, MZDS, etc.)
Female:	*Iasoshi* (BD, FBSD, FZDD, ZD, MBSD, MZDD, etc.)

G-2 (AND BELOW)

Male/Female	*Laual* (SS, SSS, BSS, ZSS, ZDS, DS; SSD, BSD, ZSD, ZDD, DD, etc.)

4. Simplified Toba (Qom) Affinal Terminology

A. Immediate Affines

G+1

Male:	*Lacho'* (WF)
Female:	*Lachodo'* (WM)

EGO'S GENERATION

Male:	*Lamoxoua* (Husband)
Female:	*Ca'lhua* (Wife)
	Cadapettagua' ("With whom one argues")

G-1

Male:	*Ladonanec* (DH)

269

Female: *Ladonana* (sw)

G-2

Male: *Ca laual ladonanec* (ssw, dsw)

Female: *Aca laual ladonana* (sdh, ddh)

B. Affines of Kin, and Kin of Affines

G+2 (AND ABOVE)

Male: *Iapi* (wff, wmf; fmh, mmh; fmzh, mmzh, etc.)

Female: *Come'* (wfm, wmm; ffw, mfw; ffbw, mmbw, etc.)

G+1, EGO'S GENERATION

Male: *Ledaua* (fzh, mzh; zh, fbdh, mbdh; wb, wfbs, etc.)

Female: *Lauete* (fbw, mbw; bw, fbsw, mbsw; wz, wfz, etc.)

G-1

Male: *Iasoshic* (bdh, zdh; wbs, wzs, etc.)

Female: *Iasoshi* (bsw, zsw; wbd, wzd, etc.)

Note: The terms *Iapi, Come', Iasoshic,* and *Iasoshi* are also used for consanguineal kin (see part 3).

Indigenist Organizations
Working in the Chaco

Asociación de Parcialidades Indígenas

API, the Paraguayan Indian Association, is the Indians' own organization. It developed out of the Consejo Indígena (Indian Council) set up by the Marandú Project in 1974 and was formally constituted in 1976. The Marandú Project was started in 1973 by anthropologists from the Catholic University of Asunción and was intended to provide Indian leaders with information about their legal rights. It involved the presentation of courses in Indian communities and support for the Consejo Indígena, which met in Asunción. In 1975 Marandú came to a halt when the director, Miguel Chase Sardi, and four of his colleagues were arrested and tortured for being subversives. The university withdrew its support for the project, but after considerable international protest, the staff of the Marandú Project was released, and the council was given *personería jurídica* as the Asociación de Parcialidades Indígenas.

In 1977 API received a grant from the Inter-American Foundation for its *Plan Económico,* an ambitious program that included the purchase of land for Indian settlements, technical and financial assistance for these and other colonies, and a credit program. Two properties were acquired for the settlement program in the Chaco—Buena Vista and Diez Leguas—both of which, though still populated, have never developed the independent economic base that was originally intended. The other components of the plan, the technical assistance and credits, seem to have had little impact on the Indians' economic situation and, if anything, have stimulated the expectation that projects are another resource to be exploited by the Indians (Von Bremen 1987).

Since 1979 API has had to manage on a limited budget, without the support of any nonindigenous staff. It has concentrated on lobbying at a national level and on building up its organization at regional and local levels. It has a building in Luque, just outside Asunción, where Indians can stay when they are visiting the city, and its staff, who are elected by an assembly of indigenous leaders, spend much of their time assisting Indian leaders in their negotiations with official institutions. Some of the members of API receive salaries from INDI, and INDI provides supplies for the Indians who are visiting Asunción.

Asociación de Servicios de Cooperación Indígena y Mennonita

ASCIM is the Mennonite agency responsible for the Indian colonization schemes in the Central Chaco. The first of the agricultural colonies, Yalve Sanga, was established under the auspices of the Mennonite Mission, Luz a los Indígenas (Light for the Indians), but in 1961 responsibility for the colonization programs passed to the Indian Settlement Board, leaving the mission free to concentrate on religious matters. In 1976, in response to the growing demand for Indian participation in the administration of the programs, the organization was restructured and became ASCIM, with Indian and Mennonite representatives on the board, although Mennonites have the deciding vote. ASCIM employs over sixty Mennonite staff and is involved in health and education programs as well as economic programs, which cover technical and financial assistance for agriculture and stock raising and the marketing of handicrafts.

Asociación Indigenista del Paraguay

AIP, the Paraguayan Indigenist Association, was founded in 1942 by General Juan Belaieff. Essentially a philanthropical association, it held the title to the Colonia Mak'a and in the 1970s became a cosponsor, along with the Misión de Amistad, of Proyecto Pai Tavytera and Proyecto Guaraní, projects that were concerned primarily with securing land rights for the Guaraní of Eastern Paraguay.

In the 1980s AIP sponsored Proyecto Ayoreo and Proyecto Ñandeva Guaraní. Proyecto Ayoreo led to a settlement program for an independent group of Ayoreo, who returned to their traditional territory near Cerro Chovoreca and have now acquired title to some 20,000 hectares (50,000 acres). Proyecto Ñandeva Guaraní led to the resettlement of various groups of Ñandeva Guaraní who lived in the worker villages of the Mennonite Colonies. One group settled in Laguna Negra, a property jointly purchased by ascim and enm and another in Infante Rivarola, close to the Bolivian frontier.

aip also provides legal aid and publicity and coordinates with other groups working on behalf of the Indian population.

Equipo Nacional de Misiones

enm, established in 1979, is the agency of the Paraguayan Episcopal Conference responsible for coordinating the programs of the Catholic missions that work with Indians in Paraguay. In the Chaco these include the Franciscans, the Oblates of Maria, and the Salesians, and in Eastern Paraguay, the Divine Word Order.

enm has been funded, mainly by German church organizations, and has a small staff, including a lawyer and an anthropologist. It has taken an active role in negotiating land rights and has been directly involved in settlement programs, including Yishinachat, Casanillo, and Riacho Mosquito. enm has provided funds for the purchase of land in Casanillo, San José, and Esperanza (Angulo-kué).

Instituto de Bienestar Rural

Although not an indigenist organization, ibr, the Institute for Agrarian Reform, deserves mention, since it is responsible, along with indi, for ensuring Indian communities' rights to land. It is empowered to reserve and grant title to the fiscal (unoccupied or state-owned) lands on which Indian communities are settled. It also has the power to expropriate privately owned lands for Indian communities, using either the legislation from the various Indian laws (904/81, 1372/88, or 43/90) or the *prescripción treintenaria*. So far the only successful expropriation in the Chaco has been Riacho Mosquito, expropriated from the Casado company; other expropriations are now being negotiated on behalf of the Lengua, Sanapaná, and Angaité who live on the property of the Estancia Colón.

Instituto Paraguayo del Indígena

indi is the government agency responsible for Indian affairs. It is an autonomous agency that used to come under the Ministry of Defense but has been under the administrative authority of the Ministry of Education since 1995. It was originally established in the 1950s as the Departamento de Asuntos Indígenas, under Defense, but became the focus of international criticism for its treatment of the Aché in the Colonia Nacional Guayaki. In 1976 the institution was restructured as the Instituto Nacional del Indígena INDI and was given responsibility for coordinating all indigenist activity in Paraguay.

With the passing of Law 904/81, *Estatuto de las Comunidades Indígenas,* in 1981, the organization was once again restructured, given its present title, and became an independent body (*entidad autarquica*), financed from a series of special taxes. It now has a staff of over one hundred and an annual budget of more than US$1 million, only part of which, however, has been disbursed by the Ministry of Finance in the last few years.

INDI is responsible for registering Indian communities, soliciting their legal personality, and acquiring land for communities that lack legal title. The institution provides some basic services, including legal support, agricultural extension, and visits by medical staff, but has few trained staff and lacks the organization and resources necessary to provide effective coverage. The institution coordinates activities such as health, education, and documentation (identity cards) with the respective ministries, and is empowered to monitor the activities of the NGOs and missionary organizations that work in Indian communities. In 1981 INDI carried out the national Indian census, in collaboration with the Paraguayan census department and with financial and technical assistance from the United Nations Fund for Population Activities.

Notes

1. Victor Hugo Cárdenas was vice president of Bolivia from 1994 to 1998 and was later president of the Indigenous Peoples Fund. He is Aymara, from the department of La Paz.

2. For information on infant mortality, see Fulvia Brizuela de Ramírez in INDI 1982.

3. For example, Volker von Bremen 1987. This is a thoughtful, well-written paper, but it is often unfairly cited as a justification for not attempting to implement development programs in indigenous communities. Von Bremen is generally believed to have argued that the Indians of the Chaco view development projects as yet another resource to be exploited.

4. See Geertz's (1998) review of Paul Auster's translation of Clastres's *Chronicle of the Guayaki Indians* (1972; trans. 1998). Geertz describes Clastres as "a romantic pilgrim on a self-testing Quest, confronting the Ultimate Other down deep in the jungle ('I had really arrived among Savages,' Clastres writes, 'The enormous gap . . . between us . . . made it seem impossible for us ever to understand one another')."

5. The Chiripa-Guaraní of Itanaramí, for example, have close relatives living in the Guaraní communities on the Brazilian side of the border. Richard Reed, personal communication.

6. These are fairly neutral terms and are used by Indians and Paraguayans. The term *indígena* is more formal, while the term *paisano,* literally "fellow countryman," is more likely to be heard in rural areas. In contrast, the word *indio* is derogatory and is regarded as an insult among Paraguayans.

7. I use "ethnic Paraguayan" to translate the idea of *Paraguayo* as used by most Indians and Paraguayans. It refers to the largely bilingual, Spanish- and Guaraní-speaking population of Paraguay, of mainly *mestizo* origin. Unlike indigenous societies, ethnic Paraguayans are clearly divided into social classes, seen at their crudest in the Chaco, where most Paraguayans are either *pobres,* poor landless laborers, or *patrones,* wealthy landowners. People from largely endogamous immigrant groups, such as the Mennonites, Koreans,

275

and Taiwanese, are not regarded as ethnic Paraguayans, even though they may be Paraguayan nationals.

8. Despite considerable effort, the 1981 Indian census managed to locate only 150 Indians, from the Chaco and Eastern Paraguay, who were resident in Asunción. Since the 1980s the indigenous population of Asunción appears to have increased dramatically, although many families, such as the Chamococo from Fuerte Olimpo and Bahía Negra, come and go between Asunción and their communities of origin.

9. See Renshaw 1976 for a description of the Marandú course in Puerto Casado and subsequent events.

10. There are virtually no ethnographic monographs in Spanish either. Bórmida and Califano's (1978) book on the Ayoreo is perhaps an exception, but it is based on interviews with informants and secondary sources, rather than on conventional anthropological fieldwork.

1. THE ENVIRONMENT AND POPULATION

1. The figures are 0.8 persons per square kilometer (2 persons per square mile) in Presidente Hayes, 0.29 persons per square kilometer (0.75 persons per square mile) in Boquerón, and 0.14 people per square kilometer (0.36 people per square mile) in the Alto Paraguay.

2. See López et al. 1987. The scientific names of the flora and fauna are shown in appendix 1.

3. *Ley 904/81, Estatuto de las Comunidades Indígenas.*

2. THE SUBSISTENCE ECONOMY

1. Redford and Eisenberg 1992.

2. Kempff Mercado 1985.

3. AGRICULTURE AND LIVESTOCK

1. Yalve Sanga, Campo Alegre, Campo Largo, La Esperanza, Nich'a Toyish, Paz del Chaco, and Pozo Amarillo. Since 1981 other colonies have been established at Armonía Laguna (Laguna Millón), Laguna Negra, and Campo Loa.

6. HOUSEHOLD AND KIN

1. The conventional kinship abbreviations are F = father, M = mother, B = brother, z = sister, s = son, D = daughter, w = wife, and H = husband. Thus FBS would be father's brother's son, FFBSS would be father's father's brother's son's son, and so on.

2. This contrasts with the Gê-speaking societies of Central Brazil, such as the

Shavante (Maybury Lewis 1967) and the Kayapo (Turner 1979), among whom uxorilocal residence is described as an obligatory practice. In the Gê societies the father is described as having considerably more control over his daughter and son-in-law than in the Chaco.

3. See also Clastres 1972:179 on the Aché.

4. The terminology is based on Wicke and Chase Sardi 1969 and was checked with informants from Filadelfia and Mistolar. The terms are given in the first person singular possessive ("my father . . . etc.") and are the terms used by men. They do not include the "mourning terms" used to address certain categories of kin and affines when they have lost a child, nor the terms used by coresident affines.

7. THE COMMUNITY AND POLITICAL LEADERSHIP

1. Story told by Pedro Ozuna, March 1978.

2. I believe the minister of defense, General Marcial Samaniego, was responsible for the change of name. The idea was to prevent API from becoming an organization that would formally represent the Indians of Paraguay. However, by the time Law 904 was approved in 1981, API was accepted as the organization that represented the Indian population, and the president of API was given a seat on the council of INDI.

Glossary

The orthography of Guaraní follows Melia, Farré, and Pérez 1992. The orthography of Ayoreo follows the New Tribes Mission's "Ayoreo Pedagogical Grammar" (n.d.).

Anabsonro (Chamococo)	The mythical beings who taught the Chamococo how to initiate young men. They are reenacted by masked dancers in the initiation ceremony.
anco (Spanish)	A variety of pumpkin.
anda'í (Guaraní)	A variety of pumpkin.
aphangak (Lengua)	A term used by Grubb (1911) to refer to the Lengua concept of the soul or spirit of the dead.
Aristócrata (Spanish)	An upmarket brand of *caña* (rum).
asuté (Ayoreo)	A leader whose status is acquired through killing.
baja (Spanish)	A military discharge book, often used as a personal identity document.
barrio (Spanish)	An urban neighborhood. In the Mennonite Colonies the *barrios obreros* are urban Indian settlements, referred to in English as "worker villages."
cacique (Spanish)	A "chief," usually a political leader.
caña (Spanish)	Cane spirit.
cañada (Spanish)	A dry riverbed.
capataz (Spanish)	A foreman.
capitán (Spanish)	A "captain," a leader of a work party in the cane fields or sugar mills of Argentina.
caraguatá (Guaraní)	Spiny-leaf plant of the *Bromelia* genus; the fibers are used for making string.
caranday (Guaraní)	Species of palm (*Copernicia alba*), typical of the grasslands of the Lower Chaco.
catre (Spanish)	A bed sprung with wire or rawhide.

cecina (Spanish)	*Charqui.* Meat cut into strips and dried.
cédula (Spanish)	A national identity card.
cerco (Spanish)	A garden enclosure, built of poles or brushwood.
chacheriñane (Ayoreo)	Literally "playing together"—a team game that mimics the use of the lance and club.
chamamé (Spanish)	An Argentine folk dance with a slow rhythm believed to be derived from indigenous harvesting songs.
changa (Spanish)	Any temporary wage labor; usually paid on a piece-rate basis. A *changador* is a person who lives from temporary wage labor.
cheque (Ayoreo)	An adult woman.
chicha (Spanish)	Fermented drinks of algarrobo, maize, or honey.
CODEBANE (acronym)	Comisión de Desarrollo de Bahía Negra. The Bahía Negra Development Commission.
comisario (Spanish)	A police chief.
consejo local (Spanish)	A local community council. Most were established under the auspices of API.
contratista (Spanish)	Literally a subcontractor. Often used to describe any temporary contract laborer paid on a piece-work basis.
criollo (Spanish)	In the Paraguayan Chaco the term is used to describe the Argentine settlers who live along the Upper Pilcomayo.
cuchárai, pl. *cucharane* (Ayoreo)	
	An Ayoreo patriclan (described in chapter 6).
disiode (Ayoreo)	Boys' peer group (6 to 15 years old).
edopasai, pl. *edopasade* (Ayoreo)	
	A clan "possession."
espartillar (Spanish)	An area of natural grassland covered by espartilla grass (*Elyonurus adustus*).
estanciero (Spanish)	Ranch hand who works on horseback, usually paid monthly.
faja (Spanish)	A wide woolen or cotton belt worn around the waist for support and protection.
fariña (Spanish)	Coarse manioc flour.
fija (Spanish)	A lance or harpoon, usually tipped with a steel point.
Fisoc'oyich (Nivaclé)	The Creator.

Glossary

gapu (Ayoreo)	Adolescent girls and young unmarried women.
-gosode (Ayoreo)	Literally "people." As a suffix it usually refers to a territorial group or community such as the Garaigosode ("people of the grasslands").
guebe (Ayoreo)	Literally "iron." A lance tipped with a machete blade.
guiguijnai, pl. *guiguijnane* (Ayoreo)	
	Traditional dwelling of the Ayoreo, constructed in their semipermanent summer villages.
hi-arandú-ha (Guaraní)	Shaman. Literally a "person of knowledge."
iguios (Ayoreo)	Fellow clan member (see chapter 6).
indígena (Spanish)	Indigenous person, Indian.
indio (Spanish)	Indian. The word is offensive and is used as an insult.
jangauck (Lengua)	Soul or shade (Loewen 1964).
jnacariode (Ayoreo)	Adolescent and young unmarried men.
Jnani Bajade (Ayoreo)	The "First People"—beings that were both Ayoreo and animal or plant species, material objects, and so on.
jnanione (Ayoreo)	Mature adult men.
Jopará Guaraní	The Guaraní spoken by the Paraguayan population and many of the Indians of the Chaco, with its intermixture of Spanish loan words (*jopará* means "mixed").
lecheguana (Spanish)	Wasp honey.
lenguaraz (Spanish)	Assistant to a *capitán* in the cane fields of Argentina.
lhavelh (Nivaclé)	Kindred or a kinsman.
lhcaanvaclé (Nivaclé)	Traditional warrior leader whose status was achieved by taking scalps.
libre (Spanish)	Mode of payment that includes either meals or a weekly ration.
locro (Spanish)	A variety of white maize, dried and used in soups or stews, which are also called *locro.*
mayor (Spanish)	"Major." A title adopted by some Nivaclé leaders.
mboriahú (Guaraní)	Poor. *Mboriahú porte:* "the way the poor behave."
minifundia (Spanish)	Smallholdings.
mochapi, pl. *mochapiode* (Ayoreo)	
	A raised platform of poles for sleeping.

281

Glossary

monte (Spanish)	Scrubland or forest.
ojnai (Ayoreo)	Literally "needle." A throwing spear tipped with a sharpened steel rod.
paisano (Spanish)	Literally "fellow countryman." Used in the sense of "Indian" by rural Paraguayans and Indians.
pariente (Spanish)	Kin or kinsman/woman.
partija (Spanish)	An arrangement whereby the owner of livestock leaves his animals in the charge of another, who in payment receives a portion of the offspring.
patrón (Spanish)	"Boss" or employer.
pedopicaidie (Ayoreo)	A clan mark of the Cutamoraja: a series of parallel lines, frequently used as a design on string bags.
personería jurídica (Sp.)	Legal personality.
playero (Spanish)	Ranch hands who do not work on horseback but who are engaged in menial tasks: collecting firewood, milking cows, or preparing equipment.
pochy (Guaraní)	Anger or a lack of self-control.
polverín (Spanish)	Species of tiny sandfly.
poncho (Spanish)	Describes a kind of camouflage, of vines or leaves, worn when hunting.
prescripción treintenaria (Sp.)	
	A law that entitles anyone who has continuously lived on and worked a plot of land for 30 years.
seccional colorado (Spanish)	
	The local-level headquarters of the ruling Colorado Party. It plays a major role in the economic and social life of most small towns and urban neighborhoods.
sub-oficial (Spanish)	Noncommissioned officer.
tereré (Guaraní)	An infusion of yerba maté and cold water, drunk through a metal straw (*bombilla*).
tierras fiscales (Spanish)	State-owned land (i.e., all land that is not privately owned).
troja (Spanish)	Store for maize, raised off the ground and usually constructed of poles.
vale (Spanish)	Credit note.
vanmongcama (Lengua)	The "living soul" of a person (Loewen 1964).
velha tolh'e (Nivaclé)	Group of coresident kin or affines.

yacote (Ayoreo)	"My wife." Used reciprocally between members of certain paired clans.
yerba maté (Spanish)	Dried and crushed leaves and stems of *Ilex paraguayensis*. Used as an infusion with hot or cold water (maté or *tereré*).

Bibliography

Alvarsson, Jan-Åke. 1988. *The Mataco of the Gran Chaco: An Ethnographic Account of Change and Continuity in Mataco Socio-Economic Organization.* Uppsala Studies in Cultural Anthropology. Uppsala.

Anderson, Norman. 1984. "The Form of Chiripa Behaviour: A Beginning." Mimeographed.

Belaieff, Juan. 1963. "The Present Day Indians of the Gran Chaco." In Steward 1963.

Bernand, Carmen. 1970. "Les Ayoré du Chaco Septentrional." Ph.D. thesis, Collège de France, Paris.

Bórmida, Marcelo, and Mario Califano. 1978. *Los Indios Ayoreo del Chaco Boreal.* Buenos Aires: Fundación para la Educación, la Ciencia y la Cultura.

Cadogan, León. 1971. *Ywyra Ñeery: Fluye del árbol la palabra.* Asunción: Centro de Estudios Antropológicos de la Universidad Católica "Nuestra Señora de la Asunción."

Cárdenas, Victor Hugo. 1997. "Indigenous Peoples, Development and Democracy in Latin America." Address given at the Inter-American Development Bank, Washington DC.

Chase Sardi, Miguel. 1970. "El concepto Nivaclé del alma." *Suplemento Antropológico* 5, nos. 1–2.

———. 1971. "La situación actual de los indígenas del Paraguay." *Suplemento Antropológico* 6, nos. 1–2. English translation in Dostal 1972.

———. 1981. *Pequeño decamerón Nivaclé.* Asunción: Ediciones NAPA.

———. 1990. *Situación sociocultural, económica, jurídico-política actual de las comunidades indígenas en el Paraguay.* Asunción: CIDSEP.

Clastres, Pierre. 1962. "Échange et pouvoir: Philosophie de la chefferie indienne." *L'Homme* 2, no. 1.

———. 1972. *Chronique des indiens Guayaki.* Collection Terre Humaine. Paris: Plon. Published in English as *Chronicle of the Guayaki Indians.* Translated by Paul Auster. London: Faber and Faber; New York: Zone Books, 1998.

———. 1977. *Society against the State.* Oxford: Basil Blackwell. Originally published as *La société contre l'état.* Paris: Editions Minuit, 1974.

Collier, Jane F., and Michelle Z. Rosaldo. 1981. "Politics and Gender in Simple Societies." In *Sexual Meanings*, ed. Sherry B. Ortner and Harriet Whitehead. Cambridge: Cambridge University Press.

Cristaldo Montaner, J. D. 1992. *Nueva política con la constitución nacional.* Asunción: Universidad Católica.

Crocker, John Cristopher. 1985. *Vital Souls.* Tucson: University of Arizona Press.

Dirección General de Estadistica, Encuestas y Censos (DGEC). 1992. *Censo nacional de población y viviendas 1992 (cifras provisorias).* Asunción: DGEC.

Dobrizhoffer, Martin. 1822. *An Account of the Abipones, an Equestrian People of Paraguay.* Translated by Sara Coleridge from the Latin original of 1784. 3 vols. London. Also published in Spanish as *Historia de los Abipones.* Translated by Edmundo Wernicke. Resistencia, Argentina: Universidad Nacional del Nordeste, 1967.

Dostal, W., ed. 1972. *The Situation of the Indian in South America: Contributions to the Study of Inter-ethnic Conflict in the Non-Andean Regions of South America.* Publications of the Department of Ethnology, University of Berne, no. 3. Geneva: World Council of Churches.

Escobar, Ticio. 1988. *Misión: Etnocidio.* Comisión de Solidaridad con los Pueblos Indígenas. Asunción: RP Ediciones.

Fischermann, Bernd. 1976. "Los Ayoreode." Pp. 67–118 in Riester 1976.

Foley, Robert. 1982. "A Reconsideration of the Role of Predation on Large Mammals in Tropical Hunter-Gatherer Adaptation." *Man* 17, no. 3.

Fortes, Meyer. 1969. *Kinship and the Social Order.* Chicago: Aldine.

Freire, Paulo. 1970. *Pedagogy of the Oppressed.* New York: Herder and Herder.

———. 1973. *Education for Critical Consciousness.* New York: Seabury.

Geertz, Clifford. 1998. "Deep Hanging Out." Review of Clastres's *Chronicle of the Guayaki Indians. New York Review of Books,* 22 October.

Gonzalez, Gustavo. 1968. "Entre los Guaraní-Chané (o Ñanagua) del Noroeste Chaqueño." *Suplemento Antropológico* 3, nos. 1–2.

Gorham, J. Richard, ed. 1973. *Paraguay: Ecological Essays.* Miami: Academy of the Arts and Sciences of the Americas.

Grubb, W. Barbrooke. 1911. *An Unknown People in an Unknown Land.* London: Seeley and Co. Citations are to 4th ed., 1925.

Grunberg, Georg, and Friedl Grunberg. 1974. "Los Chiriguanos (Guaraní Occidentales) del Chaco Central Paraguayo." *Suplemento Antropológico* 9, nos. 1–2.

Hack, Henk. 1978–80. "Indios y Mennonitas en el Chaco Paraguayo." *Suplemento Antropológico* 13, nos. 1–2; 14, nos. 1–2; 15, nos. 1–2.

Henley, Paul. 1982. *The Panare: Tradition and Change on the Amazonian Frontier.* New Haven: Yale University Press.

Holmberg, Allan R. 1950. *Nomads of the Long Bow: The Siriono of Eastern Bolivia.* Washington DC: Smithsonian Institute.

Hunt, R. J. 1915. *El Choroti o Yofuaha.* Revista del Museo de la Plata, Tomo 23. Reprint ed. Liverpool: Henry Young and Sons.

Instituto Paraguayo del Indígena (INDI). 1982. *Censo y estudio de la población indígena del Paraguay 1981.* Asunción: INDI.

Jackson, Jean E. 1983. *The Fish People.* Cambridge: Cambridge University Press.

Kempff Mercado, Noel. 1985. *Aves de Bolivia.* La Paz: Editorial Gisbert.

Kidd, Stephen. 1992. "Informe sobre las comunidades indígenas Lengua-Sanapaná-Angaité (Zona Anglicana)." Asunción: CEDHU. Mimeographed.

Klein, Harriet E. Manelis, and Louisa R. Stark. 1977. "Indian Languages of the Paraguayan Chaco." *Anthropological Linguistics,* November.

Laino, Domingo. 1989. *De la independencia a la dependencia.* Asunción: Inter-Continental Editora. First published in 1976.

Lévi-Strauss, Claude. 1964. *Totemism.* Translated by Rodney Needham. London: Merlin.

Loewen, Jacob A. 1964. "The Lengua: The People of the Innermost." Ph.D. thesis, University of Kansas.

López, Juan Alberto, et al. 1987. *Arboles comunes del Paraguay: Ñande yvyra mata kuera.* Asunción: Cuerpo de Paz.

Lussagnet, Suzanne. 1961–62. "Vocabulaires Samuku, Morotoko, Poturero et Guaranoca precédés d'une étude historique et géographique sur les anciens Samuku du Chaco bolivien et leurs voisins." *Journal de la Société des Americanistes* 50, 51.

Maybury Lewis, David. 1967. *Akwë-Shavante Society.* Oxford: Clarendon Press.

Maybury Lewis, David, and James Howe. 1980. *The Indian Peoples of Paraguay: Their Plight and Their Prospects.* Cultural Survival Special Report no. 2. Cambridge MA: Cultural Survival.

Meillassoux, Claude. 1981. *Maidens, Meal and Money.* Cambridge: Cambridge University Press.

Melia, Bartomeu. 1991. *El Guaraní: Experiencia religiosa.* Biblioteca Paraguaya de Antropología. Asunción: CEADUC-CEPAG.

Melia, Bartomeu, Luis Farré, and Alfonso Pérez. 1992. *El guaraní a su alcance.* Asunción: Centro de Estudios Paraguayos.

Metraux, Alfred. 1963. "Ethnography of the Chaco." In Steward 1963.

Miller, Elmer S. 1967. "Pentecostalism among the Argentine Toba." Ph.D. thesis, University of Pittsburgh.

———. 1995. *Nurturing Doubt: From Mennonite Missionary to Anthropologist in the Argentine Chaco.* Urbana: University of Illinois Press.

Miraglia, Luigi. 1975. "Caza, recolección y agricultura entre los indígenas del Paraguay." *Suplemento Antropológico* 10, nos. 1–2.

Nash, June. 1979. *We Eat the Mines and the Mines Eat Us: Dependency and Exploitation in Bolivian Tin Mines.* New York: Columbia University Press.

Nimuendajú (Unkel), Curt. 1978. *Los mitos de creación y de destrucción del mundo como fundamentos de la religión de los Apapokuva-Guaraní.* Edited by Jürgen Riester, based on an unpublished translation by Juan Francisco Recalde. Lima, Peru: Centro Amazónico de Antropología y Aplicación Práctica. Originally published in German in *Zeitschrift für Ethnologie*, 1914.

Nordenskiöld, Erland. 1912. *La vie des indiens dans le Chaco.* Translated by H. Beuchat. *Revue de Géographie* 6, no. 3. Originally published in Swedish as *Indianlif i El Gran Chaco (Südamerika).* Stockholm, 1910. Also published in German as *Indianerleben, El Gran Chaco (Südamerika).* Leipzig, 1912.

———. 1919. *An Ethno-geographical Analysis of the Material Culture of Two Indian Tribes in the Gran Chaco.* Comparative Ethnographic Studies, vol. 2. Göteborg.

Overing Kaplan, Joanna. 1975. *The Piaroa.* Oxford: Clarendon Press.

Perafán, Carlos César. 1999. *Impacto de cultivos ilicitos en pueblos indígenas: El caso de Colombia.* Washington DC: Inter-American Development Bank (SDS/IND).

———. 2000. "Adecuación de servicios financieros a las economías tradicionales indígenas." Washington DC: Inter-American Development Bank (SDS/IND).

Proyecto Marandú. 1975. *Por la liberación del indígena.* Buenos Aires: Ediciones del Sol.

Redford, Kent H., and John F. Eisenberg. 1992. *Mammals of the Neotropics.* Vol. 2: *The Southern Cone.* Chicago: University of Chicago Press.

Reed, Richard. 1987. "Indians' Work in the White Man's World: Chiripa Communities and Paraguay's Extractive Frontier." Ph.D. thesis, Harvard University.

———. 1991. "Household Ethnicity, Household Consumption—Commodities and the Guaraní." Paper presented at the AAA Annual Meeting, Chicago.

Reichel-Dolmatoff, G. 1976. "Cosmology as Ecological Analysis: A View from the Rain Forest." *Man* 11, no. 3.

Renshaw, John C. 1976. "The Marandú Project." *Survival International Review,* Summer.

———. 1988. "Property, Resources, and Equality among the Indians of the Paraguayan Chaco." *Man* 23, no. 2.

———. 1997. *Encyclopedia of Vernacular Architecture of the World.* S.v.v. "Gran Chaco," "Ayoreo," "Guaraní," "Nivaclé," and "Toba." Oxford: Basil Blackwell.

Ribeiro, Darcy. 1971. *Fronteras indígenas de la civilización.* Siglo 21. Mexico City: Editores SA. Originally published as *Os índios e a civilizacão: A integracão das populacões indígenas no Brasil moderno.* Rio de Janeiro: Civilizacão Brazileira, 1970.

Riester, Jürgen. 1976. *En busca de la Loma Santa.* Cochabamba: Los Amigos del Libro.

Rivière, Peter. 1984. *Individual and Society in Guiana.* Cambridge: Cambridge University Press.

Rosen, Eric von. 1904. "The Chorotes Indians in the Bolivian Chaco." *International Congress of Americanists,* 14th session, vol. 2. Stuttgart: W. Kohlhammer.

Sahlins, Marshall. 1974. *Stone Age Economics.* London: Tavistock Publications.

Sanchez Labrador, José. 1910–17. *El Paraguay católico.* 3 vols. Buenos Aires: Coni Hermanos.

Seelwische, José. 1974. "La organización socio-económica de los indígenas frente a los sistemas coloniales." *Suplemento Antropológico* 9, nos. 1–2.

Service, Elman R., and Helen S. Service. 1954. *Tobati: Paraguayan Town.* Chicago: University of Chicago Press.

Siffredi, Alejandra. 1973. "La autoconciencia de las relaciones sociales entre los Yojwaha-Chorote." *Scripta Etnologica,* no. 1.

Stahl, Wilmar. 1974. "Cinco establecimientos agrícolas en el Chaco Central." *Suplemento Antropológico* 9, nos. 1–2.

———. 1982. *Escenario indígena chaqueña, pasado y presente.* Filadelfia, Paraguay: ASCIM.

Steward, Julian, ed. 1963. *Handbook of South American Indians.* Vol. 1: *The Marginal Tribes.* Smithsonian Institution, Bureau of American Ethnology, Bulletin 143. New York: Cooper Square.

Susnik, Branislava J. 1961. *Apuntes de la etnografia Paraguaya, primera parte.* Manuales del Museo Etnográfico Andrés Barbero, Asunción.

———. 1962. *Vocabularios inéditos de los idiomas Emok-Toba y Choroti recogi-*

dos por el Doctor Max Schmidt. Boletín de la Sociedad Científica del Paraguay y el Museo Andrés Barbero, Asunción.

———. 1968. *Chiriguanos.* Vol. 1. Asunción: Museo Etnográfico Andrés Barbero.

———. 1969. *Chamococos.* Vol. 1: *Cambio Cultural.* Asunción: Museo Etnográfico Andrés Barbero.

———. 1971. *El indio colonial del Paraguay.* Vol. 3, part 1: *El Chaqueño.* Asunción: Museo Etnográfico Andrés Barbero.

———. 1973. *La lengua de los Ayoweos-Moros: Estructura gramatical y fraseario etnográfico.* 2nd edition. Asunción: Museo Etnográfico Andrés Barbero.

Taussig, Michael T. 1980. *The Devil and Commodity Fetishism in South America.* Chapel Hill: University of North Carolina Press.

Turner, Terence. 1979. "Kinship, Household and Community Structure among the Kayapo." In *Dialectical Societies,* ed. David Maybury Lewis. Cambridge MA: Harvard University Press.

Von Bremen, Volker. 1987. "Fuentes de caza y recolección modernas." Servicio de Desarrollo de las Iglesias, Stuttgart. Mimeographed.

Watson, James. 1952. "Cayua Culture Change." *American Anthropologist* 54, no. 2.

Wicke, Charles R., and Miguel Chase Sardi. 1969. "A Componential Analysis of Chulupi (Ashluslay) Kinship Terminology." *Ethnology* 8, no. 4.

Woodburn, James. 1982. "Egalitarian Societies." *Man* 17, no. 3.

Index

Page references for illustrations appear in italics.